The Violence of Recognition

THE ETHNOGRAPHY OF POLITICAL VIOLENCE

Series Editors: Daniel J. Hoffman, Tobias
Kelly, Sharika Thiranagama

A complete list of books in the series
is available from the publisher.

THE VIOLENCE
OF RECOGNITION

Adivasi Indigeneity and Anti-Dalitness in India

Pinky Hota

PENN

UNIVERSITY OF PENNSYLVANIA PRESS

PHILADELPHIA

Copyright © 2024 University of Pennsylvania Press

All rights reserved. Except for brief quotations used for
purposes of review or scholarly citation, none of this
book may be reproduced in any form by any means
without written permission from the publisher.

Published by
University of Pennsylvania Press
Philadelphia, Pennsylvania 19104-4112
www.upenn.edu/pennpress

Printed in the United States of America on acid-free paper
10 9 8 7 6 5 4 3 2 1

Hardback ISBN 978-1-5128-2484-1
Paperback ISBN 978-1-5128-2485-8
eBook ISBN 978-1-5128-2486-5

A catalogue record for this book is available
from the Library of Congress.

For Monali and Rupali Hota

CONTENTS

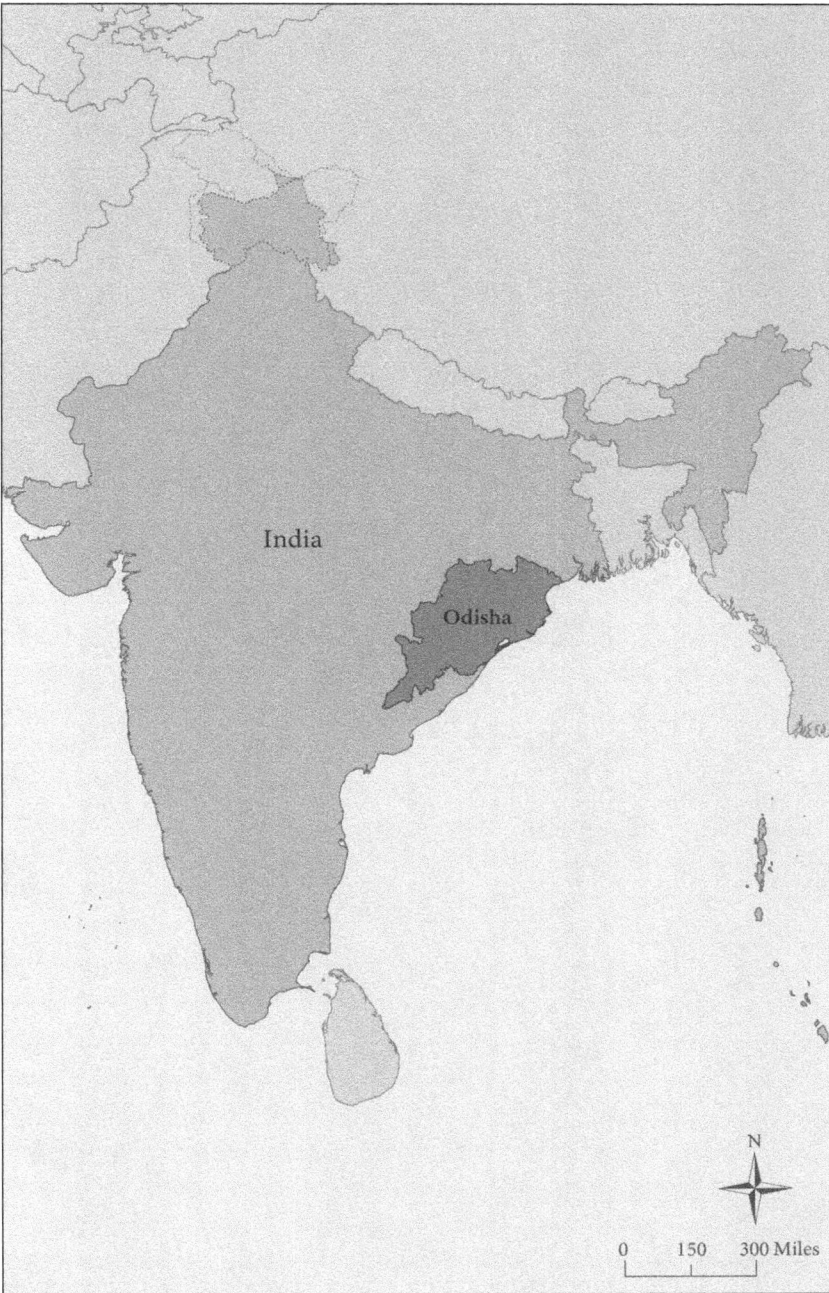

Map 1. Odisha (formerly known as Orissa) state on the eastern coast of India.

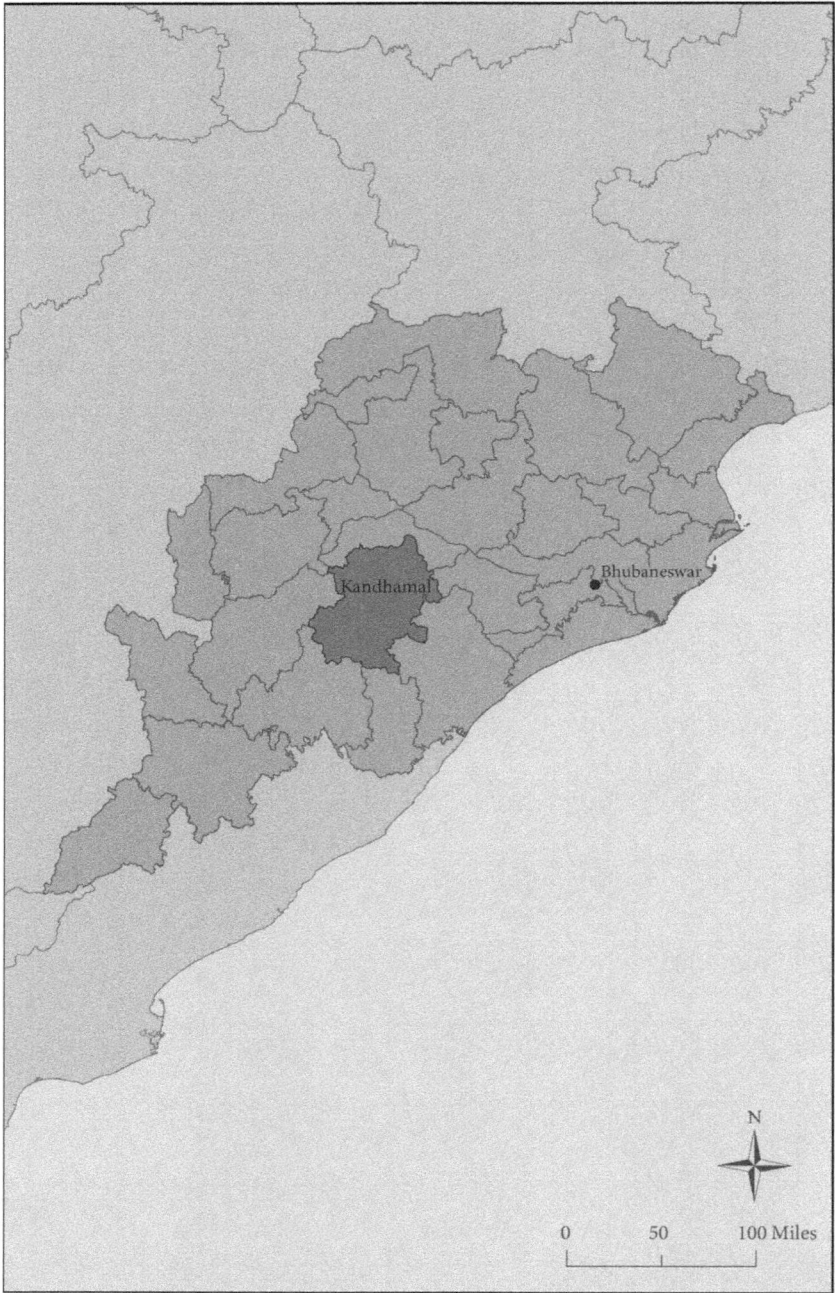

Map 2. Kandhamal district in the central highlands of Odisha.

Introduction

I n January 2008, an incident of church burning and rioting was reported in the Kandhamal district of the eastern Indian state of Odisha. Kandhamal is an Adivasi-majority district in the remote highlands of the state. Originally known as Phulbani, the district was renamed in 1992 after the Kandha tribe, whose members identify as Adivasis—literally, original settlers—one of several groups occupying the de facto indigenous slot within the Indian state. The district is also home to a significant minority population of Panas, a Dalit group that has converted to several denominations of Christianity. The violence, implicating two adjacent Hindu Kandha and Christian Pana villages, signaled that long-simmering ethnoreligious hostilities between both groups were coming to a head.

The villages' relative proximity to Baliguda, the district subdivision where I was based while I did my fieldwork in Kandhamal, meant I could visit the site before curfew restrictions were imposed. Having hiked up the rocky dirt path to the Hindu village, I saw that an angry crowd had gathered. When I spoke with them, Hindu Kandhas insisted that the Christian Panas were liars and that I should speak with Kandhas first because the Panas would try to influence me and gain my sympathy by lying about who was, in fact, responsible for the incident. I inquired after the *sarpanch*, or village councilman. After a long wait, he appeared, seeming hesitant and afraid. When he said his name, the reason for his trepidation became clear: he was Christian. The constraints that his religious identity as a Christian sarpanch of a Hindu village placed on his official authority were immediately visible. He timidly implored the crowd to not forget that I was a woman and that I had taken time to come speak with them. The crowd pushed him aside.

Anxious about these mounting tensions, I agreed to be led to the Christian village, hoping that the Hindu crowd would quiet down in the meantime.

Upon my arrival, a woman told me about waking up to see the shanty church a few yards from her house ablaze, along with the houses of the village pastor and his neighbor. She had not seen who had started the fire, but villagers said it was a Hindu man from the adjoining village. When I walked back to the Hindu village, several hostile villagers were waiting for me. Attempting to establish my caste provenance, they angrily inquired if I was Hindu and where my village (*gaan*) was in Odisha. They demanded to know if Panas had accused them of burning their churches and houses. They insisted that Panas must have concealed from me their own illegal and materialistic machinations that had provoked these actions—their encroachments upon the Kandhas' tribal status as attempts at usurping Adivasi land and resources.

They said, "You don't know the truth, do you? They are trying to make a fool of you. The truth is they did it themselves. They are so greedy; it is just another way that they can get some money out of you."

Some Kandhas justified their torching of Pana houses by accusing Panas of being instrumental in Kandhas' continuing economic disenfranchisement: "They had this coming. For a long time, we were quiet. They took everything from us. Our land, our money. We did not say anything. We suffered and bore it in silence. But now, no more. Let them not think that we are so stupid that they will continue to swindle us, try to claim that they are *Adibasi*[1] like us to try to take our jobs, our land and keep living next to us as if nothing has happened."

They continued, "We are not like them, we will not even touch a grain which belongs to someone else. We are simple, we do not cheat anyone. We have some pride, we know we are, unlike them. They are scavengers who will eat even the flesh of their own dead. We will go hungry, we prefer to die, before we betray our *dharma*, our *sanskruti*."

I reiterated my desire to consult the sarpanch, who seemed to have disappeared after his initial attempts to mollify the crowd. "Why do you want to speak to him?" they demanded. "He is with them, don't you know? He is Christian. He has been plotting with them. He is a traitor among us, he tells them what we will do, he warns them in advance."

Seeing that the angry Hindu crowd seemed unwilling to trust and candidly speak with me at such a tense time, I attempted to leave, but the villagers stopped me to demand that I give them *chanda*, money to erect a Hindu shrine in their village. "If you are Hindu, you will give the money," a young Kandha man said, his gaze challenging and direct, with more than a hint of a threat in his voice. I produced a note and slid it into the slotted box he held in his hands. He appeared placated. "*Hau*, O.K. Go your way. Go safely. And do not talk to Christians again. They will only fill your head with their lies."

I returned from Kandhamal in May 2008 as my fieldwork became restricted by curfews imposed by law enforcement to curb the violence. The mission and ethnonationalist workers I had shadowed for several months fell silent. Local Kandhas, who had warmly welcomed me into their homes only months earlier, became suspicious and uncertain of my allegiances. Panas, many of whom would seek me out repeatedly for conversations, fell silent and rarely ventured out of their villages. Tensions between Hindu Kandhas and Christian Panas became so palpable that the state began restricting the activity of journalists, religious workers, aid workers, and others like myself whose probing questions could become incitements to violence.

In August 2008, Swami Laxmananda Saraswati, a charismatic religious leader affiliated with the ethnonationalist outfit Vishwa Hindu Parishad, an important interlocutor who had secured my access to local ethnonationalist officials and institutions, was shot dead by Maoist insurgents. Soon after the incident, Kandha Adivasis began torching churches and assaulting Christian Panas, certain that they were, in fact, responsible for Laxmananda's murder. Within hours, the incident sparked anti-Christian hostility in other parts of the nation. As the violence grew, at least fifty-four thousand Pana Dalit Christians were displaced in the biggest incident of anti-Christian violence documented in the Indian nation-state's history. More than a decade later, thousands of landless Dalit Christians displaced by the violence continue to be housed in shanty relief camps, with no official claims to their homes.

A decade before Kandhamal, Odisha state gained national visibility as a site of ethnonationalist violence in reaction to religious conversion in 1999, when members of Bajrang Dal burned alive an Australian Christian missionary, Graham Staines, for his alleged forced conversion of Adivasis. The riots in Kandhamal were also attributed to, and even naturalized as, Hindu ethnonationalist retribution for Christian conversion. Anti-Muslim violence is considered the master narrative of Hindu ethnonationalist politics; since the 1990s, however, Christians have also been targets of xenophobic Hindutva violence, motivated by a long history of Hindu nationalist thought that sees conversion as a threat to Hinduism.[2] As Nathaniel Roberts has persuasively shown, a long tradition of Indian nationalist thought, including the views of stalwarts like Gandhi,[3] has framed conversion as inherently violent toward Hinduism, which makes clear the Hindu majoritarian undergirdings of the nationalist project in India even prior to Hindu ethnonationalism.

The advent of anti-Christian violence has coincided with economic liberalization initiated by market-oriented economic reforms in the 1990s that expanded the role of private and foreign investment in India. This connection between the economic and the religious in Kandhamal became acutely visible during my fieldwork from 2006 onward. As I observed in two ethnonationalist institutions that worked in tandem in Kandhamal—the Vanvasi Kalyan Ashram and the Vishwa Hindu Parishad, which worked on tribal-uplift development and the dissemination of upper-caste Hindu religious rituals and practices, respectively—Hindu ethnonationalism attempted a mimesis of Christian mission outreach in which material uplift and religious pedagogy were closely intertwined. Yet throughout their outreach and mobilization, Hindu ethnonationalists critiqued conversion to Christianity as a threat not just to caste or religious identity conceived in narrow terms but indeed to upper-casteness as a position of economic dominance.

As a movement, Hindu ethnonationalism is widely regarded to be an aggressive proponent of national economic growth; whereas early ethnonationalists renounced materialism and mistrusted commercial society, current Hindu ethnonationalist populism ambivalently vacillates between the embrace of neoliberal capitalism and economic nativism. When critiquing Christian conversion, ethnonationalists tend to engage in well-rehearsed tropes of Christianity as foreign to India and, as such, a bearer of Western values that endanger Hindu civilization. Scholarship on Hindu ethnonationalism separates questions of caste and religion from political economy. This has led to the ethnonationalist distrust of conversion being poorly understood in terms of ambivalences animated not just by religious-cultural fears but also by economic fears about the erosion of caste Hindu dominance. In Kandhamal, ethnonationalists critiqued Christian conversion as enabling Westernization in terms of the growing materialism among minorities prompted by access to Christian capital and services. Ethnonationalist anxieties about conversion appeared most pronounced when contending with the reach of Christian capital among minorities that challenged an otherwise straightforward relationship between caste and exclusion from capital. Ethnonationalists attempt a counterconversion of minority communities into Hinduism known as *ghar-wapsi*, literally a homecoming. Indicting religious conversion as coercion by Islam and Christianity, such a targeted "reclamation" frames minorities as always already Hindu, by recasting histories of caste and religious intimacies for marginalized low-caste and tribal communities.

In Kandhamal, religious and economic logics were inseparable, as ethnonationalists fueled debates over minority recognition that abetted damaging perceptions of Dalit converts to Christianity. Kandhas as Adivasis were recognized as de facto indigenes through the Scheduled Tribe category, while Pana Dalits who had lived with them intimately for nearly two centuries and had converted to Christianity were excluded from recognition, both through the Scheduled Caste category and through the Scheduled Tribe category. Recognition through the Scheduled Caste category remained unavailable to Dalits because of a constitutional exclusion of converts to Islam and Christianity, a mandate that underscores just how Dalits' incorporation into a majoritarian Hinduism forms a necessary condition for their patronage by the Indian nation-state.

To continue to be Christian and gain recognition, Panas were making bids to be reclassified as Kandhariya Panas, who could claim tribal recognition based on an intimate history with Kandha. These Pana attempts to access tribal recognition were met with hostility by Kandhas, as usurpation of their proprietary indigeneity, while also reviving long-standing panics about the canny materialism of Dalit converts. At the intersections of legal and ethnonationalist regimes of recognition, complexities and contradictions of Adivasi indigeneity enable it to function as a fulcrum of caste capitalism to the detriment of Dalits, as casteist and racialized scripts are imbued with new fictions to incite economic panics. These contestations over recognition illustrate the increasingly manifest violent doubleness of recognition in conditions of economic precarity—recognition's deceptive ability to reappear as a guarantor of economic commensuration despite its intimacies with capital through an entrenchment of race.

Caste violence fueled by economic anxieties in evolving Hindu ethnonationalism sheds light on how global ethnonationalist resurgences are prompted by majoritarian backlashes to uneven minority gains within neoliberal multicultural orders. Adivasi and Dalit contestations over recognition, and their deployment in ethnoreligious violence, revive casteist and racialized constructions of Adivasis as authentic indigenes and Dalits as their canny materialistic Others. Hindu ethnonationalism uses the exceptional and exclusionary recognition of Adivasi indigeneity to mobilize violence against Dalits, showing the centrality of caste in ethnonationalist animus toward proselytizing religions such as Christianity.

Since Kandhamal, violence against Dalits has dramatically escalated in India, as ethnonationalism has morphed into right-wing populism. Ethnonationalism prompts violence against Dalits, since their growing political

visibility threatens Hindu caste majoritarianism and reveals how Hindu ethnonationalism is a shadow of the Indian nation-state as a "republic of caste,"
to use Anand Teltumbde's words.[4] Indeed, anti-Dalit violence is a neoliberal
revelation of systemic exclusions foundational to the Indian nation-state
and its legal framework. Seen this way, resurgent ethnonationalisms and
right-wing populisms become visible as shadow formations of, rather than
aberrations within, liberal secular nation-states in which racial and casteist
exclusions are foundational to legal frameworks and governance. This analysis engages minority recognition as a site at which to locate ethnonationalist
politics in the long arc of caste capitalism in India. Religion, here, is both
event and process, structuring majoritarian hierarchies of recognition while
allowing for a recapture and resignification of caste and race in economic precarity. These workings of religion enable majoritarian regimes to be upheld
through unlikely political allegiances and attachments among minority communities that ultimately only continue their disenfranchisement.

Recognition through Reservations

The adoption of the Constitution of India, following the Constituent Assem-
bly debates of 1946–1949, committed India to a sovereign democratic republic
model that resolved to secure equality for all its citizens without discrimination
along the lines of caste and religion. Concomitant to the adoption of fundamental rights for its citizens, the architects of modern India delineated non-
justiciable Directive Principles of State Policy that outlined special protections
and provisions for Adivasis and Dalits through their juridical recognition as
Scheduled Tribes and Scheduled Castes, respectively. Stuart Corbridge lists key
articles of the constitution that outline the protective role of the state:

1. Article 46: "The State shall promote with special care the educational and economic interests of the weaker sections of the
   people, and, in particular, of the Scheduled Castes and Scheduled
   Tribes, and shall protect them from social injustice and all forms
   of exploitation."
2. Articles 330, 332, 334: provide for Reserved Seats for Scheduled
   Castes and Tribes in the House of the People for ten years (since
   extended by Constitutional Amendment Acts in 1959, 1969, 1980,
   and 1990).

3. Article 335: "The claims of the members of the Scheduled Castes
and the Scheduled Tribes shall be taken into consideration, consistently with the maintenance of efficiency of administration, in
the making of appointments to services and posts in connection
with the affairs of the Union or of a State."

4. Article 338: "There shall be a Special Officer [later Commissioner]
for the Scheduled Castes and Scheduled Tribes to be appointed by
the President."

5. Articles 341 and 342: allow the President, by public notification,
to specify the castes, races, or tribes which shall for the purposes
of the Constitution be deemed to be Scheduled Castes or Tribes,
and to consult with the Governor of a State where the Schedule is
to apply at a State-level.

Corbridge qualifies Marc Galanter's description of reservations as a system of "competing equalities"[5] as attempts by the state in independent India
to create a new class of "modern (ex)-Backwards" through economic and legal
interventions designed to reposition "troublesome" marginalized groups.[6] Differential logics were at play in crafting Scheduled Caste and Scheduled Tribe
as juridical categories. In the case of the Scheduled Castes, economic deprivation and low ritual status are seen as interlinked, with reservations thought
to accelerate the integration of Dalits into a modern polity organized around
class and merit rather than caste and status. In contrast, an isolationist protectionism of Adivasis as Scheduled Tribes was evident in the 1951 proposal
by the Commissioner for Scheduled Castes and Scheduled Tribes of common
elements of "tribal origin, primitive way of life, remote habitation and general
backwardness in all respects" as classificatory criteria for tribes, as well as in
Nehru's insistence that tribal groups be allowed to "develop according to their
own genius."[7] Exoticized and patronized tribal Others were to be protected,
but the temporal lack encoded in their primitivity also rendered them subjects
of development in perpetuity.[8] These interventions attempt to accommodate
the cultural and geographical distinctiveness of Scheduled Tribes while providing them opportunities for "advancement" through educational scholar-
ships and reserved jobs in central and state government positions since 1950
and in public sector enterprises since the late 1960s, alongside reserved seats
in Parliament and Legislative Assemblies.

For Adivasis and Dalits, recognition through the juridical categories
Scheduled Tribe and Scheduled Caste is firmly tied to ideas of economic

commensuration through its provisions of reservations, a system of quotas guaranteeing access to education and jobs in state institutions. Although reservations are usually glossed as affirmative action, Galanter clarifies them as more akin to positive discrimination through guarantees of access to education and employment and, thus, socioeconomic mobility and economic commensuration. The logics of protection and development embedded within the legal provisions for Scheduled Tribes and Scheduled Castes are markedly different in their fundamental conception of the Adivasi and the Dalit subject in relation to caste Hindu society. The legally encoded primitivity and isolation of Adivasis as Scheduled Tribes reproduce them as outside the caste system and unaffected by processes of economic modernization with a system of reservations that needs to be balanced by legislation that protects tribal communities from economic exploitation.[9] Dalits as Scheduled Castes, in contrast, are marked by landlessness, with economic advancement and cultural change seen not only as desirable but even mandatory for these communities.

In Kandha Adivasi and Pana Dalit claims over tribal recognition in Kandhamal, the distinction accorded to Adivasis also becomes productive of a religious exception. Adivasi groups are eligible for tribal recognition regardless of their religious affiliation to access reservations. On the other hand, Dalits, such as Panas who have converted to Christianity, are derecognized and lose Scheduled Caste status, underscoring not only that Dalits are assumed to be de facto Hindus[10] but also that conversion is seen as enabling Dalits to fully transcend caste as a category of social stigma and economic abjection. Placing these differential logics of recognition for both groups in the same analytic frame, the tribal category emerges as the sole category through which recognition may be secured regardless of religious affiliation. This religious exception further cements indigenous recognition through the Scheduled Tribe category as a position of pejorative privilege within the Indian nation-state.[11]

Even as minorities clamor for tribal recognition, Adivasis remain the most economically marginalized groups in the Indian nation-state. If tribal recognition reveals a paradox of economic commensuration for Adivasis as indigenes, Dalit recognition and its exclusion of converts illuminates a paradox at the very heart of the Indian nation-state and its legal framework: even as Dalit struggles have been crucial to the very nature of democracy in India, the law codifies and reproduces anti-Dalitness. Anupama Rao points out the paradoxical centrality of the Dalit to Indian democracy.[12] This foundational nature of Dalit claims to Indian democracy and the creation of its Constitution is also emphasized by Chinnaiah Jangam, in his analysis of how Dalit demands for the abolition of untouchability and the ending of caste inequality became preconditions for democratic independence during anticolonial nationalist struggles, emphasizing principles of justice, liberty, equality, and human dignity as foundational to the Indian Constitution under Ambedkar.[13] And yet, despite the centrality of the Dalit condition for the formation of the modern Indian nation-state itself, exclusions and contradictions in the legal recognition of Dalits show how Dalit converts in particular challenge secular minority citizenship in India, replete as it is with contradictions that attest to Indian secularism's fundamentally Hindu character.

These minority struggles over recognition show how Hindu majoritarian assumptions encoded within India's regime of minority recognition institutionalize rather than transform hegemonic forms of domination, as is argued more broadly for recognition in multicultural orders. A long history of engaging a language of shared subalternity for Adivasi and Dalit groups then obscures the distinctive and divisive role of caste, which has resulted in distinct pathways of Adivasi and Dalit political engagements within the Indian nation-state. Adivasi politics is increasingly reacting to the violence of the development state by articulating claims in terms of rights to land and forest zones. Dalits, in contrast, directly grapple with the socially embedded and casteist workings of the state and its legal framework by fighting caste biases in government schemes and protective legislation.[14] As recognition motors a differential economic casteism against Adivasis and Dalits to differentially implicate them within ethnonationalism, we see ossifying divergences between minorities' economic and political trajectories in the Indian nation-state that assert a need to recenter caste. These differences reveal a clear hierarchy of minority claims within the nation-state, making the anti-Dalitness of Indian multiculturalism acutely visible.

A Dalit Perspective on Caste Capitalism

Caste has been treated as an archaic system and a source of historical disadvantage deserving compensation and transcended through reservations in a uniquely South Asian system that secures affirmative action through legal recognition.[15] Yet caste persists as a structure of advantage and discrimination in the modern Indian economy in ways that have deepened post-liberalization in the 1990s, while being framed within the nonmodern realm of religion and "caste politics." This treatment renders it peripheral or incidental within a caste-erasing market economy, reflecting an elision of caste in contemporary economic conditions also mirrored in conversations about race, or the lack thereof, in neoliberalism. As the economic claims of derecognized Dalits making bids toward tribal recognition are invoked to justify ethnonationalist violence against them, contemporary neoliberal configurations, including emergent forms of right-wing politics, demand to be understood within the long durée of racial and caste capitalism.

Despite an earlier insistence on the singular nature of caste and its distinction from race, scholarly and popular debates are increasingly acknowledging uncanny similarities between caste and race as systems of inequality and stratification. The cross-pollination and lamination of casteism and racialization as well as colonial, mission, and legal governance of minorities within caste society emphasize that the Adivasi and Dalit conditions cannot be wholly understood in terms of the singularity of caste and have, in fact, critical resonances with racialized formations elsewhere. This dialogue between caste and race does not aim to simply make race paradigmatic in order to subsume caste within race. Rather, it emphasizes how a Dalit perspective foregrounds the continuing role of religion in the violence wrought by caste capitalism, usually occluded in secular accounts of political economy, including those foregrounding racial capitalism.

The domain of the religious, I emphasize here, is not separate from political economy and has been critical in consolidating economic dimensions of caste and race. Religion renews caste capitalism's violence through a resignification of caste and race that lead minorities to participate in a politics that only furthers their economic exploitation. Ultimately, a Dalit reformulation of caste capitalism resists accounts of caste and race as fixed within feudal, precapitalist understandings.[16] Instead, it emphasizes the capacious nature of caste and race as modern phenomena[17] that make them endure, shape-shift, and ultimately flourish in order to reproduce and entrench caste and racial inequality in neoliberal conditions.

In their inaugural volume that outlines a manifesto for Dalit studies, Ramnarayan Rawat and K. Satyanarayana mark five broad developments that have provided the conditions of possibility for the rise of Dalit studies: the political and intellectual controversy in the 1990s over the expansion of constitutionally mandated reservations in public education and employment for low-caste Hindu groups, the rise of new Dalit activism, political and electoral interventions by new Dalit political parties, the rise of Dalit feminism, and global discussions on caste and race that assert them to be comparable systems of social stratification and exclusion.[18] Together these developments have compelled a powerful area of study on the Dalit condition that foregrounds issues of human dignity as central to the study of Indian history, examines discursive practices that perpetuate caste discrimination, and moves beyond the conceptual obsession with the framework of colonialism versus nationalism to center Dalits as active participants in the project of imagining new visions of modern India.[19]

Firmly locating my analysis within a Dalit Studies approach, I emphasize caste and race as distinctly modern phenomena that have been strengthened rather than erased in the age of the market. Caste, much like race, as Nikhil Pal Singh argues, demands to be engaged not in terms of ascriptive fixity and static notions of precapitalist particularity but rather as "the modern, uniquely fabricated quality of racial distinctions as domains for the elaboration of institutionalized coercion and extraction that persistently shadow normative processes of value within contemporary capitalist societies."[20] This assertion is echoed in David Mosse's articulation of caste as not one thing or anything, as a script that accrues novel economic and political valences to become a persistent, durable fiction.

This reading of caste capitalism's continuities within neoliberal ethnonationalist violence builds on Mosse's assertion that although caste was first enclosed within religion, it can only be understood as political by engaging it as fundamentally economic. Anupama Rao argues, drawing on Nicholas Dirks, that Louis Dumont's totalizing and ahistorical treatment of caste rendered caste from a colonial category to an "ethnographic real," denying its politics.[21] As Mosse argues, Dalitness is increasingly engaged in terms of identity politics, enclosing caste within politics, which is paralleled by contemporary neoliberal claims to the modernity of the market economy that render caste a matter of politics by denying caste capitalism. Thus, while Brahminical and Orientalist ideological effects made caste visible in problematically apolitical ways, economic knowledge and derivative development discourse make caste phenomena disappear through discursive exclusion.[22]

Joining scholars such David Mosse, Anand Teltumbde, Rupa Viswanath, and Nathaniel Roberts, I remediate the neglect of the economic character of caste by illustrating the persistent economic valences of the landless Dalit condition through religious conversion, emphatically underscoring a caste-religion-state nexus.[23] Rupa Viswanath and Anand Teltumbde emphasize that the transcendence of caste hierarchy fundamentally needs to engage labor relations and Dalit landlessness. Historian Navyug Gill argues that Dalit

conversion is unable to resolve an antinomy between emancipatory discourses and exploitative economic relations.[24] When we engage with caste as
an economic phenomenon, in contrast to its prior representations as primor-
dial, backward, and reactionary, caste can be clearly seen as a modern and living political category that resolutely refuses shopworn distinctions between
the social and the religious, the religious and the political, and the religious
and the economic.[25]

Developing a framework of caste capitalism, I show how a modern and
nonreductive understanding of caste as durable yet shape-shifting allows us to
see continual economic coercion and value extraction in the reconstruction of
caste dominance and hierarchy. A rereading of a history of Adivasi-Dalit relations and their charged reinvigoration in struggles over recognition illustrates
the differential construction and management of Adivasi and Dalit formations
within caste capitalism. Bringing a Dalit perspective to the Adivasi condition,
a racialized condition bracketed in discussions of caste, emphasizes its constructed nature and its ability to acquire novel valences, rather than insists
on it as a set of immutable essences and unproblematic claims. Adivasiness
and Dalitness emerge as far from static, far from assumed, and far from stable
positions. From a Dalit vantage point, we see indigenous recognition's violence
not just in its exclusion of landless minorities but also its failure to secure economic commensuration for indigenous communities themselves. To precisely
engage the violence of recognition in motoring caste capitalism, as Indigenous
Studies scholar Glen Coulthard suggests, we must contemplate how the structural impact of recognition is furthered through psycho-affective dimensions
of colonial power that secure hierarchical relations of recognition. Coulthard
emphasizes that it is only through Frantz Fanon's "stretching" of a conventional
Marxist analysis that we see how the axes of domination historically relegated
by Marxism to the realm of the superstructure, such as racism, substantively
configure the character of social relations alongside capitalist economics.[26] A
Dalit perspective foregrounds this churning of the structural alongside and
indeed through the affective-aesthetic, asserting religion to be foundational to
their interrelationship. Through this perspective, we see indigenous recognition motoring caste capitalism by reproducing Adivasi authenticity and Dalit
materialism to continually reengineer relations between both groups. As (neo)
colonial regimes of recognition and ethnonationalism converge and pivot on
Adivasi indigeneity to reveal the vulnerability of Dalits as their landless Others, it becomes necessary for us to interrogate India's exclusion from settler
colonial geographies.

Theorizing Recognition in Economic Precarity from Odisha

When the British took over territories now within the state of Odisha from Maratha rule, parts of the state were variously under the British colonial administration's Bengal Presidency, Madras Presidency, and Central Provinces. Throughout Odisha's colonial history, tribal groups featured prominently in colonial and missionary accounts as indigenes to be pacified, civilized, and converted, as well as key figures in anti-colonial uprisings. These included movements led by Kandhas, known as the Ghumsur uprisings, motivated by Kandha resistance to British interference in meriah human sacrifice, alongside economic exploitation by coercive collection of nearly 50 percent of all Kandha land revenue by the colonial administration. In 1903, the organization Utkal Sammilani led by Madhusudan Das was founded to demand the unification of Odia-speaking regions into one state, contributing to the formation of the Bihar and Orissa Province. In 1936, Bihar and Orissa were split into separate provinces, when claims to the linguistic integrity of the Odia language that argued against its classification as a dialect or variant of Bangla cemented the demand for the new province of Orissa.[27] Following India's independence, Orissa's territory further expanded when twenty-seven princely states joined it. In 2011, Orissa was formally renamed Odisha with approval from the Central administration, influenced by growing calls to substitute colonial names of states and cities throughout the country with vernacular, and often archaizing, monikers.

Since the inception of the modern Indian state, Odisha state has become associated with economic marginality in the national imagination. But for at least two decades a seemingly straightforward narrative of economic abjection has been complicated by rapid socioeconomic change in Odisha. The state has emerged as a highly visible site of foreign direct and domestic investment for the mining and extraction industries. Odisha's Adivasi population, nearly 25 percent of its total population and the third highest of any Indian state, is often scapegoated for the state's lack of economic progress, while Dalits are conspicuous in their exclusion from any such narrative.

Kandhamal, a remote highland in central Odisha, was renamed in 1992 after members of the Kandha Adivasi community who are seen as the proprietary claimants of the district's territory. Kandhas, one of the most populous Adivasi groups in the Indian state, also have a presence in the states of Andhra Pradesh, Bihar, Chhattisgarh, Madhya Pradesh, Maharashtra, Jharkhand, and West Bengal. Traveling from Phulbani, the district headquarters, to Baliguda, the district subdivision, Kandhamal's profound physical beauty—seen in its waterfalls, forests, and verdant green hills—becomes visible. Also visible are the extreme infrastructural neglect and economic marginalization of its residents, more than 65 percent of whom are Adivasis and Dalits. Kandhamal's geography is intimately identified with Kandha Adivasi identity and economic marginality; caste Hindus describe the beauty of Kandhamal's geography as wasted. Kandhamal, they lament, is ripe for development for ecotourism but stymied by the crushing poverty of its minority residents. These claims echo colonial tropes of insufficient and inefficient land use by indigenous groups that justified colonists taking over indigenous lands to ensure the maximization of their productive value.

Odisha's embrace of aggressive neoliberal capitalism has barely been thwarted by Adivasi struggles against mining and extraction. Coast-dwelling caste Hindu Odias have long extracted value from Adivasi lands through the forcible removal and resettlement of Adivasis for dam building and mining and industrial development.[28] Adivasis constitute the main labor force for the extraction industries, and they serve as migrant labor in agriculturally underdeveloped regions such as Kandhamal. Yet caste Hindus and state development workers engage an opposition between Adivasis and industry to lament the Odisha's halting industrial growth as market logics are increasingly upheld as paramount for economic progress. Caste Hindus and officials from coastal Odisha describe the labor and lifeworlds of minority populations as entirely valueless and as "going nowhere." These iterative laments speak to the contempt for, and neglect of, rurality in an urban-centered world, in which the rural is a void that is not only "empty" or "desolate" but also "ineffective" and "useless."[29]

State economic neglect has led to a proliferation of development discourses and institutions spanning state and nonstate actors, a number of which specifically focus on tribal as indigenous development. These development discourses effectively depoliticize questions of resource allocation and strengthen the bureaucratic power of the state.[30] Such depoliticization reproduces Kandhamal as a zone of abandonment[31] in which the exclusion and abandonment of minority citizens is instrumentally forged through state neglect. Indicted as failed subjects of development imperatives, rural Adivasis and Dalits are relegated to marginal zones of collective amnesia, social erasure, and annihilation, a state of abjection explained by naming those in this zone "hopeless cases."

Odisha is then metonymic of rural India—an India not on the incomplete periphery of capitalism but rather exemplifying a dominant capitalist mode.[32] Adivasis are a "footloose proletariat," a neo–bonded workforce trapped in an ongoing state of casualization yet centered to the land, if only through dispossession and displacement. On the other hand, Dalits, also economically precarious, are almost entirely erased from questions of labor, land displacement, and forest rights. Amid such deepening caste-based economic inequalities, Odisha showcases the aggressive proliferation of the imperatives of economic development in the neoliberal Global South by a dizzying plurality of actors, including missions and nongovernmental and faith-based organizations. In this context, indigenous recognition through the tribal category emerges as an omnipotent and omnibenevolent guarantor of political and economic uplift.

Two states, Jharkhand and Chattisgarh, have been carved around Adivasi claims to land rights and territorial autonomy, which attests to the momentum gained by Adivasis through indigenous politics in India. Unlike in these states, however, Adivasis in Odisha are encapsulated within a caste Hindu–majority state, which has strengthened Adivasi indigeneity's incorporations into majoritarian Hinduism and, thus, into ethnonationalist politics. A deep exchange between Hindu and Adivasi traditions has formed the distinctive Hindu identity of the Odisha State.[33] For instance, Pralay Kanungo points out that Odisha's Jagannath cult, which forms the center of high Hinduism in the state, has grown by incorporating Adivasi traditions.

Despite a few muted critiques of caste, including through religious reform movements such as the Mahima and Brahmo movements, the Hindu majoritarian character of the state has stunted the development of Dalit identity and politics. Building on mission presence predating British colonialism,[34] Christianity, as the most significant minority religion in the state, continues to be a major force among low-caste and tribe groups. Adivasi-Hindu imbrications sharply contrast with underdeveloped Dalit self-assertion and politics, heightening conversion's salience for Dalits.[35] Odisha, then, shows the conditions under which Adivasiness emerges as a complex condition of political-economic abjection and religious-cultural intimacy capable of throwing the anti-Dalitness of Indian multiculturalism into sharp relief.

Mapping Adivasi Authenticity and Dalit Materialism

I conducted ethnographic fieldwork in Kandhamal during 2006–2008 to document how minorities intimately and viscerally experience legal regimes, the unanticipated social consequences of the law, and resulting reorientations within identity politics.[36] During this time, I engaged with Adivasis and Dalits demanding recognition, rights, and entitlements; ethnonationalists and mission workers advocating on their behalf; and state and nonstate actors who debated the law and its entitlements without expert knowledge. After receiving permission from the Rashtriya Swayamsevak Sangh headquarters in Nagpur in the summer of 2005, I observed the outreach of the two major ethnonationalist outfits that worked in concert in the region: the Vanvasi Kalyan Ashram, an ethnonationalist organization that purports to engage Adivasi communities through projects of community development, and the Vishwa Hindu Parishad, whose religious pedagogy and mobilization were largely responsible for the exponential growth of ethnonationalism in Kandhamal. I also interviewed officials of state tribal development agencies, including the Integrated Tribal Development Agency, the Kutia Kandha Development Agency, the district magistrate, and local state and law enforcement officials. To excavate a longer history of the differing racialization of Kandhas and Panas under British colonialism with regard to human sacrifice, I also conducted additional archival work until 2014. Through these processes, racialized and casteist constructions of Adivasis and Dalits emerged, as did minority claims over and disavowal of these constructions, as well as how these sociolegal scripts accrued new valences as they circulated in caste society.

A note on the gendered nature of the politics here. Though I interviewed roughly equal numbers of Kandhas and Panas, missionaries and ethnonationalist workers, most interlocutors featured on these pages are men. Kandha and Pana discussions about politics were usually among men in the public domain while women from both communities continued to be identified with the "private" domain of household and family and were likely to be implicated through their participation in religious piety and ritual. Following the circulation of nationalist processes, we see the contours of a masculinist ethnonationalism, in which caste and gender were invoked to do crucial material-symbolic work, such as figuring the Hindu nation and Kandha land as maternal figures to suture a Hindu and Kandha masculinist protectionism in order to reprovoke violence toward Dalits, notably women, by casting their sexuality as endangering the nation.

The first chapter of this book describes how and why debates over recognition reared their head in the district as Panas were making bids toward reclassification. To continue to practice Christianity while being eligible receive positive discrimination quotas from the state, Panas, derecognized as Scheduled Castes upon converting to Christianity, were petitioning for tribal status by demanding reclassification as *Kandhariya* Panas (Panas akin to Kandhas). This chapter illustrates the differential economic racialization of Adivasis and Dalits, and its reemergence in minority claims over recognition.

The second chapter describes how tribal recognition appears to have secured political ascendency without economic commensuration for Kandhas. Caste Hindus and minority residents of Kandhamal discuss the privilege of Adivasi status but also denigrate Kandhas as incapable of fully realizing the potential of their recognition because of their "simplicity." Kandhas struggle with such a characterization and engage a language of rights and entitlements aided by recognition to articulate their political power and economic dues.

The third chapter describes how the constitutional derecognition of Dalit converts as Scheduled Caste and Odisha state's anti-conversion statute reinforce each other to configure Dalits as materialistic, and spurious converts whose motives for conversion are to be constantly interrogated. Panas insist that their legal derecognition upon conversion has led to Pana and Dalit identities becoming increasingly disarticulated from each other, enervating a burgeoning Dalit politics. At the same time, invoking anti-conversion legislation, Pana attempts to gain recognition are seen as deceptions that prove them to be duplicitous traitors to their own heritage and religion. This chapter shows how conversion differently implicates Adivasis and Dalits, seeking from them different burdens of proof both within faith and within law, and solidifying distinction between both communities.

The fourth chapter illustrates how Adivasi indigeneity operates as a privileged savage slot within Hindu ethnonationalism. Despite how ethnonationalist engagements of Kandhas seem to be culturally hegemonic, civilizing efforts that undermine Adivasi claims to indigeneity, Kandhas discuss these practices as affirming their indigenous distinction while echoing ethnonationalists that "Adivasis have always been Hindu." This chapter shows how a longer history of Adivasi assimilation through religion enables Adivasis to be claimed as Hindus.

The fifth chapter demonstrates how Adivasis and ethnonationalists claim affinities over ontological beliefs about land as a nature-culture figure in order to naturalize Adivasi claims to tribal recognition while excluding Dalits from worship and regard of land to justify their exclusion from indigenous recognition. A long history of Adivasi religious osmosis and exchange with Hinduism is crystallized in ethnonationalist valorization of Adivasi devotion to land, showing how indigenous religious cosmologies unevenly support dominant Hindu control over, and continue to further, indigenous dispossession.

The sixth and final chapter details how Hindu ethnonationalists give discontents over recognition visceral charge through the circulation of moral panics linking Dalit materialism and Christian capital to mobilize animosity against Dalits. As minorities desire yet disavow material advancement, ethnonationalists employ charged imagery to suture carnality to capital by linking Panas' alleged involvement in sexual and bodily excesses to their accrual of illicit Christian capital.

I conclude by drawing out the national—and indeed global—implications of the struggles over recognition in deepening economic precarity in India. As right-wing and populist politics reanimate racialized and casteist economic anxieties, contemporary conservative politics and their reinvigoration of racialized violence must be understood with recourse to recognition as a motor of racialized and caste capitalism. This clamor for recognition in the Global South portends the reinvigoration of recognition and race in economic precarity as uneven minority advancements deepen in late capitalism.

CHAPTER 1

Crafting Indigeneity and Its Other

In Raikia village, about a hundred kilometers from Baliguda, I was walking toward a schoolhouse when I saw a fight break out in a shanty hut. Two Kandha men dragged a young Pana man out of the hut and beat and kicked him. A crowd gathered to witness the fight, but no one intervened. An old man standing in the crowd shouted, "If you lie about your heritage, this is what happens!" And he then spat on the ground to underscore his disgust. After the sarpanch of the village arrived to break up the fight and disperse the crowd, he went on to explain that the young Pana man being beaten was involved in circulating a petition for the reclassification of Panas as tribal by claiming similarities with Kandhas.

Tribal recognition circulated in social discourses in rural Kandhamal as a perverse privilege, one audaciously and volubly coveted even by upper castes because of its perceived entitlements to land. And yet when Panas, a group of Dalits who had lived in close proximity to Kandhas for centuries, made bids to gain tribal status, their claims were met with hostility and resentment, both by caste Hindus and by Kandha Adivasis. These struggles over tribal recognition between Kandhas and Panas brought to the fore foundational histories of the differential casteist racialization of Kandhas as indigenes and Panas as indigeneity's Others.

The Pana bid for reclassification was fundamentally necessitated by the fact that while Kandhas received recognition and consequently affirmative action benefits regardless of their religious affiliation as Hindus or Christians, Panas who had converted to Christianity were derecognized as Scheduled Castes and did not receive recognition or its affirmative action in any form. Increasingly Panas were arguing that the Pana condition was an unusual one: it was so inextricably tied to the Kandha condition that it meant that Panas also suffered socioeconomic marginalization much like Kandhas and, thus, were in need of uplift through recognition. Local state officials described these attempts by reverting to deeply entrenched scripts of Pana wiliness and chicanery. According to officials, Panas' attempts to gain recognition were motivated purely by material greed. Kandhas, at first, hesitated to describe Panas as motivated by a savvy materialism because they felt burdened to explain a difficult past of meriah sacrifice, which a caste Odia audience who would only reengage to cement Kandhas' continuing characterization as primitive and savage indigenes. And yet while they avoided speaking about Kandhas' historical engagement in meriah sacrifice with me and other caste Odias, they remained emphatic that it was dishonest and a *paapa* (moral sin) for Panas to claim that they had a shared heritage with Kandhas and insisted that they had differing origins and heritage.

By 2007, a Kandha tribal political platform known as Kui Samaj had become well consolidated in Kandhamal. The movement had been started as early as the 1960s by some accounts (it certainly was in existence in the 1980s) for the preservation of Kandha cultural practices and rituals. During my fieldwork, several Kandha elders continued to express concerns that Kandha youth were growing up with diminishing interest in Kandha heritage. Kandhas hoped that Kui Samaj would enable the formalization of the preservation and transmission of Kandha heritage and cultural practices and of Kui as a language. It was also increasingly a platform that groomed young Kandha men to run for local political positions, guided by the reasoning that Kandhas should participate in state and local politics to be able to model their sovereignty while securing change for the community.

Kui, identified as the language of Kandhas, is a southeastern Dravidian language written using the Odia script and is spoken by both Kandhas and Panas. Panas gained fluency in both Odia and Kui while acting as liaisons between Kandhas and caste Odias, while Kandhas were slower to embrace Odia. Now Desia Kandhas are fluent in Odia, speaking it with a distinct intonation as Dravidian speakers, and they continue to use Kui to communicate within their community. Panas are also fluent in both Kui and Odia, speaking Odia in ways that are not marked by the distinctive Kandha intonation and using both Kui and Odia to communicate with one another. Thus, even as Kui is a shared language between Kandhas and Panas, the language serves as important marker of Kandha Adivasi distinction, even as these Adivasis have mainstreamed into caste Odia society.

Since Kui Samaj's earliest stages of inception, Panas began to advance the argument that Kui Samaj should also include Panas, since they were also part of a linguistic community of Kui speakers, though with critical differences. These claims had been met with hostility on the part of Kandhas, who were emphatic that while Panas spoke Kui, it was *the* language that originated in the Kandha community and, thus, distinctive of and foundational to their identity. Kandhas contrasted this with Panas' purely imitative use of Kui, which they acquired to facilitate their dealings with Kandhas. Pana claims on Kui as a shared linguistic heritage were then dismissed as attempts at usurping the Kandhas' distinctive history, customs, and identity.

When asked about three decades, if not more, of assertions of shared affinities and vulnerabilities with Kandhas, Panas emphasized the singularity of the Pana condition as a condition of intimacy inextricable from that of Kandha Adivasis. Pana identity could never be extricated from Kandha identity, because no one could narrate the history and social position of Panas without explaining their role in the Kandha community. Saying this, Panas engaged in a vernacular articulation of a project of racialization undergirding the differential construction of both groups—indigeneity was foundational in the formation of Kandha identity but also that of Panas in a way that did not allow for a simple separation of Pana and Kandha cultural history and economic conditions. Through recognition, Panas would also gain access to local land through the tribal identification as a condition with perceived entitlements to land, which would work against the landlessness inherent in their condition as Dalits, as well as mitigate their characterization as outsiders to the district. Local residents, however, met these Pana bids for tribal recognition with violent suspicion. Caste Hindus and even Kandhas dismissed the Panas' claims as spurious and merely signs of their long-standing duplicitous and clamorous nature.

Legal scholar Marc Galanter has used the phrase "competing equalities" to explain India's system of reservations as a program of positive discrimination. Laura Dudley Jenkins and Stuart Corbridge each amend this formulation to "competing inequalities" to engage just how these legal categories and processes spur competition between minority groups that might otherwise work together to fight inequality.[1] Such fragmenting and divisive consequences of legal recognition can be seen in an Adivasi embrace of a politics of difference/protection rather than sameness, which has only furthered greater class stratification and inequality within Adivasi communities, contributing to emergence of vernacular Adivasi elites with greater political-economic aspirations and control over resources.[2] These divisive consequences also become visible as a distinct hierarchy of minority claims emerges when the logics

of recognition involved in the Scheduled Tribe and Scheduled Caste categories are placed within the same analytic frame, as claims to tribal status and
recognition end up trumping the mandates associated with the Scheduled
Caste category for Dalits.[3] This hierarchy of categories of recognition and the
claims they secure reveal just how legal categories do not resolve but rather
carry within them the material-symbolic weight of casteist valences. Indeed,
in Kandhamal processes of recognition reinscribed casteist and racialized
scripts about Adivasis and Dalits. They also continually reengineered economic and social relations between both groups to ossify their differential
trajectories through circuits of capital in caste society.

In this chapter, I revisit historical and ethnographic accounts of Kandha
and Pana relations to bring to the fore their differential casteist racialization
with recourse to indigeneity. My use of the term *casteist racialization* throughout this analysis, and indeed this book, emphasizes how Adivasi indigeneity is
a lamination of precolonial and colonial epistemological and historiographic
practices. This lamination illustrates how Adivasi indigeneity was created and
consolidated through a fusion of existing notions about plains-dwelling Adivasis in Hindu caste society, to which colonists added further valences drawing
on indigeneity as a condition of primitive savagery. Exploring this dynamic
highlights how and why Adivasi indigeneity has critical similarities with racialized constructions of indigeneity beyond South Asia and accordingly can be
fruitfully held up in the same analytic frame as them. Taking cues from Dalit
Studies' aim to make interventions that are not merely political but also historiographic and epistemic in nature, my account flips the conventional ana-
lytical gaze[4] to focus not just on how Kandhas were constructed as indigenes
but also on how their indigeneity became critical for the construction of Pana
Dalits as indigeneity's Other.

Such an attention to larger epistemological and historiographic practices
undertaken in historical and anthropological accounts of Kandhas, accounts
in which Panas always make an appearance but are relegated to the margins,
is motivated by the silences, erasures, and accusations that came to the fore
in my encounters with my Kandha and Pana interlocutors. These accounts
wittingly and unwittingly reproduce key tropes in the romanticized primitive
indigeneity of Kandhas, whose seemingly barbaric endorsement of human
meriah sacrifice becomes a critical site of their recognition, or rather mis-
recognition, under British colonial rule. These differential mobilization of
indigeneity in crafting Kandhas and Panas offers a window onto how notions
of indigeneity have been critical to the classification and governance of

Adivasi groups prior to and extending through colonialism as well as groups who claimed Dalit status in the modern Indian state.

Cultural Mimesis and Economic Alterity

In the early days of my fieldwork, I sat down with my Adivasi and Dalit interlocutors together and separately over cups of milkless red tea. A complicated history of the relations between Kandhas and Panas emerged as months passed, one in which indigeneity as a project of caste and racial minoritization emerged as critical to their differential interpellation within feudal, colonial, and contemporary political economies. Kandhas understood themselves as indigenous or prior to Hindus, predating their British colonial figuration as tribal. As such, they saw themselves as original inhabitants with proprietary claims to local lands and as valuable patrons, rather than merely subjects, of Hindu kingship. But another significant aspect of their indigeneity became crucial to cementing their status as indigenes under colonial rule: their religious cosmology rooted in the practice of meriah human sacrifice.

Long subject to pacification under Hindu kingship as violent and warring savages, Kandhas became particularly targeted under the British to brutal censure of their engagement in human sacrifice, which also significantly shifted their relations with Panas, who procured the humans to be sacrificed. Panas, the most populous Dalit group in Odisha, have a significant presence in several Adivasi-majority regions. Cast as outsiders in Adivasi territory, Panas have lived in close proximity to Adivasi groups for generations. Some recall that their ancestors were brought into Adivasi regions in precolonial times to serve as go-betweens between Hindu kings and Adivasis who were framed as aggressive martial groups whose pacification and patronage were vital for Hindu control over Adivasi lands. Other Panas emphasize their role as social and economic liaisons between Kandhas and caste Hindus, in which their presumed facility with materialism and commerce in distinction to the materially unsavvy ways of Kandhas became critical to their casteist racialization.

A complicated and vexed history of intimacy and hostility, and indeed mimesis and alterity, between Kandhas and Panas opened up a fascinating and somewhat singular portrait of indigeneity as a project of racialized minoritization that informed not just the formation of Adivasi identity and political-economic claims but also that of other minorities who claimed Dalit status and their political-economic trajectories within the modern Indian state. Bhrigupati Singh uses the term "agonistic intimacy" to describe how tribe and caste groups relate to their neighbors "whose coordinates are not predisposed entirely toward either oppositional negation or communitarian affirmation," using Michael Herzfeld's idea of how a proximate hostility can serve as a form of cultural intimacy.[5] An alternate reading of Kandha and Pana relations might belabor their shared subalternity and cast their hostilities in terms of a Freudian narcissism of minor differences, now dangerously weaponized by Hindu ethnonationalism. Such a thesis of minor differences is also echoed in terms of the preservation of distinction, in Pierre Bourdieu's terms, in which the maintenance of distinction becomes crucial in similar groups that are in greatest proximity to one another and therefore represent the greatest danger through the threat of sameness.

Even as Adivasis and Dalits are so often discussed in terms of a shared subalternity and marginality in caste society, scholars within Dalit Studies emphasize the need to recenter caste in a departure from the trope of subalternity that has proven so dominant. Taking cues from such scholarship, I reach into a longer history of the differential construction of both groups through casteism and its fusion with a colonial racialization to recenter caste to an analysis of their relationship. As the authors of a study that revisits F. G. Bailey's work in Kandhamal as well as his peers David Pocock and Adrian Mayer also allude to, anthropologists who reported a peaceful civility and tolerance of differences between rural communities in the 1950s onward naturalized the oppression and discriminatory practices of the hierarchical caste order and underplayed gendered domestic violence, rendering these ubiquitous forms of violence in village life as unworthy of analysis.[6] Reexamining rural life, the authors point to the persistence of caste but point also to the emergence of more charged religious hostilities, with unequal minority relations appearing newly unsettled with the influx of caste politics, categories of recognition, and ethnonationalism within the modern Indian state.[7]

While these forces were certainly major vectors in Kandhamal, this analysis recenters a longer history of racialization in caste society as a project of social engineering and violent transformation of relations between minority groups to bring to the fore continuities and disruptions in the economic dimensions of caste within the modern Indian state. Doing so, despite the mimetic movement of Panas toward Kandhas, claims of cultural similarity and shared subalternity between both groups become insufficient. As we recenter caste in the differential construction and governance of both groups, a long history of fraught hierarchical relations and differing economic racialization of both groups comes to the fore: one in which Kandhas became identified with the positive, concrete dimensions of capital as indigenes and Panas came to personify the negative, abstract dimensions of capital, including abstraction, invisibility, and impersonal domination, as indigeneity's Other.[8]

Kandhas as Authentic Indigenes

The Kandhas are a tribal group in the central highlands of the Odisha state, forming 52 percent of Kandhamal district's population. In the historical and anthropological record, Kandhas became identified through their engagement in meriah human sacrifice.[9] British colonial authorities instituted the Meriah Agency specifically to stop the "barbaric savagery" of human sacrifice.[10] Colonial accounts depict meriah sacrifice as being at the center of a Kandha religious cosmology in which the appeasement of land with human blood was seen as ensuring fertility for a community that sustained itself through agriculture. Humans feed personified aspects of nature through blood sacrifices, which in turn "feed" the community, assuring villagers good health and harvest, and social harmony. If this cyclic relationship breaks and crops fail or disease breaks out, villagers view this as a sign of Dharini Pennu's displeasure, dissatisfaction, or even anger that can only be assuaged through ritual, accompanied by an appropriate sacrifice prescribed by the *jani* (village priest). The Kandha relationship with Dharini Pennu, the Earth Goddess, then, does not install a divide between nature and culture, placing humans and nonhuman actors in a cycle of reciprocity and mutual dependence.[11] Colonists vacillated in their stance toward meriah sacrifice even as they emphasized it—sometimes they denigrated it as superstition without substance, while at other times they attempted to engage the complexity of Kandha cosmologies and its collapse of nature and culture[12] seen in the worship of the earth and a belief that it can be adequately sustained through human blood. In fact, Kandhas did not, and could not, see the earth itself as firm and solid, and as having integrity, until human beings were sacrificed to Dharini Pennu.[13]

Even after the ban on human blood instituted after the British colonial administration's installation of the Meriah Agency, Verrier Elwin noted in 1944 the continued centrality of the desire for human sacrifice to Kandha "psychology."[14] During my fieldwork, I observed the harvest festival, which now centered on the sacrifice of a rather expensive *podha* (ox) by Desia Kandhas whose blood is offered to Dharini Pennu.[15] My closest interlocutors, however, conspiratorially spoke of times when the ox would be released from its enclosure and the gathered crowd would become unruly. In the scramble of human bodies, they suggested that the blade of the sacrificial knife would "accidentally" make a deep cut on the body of a member of the crowd such that "enough" human blood would fall to the earth to restore the ritual to what "it ought to be." Dharini Pennu could only be adequately appeased with human, and not ox, blood. Describing these subversions with a wink and sometimes a knowing smile, my Desia Kandha interlocutors conveyed their pride at their ability to recoup ritual from juridical sanctions and their successful subversion of the censure of their beliefs.

Meriah sacrifice also implicated the Panas, believed to be a subgroup of an ethnic community known as the Doms, who have lived in close proximity to the Kandhas since at least the 1830s. Frederick Fawcett describes them as a pariah group, with a "propensity for thieving," living in poor conditions as outcasts in caste society.[16] Historical accounts attribute their poor economic and living conditions to their inability to sustain themselves through productive labor, especially in contrast to hunter-gatherer Kandhas, who achieved self-sufficiency by using the natural world around them through their labor. The Panas lived in separate settlements on the fringes of Kandha villages. By all Kandha and Pana accounts, Kandhas historically observed spatial distancing, purity, and pollution taboos against Panas, including preventing them from entering the thresholds of Kandha houses, not sharing meals or accepting water from them. In so doing, Kandhas observed untouchability against Panas to cement their status as lower and ritually polluting in relation to them, even as caste Hindus considered Kandhas themselves to be ritually impure because they were consumers of animal meat and prohibited them from spaces of Hindu worship. Panas were, however, critical for Kandha practice of meriah, as they were paid by Kandhas to go from the highlands to plains to procure human victims, whom they would then sacrifice. Panas were then middlemen who procured victims for meriah sacrifice, which also led them to act as economic liaisons between Kandhas and caste Hindu society.

The anthropologist Felix Padel offers the most sustained account of Kandha engagement in meriah sacrifice and its violent censure by British colonists. Here I rely largely on his account of meriah sacrifice, not only because my own interlocutors were reluctant to volunteer their own take on meriah sacrifice, but also to show how Padel's critical reading of the reductive ways in which meriah sacrifice was understood by colonists still valorizes Kandha cosmology as indigenous, while bracketing how the practice became implicated in demonizing Panas. Padel notes the duality of the British engagement of Kandhas as primitive noble savages, where, on the one hand, Kandhas were understood to be courageous, gallant, and hospitable and, on the other hand, the British commented on their degenerate natures, animality, ignorance, and superstition, rendering them the primitive Other of British rationality.[17] Padel contextualizes Kond religion to fundamentally point to a reductive misreading of Adivasi religion: one that reads meriah sacrifice as purely religious, rather than cosmological in a way that is deeply political and fundamentally inseparable from political economy, including control over material circumstances and resources.[18] Padel cautions against any simplistic readings of meriah sacrifice, emphasizing the need for a committed agnosticism regarding Kandha practices of human sacrifice. Not only does the untranslatability of the act challenge the analytic division between religion and politics, cosmology and political economy, but any capacious translations are further impeded by tropes of barbarism and savagery that overwhelm the colonial archive.

To provoke a skeptical reading of Kandhas' endorsement of human sacrifice, Padel suggests that the colonial archive documenting meriah sacrifice is animated by a charged emotive fantasy of savagery that showed colonists' preoccupation with human sacrifice as a practice that needed to be urgently pinned down and rendered sensible in order to be arrested. Padel is emphatic about the humanity of Kandhas, both in the treatment of their victims, who he stresses were nurtured and well-fed captives until the moment of sacrifice,[19] and also in the way that, after being killed, victims would be collectively mourned for several days by villagers through a series of rituals.[20]

While Padel teases out the motifs of savage barbarism that undergirded British attempts at stamping out meriah sacrifice, he makes passing mention of the Panas as Dom traders, who acted as economic liaisons between Kandhas and caste society who procured the meriahs to be sacrificed, either by kidnapping or purchase—usually children sold by parents, whom the Panas brought to the highlands from distant plains. Oftentimes, if they failed to procure victims, Panas pledged their own children for sacrifice. Padel also notes that when the British found and rescued meriah victims and thus disrupted the ritual, Kandhas would insist on sacrificing Pana children, as they feared the consequences of failing to please Dharini Pennu.

Padel reminds us that very act of interpreting meriah human sacrifice is a political act.[21] And yet even as he invites us to suspend judgment about a practice overwhelming portrayed as motivated by barbarism and savagery, it would be somewhat remiss not to note Padel's own desire to insist on the humanity of Kandhas in ways that elide their subscription to caste hierarchy and their desire to retain economic control in the region. This happens even when he himself notes the political, and I would add economic, implications of meriah as a sacrifice of the outsider in the context of increasing "external" domination, politically through Hindu rajas and economically through the Dom traders who sold the meriahs. The meriahs' status as slaves, Padel insists, became analogous to Kandhas' own increasing subjection to outsiders and a kind of "symbolic recompense"[22] against this external control and implied growing powerlessness.

Padel's account emphasizes the autonomy of Kandhas as indigenes but ends up justifying a violent nativism that seeks a purification from outsiders, as he underplays Kandhas' economic subjection of and hierarchical distancing from Panas. Despite his nuanced and complicated reading of Kandhas' cosmologies and motivations about meriah sacrifice, Padel furthers a vision of Adivasi communities as egalitarian and free of hierarchy, underplaying Kandhas' imposition of servitude on Panas and engagement in the ritual practice of untouchability. A number of accounts characterize Kandhas as exploited by Panas as "outsiders" but occlude a perspective on Kandhas as practitioners of caste hierarchy through their observance of untouchability and servitude toward Panas. It would be facile to point out that Kandhas were not endorsing liberal, and indeed historically impossible, ideas of equality; yet it is worth reiterating the extent to which caste hierarchy was central to Kandha political, economic, and religious cosmology. Consequently, interpretations that elide Kandha observation of hierarchy and dominance over Panas underplay just how Kandha economic and political dominance in a local hierarchy began to fray under colonial intervention to significantly disrupt the economic hierarchy between the two groups.

The unequal yet symbiotic relationship between Kandhas and Panas began to sour with British colonial censure of meriah human sacrifice among Kandhas. Barbara Boal mentions the Kandha hatred of Panas as a product of affective displacement, suggesting that British rhetoric about the shameful barbarism of human sacrifice served as a site of shame and negative self-understanding for Kandhas, leading them to displace this shame onto Panas. Rather than characterize this animus in terms of psychic disavowal and shame in a political economic void, however, it is critical to understand the resulting shifts in the material-symbolic dimensions of ethnicities and caste identities that led to significant economic rupture and affective turmoil between both communities. Until British rule, Kandhas understood Panas to be lower than them in hierarchy as their workers, sometimes leading Kandhas to describe Panas as their *chaakaras* or servants. The British reformulation, however, unevenly associated Kandhas with the concrete dimensions of capital as naturally self-sufficient and capable of hard labor even as they lacked mastery of the material world. This lack of mastery, colonists surmised, was visible in Kandhas' inability to cordon ontological divides between nature and culture, evidenced in a religious cosmology centering on human sacrifice.

To preserve the figure of the Kandha as a savage devoted to land who was to be pacified but not reviled, the colonial indictment of Panas as canny mercenaries rendered the Kandha an economic victim, motivated only by his religious cosmology to engage in human sacrifice. In so doing, they displaced blame for the practice onto Panas who procured the human victims only for material gain. Colonists described Kandhas as duped by Panas who were motivated by commerce, rather than seeing Kandhas as themselves agentive procurers of victims who actively engaged Panas as their economic patrons. Colonists romantically recouped the indigeneity of Kandhas by insisting on their economic guilelessness and how they were ultimately motivated by a pure religious cosmology free of material desires. At the same time, colonists overwhelmingly associated Panas with an abstract, impersonal engagement in capital motivated only by commerce and materialism. Pana alterity was narrowly and insistently cast in terms of material canniness, as a result, often by being directly contrasted with unsavvy, noncommercial Kandhas who were unable to grasp true value as market value in economic exchange and were considered materially unmotivated. This vulgar anti-capitalist reading by colonists also sowed the seeds of Kandha dispossession of and alienation from land.

This typification of Panas in caste society became instrumental in an evolution in their identification as mercenary and parasitic exploiters, rather than as erstwhile economic servants of Kandhas. "All Pans are beggars," F. G. Bailey[23] remarks uncritically in his book *Tribe, Caste, and Nation*, insisting that Panas symbolized their dependent status by engaging in ritual begging, even when they did not rely on this income for their survival. Describing them as both skilled and persistent, Bailey reproduces Pana canniness as he describes them as opportunistically taking advantage of Kandhas' desire to index themselves as economically and ritually superior.

Rather than acknowledging a history of violence inherent in Kandhas' own observance of hierarchy and ritual servitude against Panas, Bailey insists on

Kandhas' innocence even when they exercise and maintain economic dominance. With the transition to market economy in the 1950s onward, as Bailey
notes, Kandhas became more habituated to settled agriculture, particularly in
the cultivation of turmeric and nutritionally dense *kandula* legumes, while
Kandhas continued to use middlemen, either Odia or Pana, in the sale and
trade of their produce, as they considered commerce and trade to be at once
beneath them and beyond their capabilities.[24] Commerce and trade maintained economic distinction between Kandhas and Panas, a distinction that
began to favor Panas with the expansion of market logics in the local economy,
while also furthering a caste hierarchy in which Kandhas remained above the
worldly undertakings of commerce. To his credit, Bailey acknowledges the
disruption of Kandhas' hierarchical dominance and the resultant unrest in his
description of a Kandha-Pana conflict in Baderi in which Kandhas' chief com-
plaint was that Panas were behaving like equal citizens rather than acknowledging themselves to be obedient, servile dependents with no ancestral right
to land and a right to earn their living that was contingent upon their continuing to be dependent on and subordinate to Kandhas.[25]

While Kandhas attempted to sustain themselves from the land, Panas
transitioned from economically serving Kandhas—first as middlemen in
commerce, including procuring human victims for meriah sacrifice for a fee,
and then after a British colonial ban on meriah sacrifice following the institution of the Meriah Agency—to becoming weavers of cloth for Kandhas, a
profession unsettled by the advent of and growing reliance on factory-woven
cloth, which caused them to transition to local, small-scale trade relationships. Jobs in administration and commerce eluded Kandhas and largely
went to Panas, who began to gain a worldly urban sophistication[26] in distinction to a Kandha habitus and comportment that continued to be marked
by rurality, primitivity, and savagery.

Although Bailey does not specify this about his Pana informants in Bisipara, in the villages surrounding Baliguda where I worked Panas had also
acquired their relatively urban sophistication through their access to mission schooling, which gave them facility in the English language and occasionally provided travel opportunities within the country through Christian
networks, affording them a cosmopolitan exposure that contrasted with
the identification of Kandhas with local lands and attendant discourses of
economic and social stagnation. The 1950s also marked the beginnings of
Kandha migration as labor, compelled by Kandhas' inability to make an adequate living in the district through enforced settled agriculture. By the time

of my fieldwork in 2007 and 2008, Kandha youth served as seasonal migrant labor in large numbers, traveling to urban centers in states such as Gujarat, where they served as daily wage laborers on construction sites. Kandhas, then, became alternately associated with agrarian toil on local lands and pure mobile labor, while Panas were funneled into more administrative and local employment to be routed into different circuits of capital.

During my fieldwork, Panas, more than Kandhas, emphasized how their condition was inextricably linked to that of the Kandhas. In early conversations, however, Pana claims to inseparability from Kandhas minimized the fundamental impasse between them in terms of caste, in both symbolic and material-economic terms. Kandhas acknowledged their relationship but laid out critical differences in their heritage.

While Panas appeared eager to cast their relationship with Kandhas in terms that mirrored the rhetoric of minor differences and hostilities stemming from minor misunderstandings, Kandhas emphatically, and sometimes violently, resisted the rhetoric of sameness with Panas. Panas insisted that their relationship with Kandhas was that of "nail to flesh" (*nakha ku mansa*), insisting that a separation between the two groups was unthinkable because of a codependence over two centuries. Kandhas denied that intimacy or resituated it as hierarchical intimacy. Kandhas practiced untouchability against Panas and also patronized them to undertake tasks that were seen as ritually polluting. For Kandhas, Panas were particularly crucial as economic liaisons between Kandhas and caste Hindu society, a role that Panas still sometimes inadvertently assumed by speaking for Kandhas when the two were present. Kandhas rejected any claims to sameness, however, insisting that Panas had served them in the past in order to resignify them as servile and lower in both caste and economic hierarchies.

Panas continued to serve as economic middlemen, becoming a recurring figure in a history of the economic exploitation of Kandhas, obscuring its genesis and entrenchment in exploitative transactions between caste Hindu landlords and merchants.[27] With their knowledge of plains geographies and communities acquired during years of procuring human victims for meriah sacrifice, Panas were well positioned for an earlier entry into the modern economy as middlemen in *haatas* (markets), acquiring cattle for their Kandha "masters," and pawning or acquiring jewelry for Kandhas.[28]

With these shifts in the local market economy, Panas began serving as economic liaisons between Kandhas and upper-caste traders in transactions of forest produce and land. Kandhas detailed such transactions as exchanges of incommensurable value that were predatory in nature. They marked their long history of economic marginalization by caste Odia traders, moneylenders, and landlords by insisting that such transactions were overwhelmingly exploitative. Kandhas did not hesitate to blame their exploitation by caste Hindu moneylenders and landowners for their continuing economic marginality, particularly in conversations when caste Odias were absent. Yet, Panas continued to be scapegoated as instrumental in Kandha economic exploitation, showing how Panas served as a site not just of displacement of Kandha shame about meriah sacrifice but also of their anger reacting to their exploitation by caste Odias.

When Kandha lands were taken away for paltry sums and Kandhas were inadequately compensated for forest produce they gathered, they attributed these unfavorable transactions to cunning Pana middlemen rather than the caste Hindus who hired the Panas and set the terms of monetary exchange. Panas' perceived natural savvy in commerce overwhelmingly associated them with the negative, abstract dimensions of capital, including abstraction, invisibility, and impersonal domination, while Kandhas were identified with the positive, concrete dimensions of capital, including land and labor. Panas were described insistently as clever, canny, and often cunning—a cluster of terms centering on wily materialism, not just by local caste Odia traders, state officials, and religious workers, but sometimes also by Kandhas themselves. As Kandhas spoke with me about their relationship with Panas, they evaded discussions of meriah human sacrifice, preferring at least in initial days to describe it as a *bhool bhujabana*, a misunderstanding. After many months of discussions, Panas, and to a lesser extent Kandhas, haltingly volunteered meager information on how human sacrifice had been implicated in securing a history of intimacy and antagonism between both groups.

A local Pana journalist, Santosh Digal, who helped me gain access to several Pana villages in my earliest days, introduced himself to me in English, using only his first name. Urbane and well educated, Santosh babu grew up in residential mission schools and worked for an Odisha state newspaper as their Kandhamal correspondent. Although he lived in Phulbani with his family, Santosh babu often traveled to Baliguda, the district subdivision, to report on local government affairs and bureaucratic failures. He insisted on inviting me to meals in a meals-ready canteen, even when I ventured that I would like to meet his family on numerous occasions. I later understood these invitations to share meals outside his home to be motivated by his desire to not offend my perceived caste sensibilities as a Brahmin Odia woman. Over these

meals, which he insisted on paying for, he spoke at length with an air of stud-
ied professional detachment. His detached demeanor, however, began to give
way when he first revealed his last name after some hesitation. The last name
Digal was the most common and distinctive Pana last name in the district,
originating from the Kui word "digaloo," alternately glossed as interpreter or
middleman.[29] One day, discussing Kandha Pana relations in the district, he
became unusually emotional.

"Sometimes," he said, "I feel ashamed of this name. Immediately when
people hear this name, they think something about you. They think you are a
cheat, a swindler, a *chora* (thief). I hate this name. For many years, I thought,
I would change it. You know, my wife, she is a Brahmin. She is a schoolteacher
in a government school in Phulbani. We met as schoolmates and ran away
from home. Otherwise, we would have never been able to get married. She
has not taken my last name, she has still kept her Brahmin last name. My
children have no last name. I gave them two first names. I know why. Because
in Kandhamal, when you are a Digal, there is no escape."

Santosh babu was one of several educated and upwardly mobile Panas
who articulated the pejorative burdens of their Pana identity, and indeed of
casteism, lamenting that their last name immediately reinscribed them not
just as Dalits but also as untrustworthy mercenaries. Panas like him despaired
that their children and grandchildren would continue to be marked and
haunted by the burdens of Pana identity. Some others engaged in a fragmen-
tation of Pana identity, which enabled them to disavow and distance themselves from the enduring construction of the cunning and canny materialism
that the Pana identity seemed to so immediately invoke.

Peter, a young Christian Pana man, said, "There are two kinds of Panas—
Kandhariya Panas who are not outsiders, who are from here, who have always
been here. And then there are the *kating* Panas. They are the bad ones, they
are the ones who come from outside, who do not have good intentions. Kating Panas are the ones who are swindlers, cheats. They are the ones who will
cut your throat and take your money, not us." I asked Peter to clarify the word
"kating." It turned out to be a vernacularization of the English word "cutting," which he emphasized by making a gesture of slashing his throat, imply-
ing that kating Panas were capable of cutting throats for material gain. "But
we are not those Panas," he insisted, "the Kating Panas. We are Kandhariya
Panas, we have always lived here, right next to Kandhas, helping them."

When I probed into the provenance of the Kating Pana identity in the
archive, it emerged that certain groups of Panas elsewhere in the state were

once notified criminal groups under the colonial administration, and were
since referred to as denotified and ex-criminal groups, including Adhuriya
Domb, Oriya Domb, Ghasi, Dandasi, and Jayantira Pano. Writing about
Jayantira Panos, Mohan Behera relates that they were brought from other districts to serve as strongmen on behalf of landlords to forcibly collect revenue
from locals in their *zamindari*.[30] Their roles as mercenaries and extortionists
were in many ways their only economic means of survival because Panas
were excluded from several other vocations because of their ritually polluting, "untouchable" status. Their feared social status was only consolidated by
their formal classification as a criminal group under the British, which also
led them to be reviled by other Panas, who wanted to distance themselves
from their perceived dangerous criminality. As anthropologist Anand Pandian has noted of another denotified criminal caste, the Kallars in Tamil Nadu,
such a construction rendered them ethically suspect subjects burdened to
constantly prove their desire to be reformed and compliant subjects within
the Indian development state.[31] Thus, as Panas in Kandhamal insisted on the
criminality of some Panas from "outside" to emphasize their own innocence
and moral and ethical strivings, they attested to the social cleavages and schis-
mogenesis that had arisen within groups that went on to claim Dalit status in
modern India because of an internalized casteism, and its hardening through
colonial law and governance.

    Peter was not the only one to split the Pana identity in order to distance
himself from the scourge of being Pana, so often cast as an immutable essence,
which in fact was a constructed and contingent casteist racialization of Panas as
Kandha indigeneity's Other, rendering them mercenary, cunning, and driven
by materialism above all else. Kandhas and Panas were cast as two opposing
economic nodes in caste society in terms of a lamented economically unsavvy
and wasteful indigeneity and Panas as Kandha indigeneity's canny mercenary
Other. Even several Panas repeated versions of this formulation: Kating Panas
as outsiders to the district were, in fact, canny exploiters capable of slitting your
throat to swindle you, but the Kandhariya Panas were not the same as them.

    With these charged characterizations of Panas still circulating, Kandhas
denied any Pana claims of similarity with them in terms of shared heritage
and cultural practices as the basis for their reclassification as Kandhariya
Panas. Yet Panas sometimes still spoke for Kandhas in public settings, laps-
ing into their historical role as spokespersons even as Kandhas were agentive
actors in a local market economy and claimed local political dominance. At
times, Kandhas chafed against being spoken for. At other times, they let Panas

explain the socioeconomic marginalization of Kandhamal and the economic condition of its minority residents as a condition of shared abjection within the development state. When I first entered local villages, these dynamics were clearly visible when villagers would congregate in groups to speak with me. In one such instance, a village crowd of Kandhas and Panas began to discuss the economic problems they faced. Several members of the crowd spoke of the problems they faced as Adivasis due to state neglect and the difficulties of eking out a living from agrarian toil in the rugged, hilly terrain of Kandhamal. When I asked some young men their names so that I could follow up with them, their names identified them as Digals, as Panas, who unhesitatingly spoke of adibasi problems as their own. As Panas continued to step up to speak of Adibasi problems as "our problems" and refer to themselves as Adibasi, over time I learned to identify them not only by their last names, with Majhi and Digal being the two most common last names used by Kandhas and Panas, respectively, but also by listening to their differing Odia *ucharana* (pronunciation), which divulged their identity without need for formal introduction. This discernability of caste through language and pronounciation emphasized the immediacy of caste as a public marker, contrary to the assertion that caste, unlike race, cannot be immediately read and fixed through embodied attributes.

A differential logic underpinning claims to tribal recognition and Dalit recognition in the social life and circulation of recognition emerged. Tribal recognition necessarily engaged the cultural distinction of Adivasis as well as the primacy of claims to land. Dalit recognition was provisionally acceptable only in terms of casteist marginalization and was not engaged in terms of a temporal "backwardness," or lag, in the same way that tribal recognition connoted the Adivasi category. Panas were more hesitant to speak of their continued stigmatization as Dalits in caste society after their conversion to Christianity, but they spoke of the particular scourge of Pana identity, which echoed casteist tropes of Dalit identity construction elsewhere—including ritual pollution, servitude, and materialism—alongside motifs of criminality, economic chicanery, and a wily, even dangerous, canniness more idiosyncratic to the local context.

Thorny issues of shared culture and claims to land remained unsettled among both communities. The fact that Pana claims hinged on a mimetic movement of their community toward Kandha language and cultural practices was particularly contentious. To Panas, this mimesis validated their claims of a shared heritage and history, which served as the basis of their understanding of themselves as Kandhariya Panas, whose history was inextricably intertwined with that of Kandhas. For Kandhas, Pana mimesis was merely canny imitation, and their adoption from Kandhas' original practices and identity was so derivative as to seem parasitic. Kandhas, in particular the leader of Kui Samaj, Purba Majhi, argued that Panas would have no identity or economic standing without Kandhas but that Kandhas had always been who they were, long before Panas had been brought into the region. Panas, they said, had lived off Kandhas, but Kandhas had never made their living or gained economically from Panas. These Kandhas insisted that they had no objection to Panas receiving recognition on their own terms, through asserting their distinction and economic claims as separate from that of Kandhas. It was the claims of sameness that angered Kandhas, claims that were grave betrayals of their forefathers and their distinct heritage. A young Pana man, Bijoy, argued, "They say Panas are outsiders here, they are not from here. But tell me where am I from? My grandfather lived here, his grandfather lived here, his grandfather lived here. We do not know anything else. Where else do we come from? All we have known is this. Anything that Kandhas have suffered, we have suffered it alongside them. We came here to work for them. Even now, we bear their burdens alongside them. Then why are we treated so differently? Our children also need opportunities, they also need economic progress and education. What will become of them?"

Bijoy was among a younger group of Panas who were vocal about their social ostracization and economic marginalization. As we saw earlier, Panas were widely understood to be outsiders who had settled among the Kandhas, but they were also notably considered rootless, in sharp distinction to the close identification of Kandhas with local lands. This notion of unrooted Panas could possibly be traced back to their purported descent from a nomadic people known as Doms, who traveled and settled in various parts of India and, by some accounts, Europe to form an ethnic group identified in the present day as Roma. Yet, Pana as rootless and thus not marked by an inalienable fidelity and entitlement to land was reproduced by the landlessness of the Dalit condition.

As Bijoy and other young Panas reminded me, unless Panas gained access to land, they would forever be seen as unlawful squatters in the district who could be subject anytime to being xenophobically expelled as outsiders. Unlike the mimetic similarities with Kandhas cited by older Panas, younger Panas highlighted their interest in being reclassified as Kandhariya Panas precisely because tribal recognition would gain them land rights. If older Panas were more muted about the economic dimensions of their casteist construction as Dalits, younger Panas were more forthright that their lack of rights to land was not just preventing them from achieving economic commensuration in a meaningful way but also continued to play into the xenophobic characterization of them as outsiders in Kandhamal with no legitimate claims to local lands.

Elizabeth Povinelli argues that the recognition of indigeneity in multicultural orders perpetuates unequal systems of power among colonized indigenous subjects by demanding that they identify with an impossible standard of authentic traditional culture, thus reifying indigenous authenticity in ways that ultimately reinforce liberal regimes.[32] Debates abound as to whether or not India's idiosyncratic system of minority recognition is in fact comparable to liberal regimes of multicultural recognition and, thus, if tribal recognition can be discussed alongside other modes of indigenous recognition. Yet, we plainly see not only that tribal recognition entraps Adivasis into indigenous authenticity but also that Adivasis invoke logics of recognition to maintain a proprietary indigenous distinction from other minorities.

When Panas pointed to their economic needs and landlessness, Kandhas returned to the continuing economic dimensions of their differing racialization with recourse to indigeneity, engaging a rhetoric that tied Kandhas with the concrete, positive dimensions of capital such as land and labor while it reinscribed Panas as tainted by abstract impersonal dimensions of capital via commerce. The leader of Kui Samaj, Purba Majhi, said, "These are ploys to attempt to become Adivasis to snatch our resources, our land that we have labored and toiled on. It was not enough that they took our money, our resources in the name of their self-interest and profit. Now they want to do it shamelessly using the law and saying that they are the same as us."

I pressed Purba Majhi on whether he thought Dalits needed recognition and uplift because of their economic circumstances. He agreed that Panas might need assistance in improving their life conditions. He was emphatic, however, that they receive that recognition on their own terms and not as Adivasis, because it would be a betrayal of history and heritage to claim Panas were similar to Kandhas, which fundamentally betrayed a history of their unequal and fraught positions in the local order. He insisted that it was egregiously dishonest on the part of Panas, a betrayal of not just Adivasi heritage but also Pana history, to claim sameness with Kandhas in order to access economic opportunities. "We are not stopping them from saying that Dalits should have jobs," he said, "and I don't understand how all this works, how and why big people decided that Dalits should not get jobs if they are Christian. But we all know one thing: Panas cannot say they are Kandhas. You do not become Adivasi after years of being something else. See, we as Kandhas have always been Adivasi. We are the original people here, that's what it means. That even before Odias, we were here, our *puruba-purusa* (forefathers) are from this soil. But everyone knows Panas are not from here, they were brought here for some reason. Where is their village (*gaan*), what is their origin, we do not know."

As these tensions around Pana claims to reclassification intensified, caste Hindus—spanning local caste Odias residents, state officials, and, less frequently, aid and NGO workers—asked me not to trust Panas or to take their claims of suffering seriously and, indeed, to never take any statement they made at face value. During a tea break on the long rocky journey from Raikia to Baliguda, I met a schoolteacher from Cuttack who expressed his surprise at my presence in remote Kandhamal, especially at a tense political moment in the district. Hearing about my interest in Kandha-Pana relations, he smiled sardonically, offering an Odia *dhaga*, a mnemonic-like aphorism: "You know what they say in Odisha—beware of three kinds of people: the Puri Brahmuna, the Katakiya Karana, and the Phulbani Pana."

In a rhythmic sequence, the schoolteacher pointed out that it was well known—in fact, common knowledge—that one should never trust three kinds of people in Odisha: Brahmins from Puri, known for their exploitation of pilgrims and devotees at the Jagannath temple; an upper-caste group of landholding scribes from Katak (known by the colonial moniker Cuttack), who are highly visible as political and economic elites in the state; and the Phulbani Panas, known to be canny and materialistic turncoats. The aphorism attempted to thread these groups together as materially canny, economically exploitative, and thus untrustworthy; but while the other two groups were upper-caste groups, Panas were hardly privileged in the caste order, as I reminded him. The teacher immediately attempted to erase caste by saying that the wily economic notoriety of these groups had nothing to do with caste: "You cannot call me casteist, you cannot say I am saying this as a caste issue. After all, I have included your kin and mine in this group. This is just common knowledge."

The traveling schoolteacher's comments showed how Panas continued to circulate widely throughout the Odisha state as materialistic and untrustworthy in the caste Odia imagination. It was hardly remarkable, then, that the dismissal and invalidation of Pana claims were particularly vociferous among state officials, who described the Panas' attempts as spurious and illegitimate, as merely another instantiation of Panas' cunning and wily ways. Kandhas did not as openly cite Pana wiliness, in part because of a reluctance to speak of the historical conditions of human sacrifice under which the relationship between both groups had soured. Instead, they reengaged the cultural and economic dimensions of their differential racialization with recourse to notions of indigeneity.

As a Kandha man, Benu, explained, "We are from here, this is our land. We have a distinct way of life different from others. That is what is means to be, that is why they give us this recognition of our distinct status. They do not give it to everyone, they do not say everyone is Adivasi. Now how can Panas say they are the same as us? We do not deny that they also might have problems and need help. But they cannot claim to be the same as us." Some older Kandhas emphasized that by claiming to have a shared history and heritage with Kandhas, Panas were, in fact, engaging in some of the gravest sins in the eyes of Kandhas—a betrayal of religion (*dharma*), heritage (*sanskruti*), and forefathers (*puruba-purusa*). Pana desire to be seen as Adivasi signaled to Kandhas that they had no regard for their own practices, their own distinct identity. In Kandha assertions, indigenous recognition through the Scheduled Tribe category had reified Adivasis' understanding of themselves as indigenes in distinction to other minorities. As Kandhas insisted that Adivasis were distinct from Dalits, not just culturally but also economically because of their entitlements to land, legal categories of recognition hardened and ossified distinctions between Adivasi and Dalit minority groups, such that Kandhas insisted that cultural distinction and social distance had to be maintained between both communities in caste society even while making claims through categories of ostensibly secular legal recognition.

Indigeneity in Caste Capitalism

As Prathama Banerjee points out, the Adivasi formation has long been regarded as a contrary critical presence within capitalist modernity while consolidating the economic processes of caste modernity.[33] Adivasis like Kandhas were banned from practicing slash-and-burn cultivation (*poddu chaasa*) and denied access to forests under the British in the early nineteenth century and onward, while their aboriginal or indigenous labor became particularly valued in a marketplace of indentured labor.[34] Land alienation and

dispossession by moneylenders and richer farmers became chronic to Adivasi communities. Concomitantly, colonial officials forcibly uprooted tribals
from their lands, glossing it as "freeing" their labor and constituting them as
particularly valuable as laboring bodies.

Adivasi exclusion from capital only deepened in the postcolonial Indian
state. When a paradigm of socialist modernity was adopted within a newly
independent Indian state, Nehruvian state policies deepened an already existing temporal lag between caste Hindus and Adivasis. Aggressively modern
in its strategies of development, the state purported a stance of isolationist
protectionism of Adivasis by advocating against their economic mainstreaming. Yet, in the 1960s and 1970s, state development projects such as dams and
industry extracted value from lands occupied by Adivasis, triggering a series
of dislocations that transformed adivasis' nomadic lifestyles into a system of
mobile, pure labor.[35] At the same time, the modern Indian state's tribal welfare policies engaged tropes of indigenous cultural preservation that emphasized the need to preserve and protect adivasi distinction. As Kaushik Ghosh
points out, a modernist discourse of primitivity established the Adivasi as
both an exotic tribal and everyday manual labor, a figuration that became
critical to crafting the Indian nation in ideological and material terms.

Despite the economic Othering of indigeneity that becomes foundational
in the consolidation of capital, Tania Murray Li questions the conceptual
opposition of indigeneity and capital; instead, she asserts that "indigeneity
was not conjured unilaterally by global capitalism with its functional requirements any more than it was conjured from the top down by technologies for
indirect rule. It has been woven from diverse threads that emerge from above
and below in entanglements with capitalism. . . . Indigeneity does not stand
opposed to capitalism as a prior state on a linear, evolutionary trajectory or as a
marker of ineffable otherness. Rather, it stands opposed to capitalism because
it coemerged with it."[36] Drawing on Murray Li, Sheetal Chhabria shows that
aboriginality and indigeneity functioned as a tactic of colonial governance
that variously contained, managed, regulated, distributed, and reorganized
entitlements as the commoditization of land, labor, and shelter in India.

In Kandhamal, indigeneity emerges as a technology of colonial governance
not just through a secular reading of its organization of access and entitlements
to capital in terms of land and labor but rather by emphasizing religion as a key
modality through which economic entitlements became adjudicated. Kandha
and Pana relations, thus, offer a historical window onto the inextricability of
religion from the economic racialization of Kandhas as indigenes and Panas

as their Other. Colonists preserved the guileless simplicity of Adivasis by asso-
ciating Dalits as their economic liaisons with the canniness of commerce[37] to
govern Kandha engagement in human sacrifice with recourse to their religious
cosmologies, which transformed relations between Adivasis and Dalits.[38] Contemporary Adivasi claims to recognition, in fact, continue to be understood by
invoking Adivasi entitlements to land, not just through labor but also through
an animistic religious cosmology free of material desires, which is valorized by
missions and caste Hindus as an abjuration of materialism.

Through Kandha and Pana reflections on their shared history, it becomes
clear that colonial practices of social classification and their epistemologies
alone did not usher in notions of indigeneity and caste hierarchy. Rather, as
Anastasia Piliavsky[39] has been careful to point out, caste cannot be understood merely as a project of colonial knowledge practices that consolidated
caste in terms of Orientalist essences akin to Ronald Inden's argument that
"Orientalists" imagined "an India kept eternally ancient by various Essences,"
which were put to "invidious uses . . . to constitute the European world's Others."[40] Sanjay Nigam also advances such a critique of British officialdom, suggesting it "reduce[d] the natives to their racial essences to suit the exigencies
of colonialism. Inherent in the production of this knowledge was the notion
of the essential type, an object without history."[41]

Piliavsky points out that postcolonialism has been exhaustively criticized
for ignoring the roles of indigenous actors, homogenizing Orientalism, and
short-circuiting the relation of knowledge and power under colonial rule.
Drawing on indigenous sources, she shows how the production of colonial
knowledge often involved a variety of Indian actors and absorbed several
indigenous concepts, practices, and institutions. Colonial uses of racialized
and casteist stereotypes, rooted in histories stretching back far beyond British
colonialism, add up to a lurid history of violence against people branded as
congenital criminals in colonial law.

Akin to Piliavsky's exhortation that we reach into precolonial histories
rather than overemphasize colonial knowledge, a precolonial history of relations between Kandhas and Panas attests to the circulation of vernacular ideas
of indigeneity about Adivasi groups predating colonialism, as well as how
Adivasis themselves endorsed caste hierarchy and observed untouchability
against other communities such as Panas. We see the existence of older ideas
of the savagery, primitivity, and inherent violence of Adivasi groups such as
the Kandhas under Hindu kingship predating colonial rule. Indeed, Kandhas
were constructed as indigenes, alternately to be pacified and subjugated, and

feared and patronized, under Hindu kingship before the arrival of British colonists in the region.

We also see the precolonial roots of caste hierarchy in the Kandha observance of hierarchy, including practices of purity and pollution taboos, ritual servitude, and untouchability against Panas. Understanding the endorsement of the social marginalization of groups, the constructions of Adivasi as indigene, and Panas as indigeneity's Others reveal how groups who came to later self-identity as Adivasis engaged, before colonial rule, in the practice of untouchability and ritual servitude against groups that were accorded Dalit identity in the modern Indian state. These motifs unevenly continued but also found distinct forms of rupture under British colonial governance as we see caste practices predate and underlie hostilities between both groups that gained new form and valence with their differential governance by British colonists. Colonial epistemologies and resulting interventions through governance cemented the differential casteism and racialization of both groups in ways that reengineered economic relations and hierarchy between them.

Mapping these laminations of caste and race allows for a number of related interventions in the theorization of Adivasi indigeneity in caste society. Racialized logics unevenly build on and disrupt existing tropes of indigeneity and its Others in a caste framework. These racialized logics emphasize that Adivasi indigeneity engages uncannily repetitive tropes of indigeneity that bear resemblance to racialized motifs of indigeneity elsewhere. Adivasi indigeneity in South Asia has been engaged as an exceptional and constructed condition rather than a condition of uncontested prior claims. Tracing the laminations of casteist and racialized indigeneity allows for South Asian indigeneity to be productively put into conversation alongside indigenous formations elsewhere. Adivasi indigeneity comes into view as a fulcrum within recognition as a motor of caste capitalism, determining access to land, engagement in labor, and access to capital for those communities identifying as indigenous as well as those excluded from indigeneity.

CHAPTER 2

Recognition Without Redistribution

Early in July 2007, I hitched a ride in a van owned by a local NGO. On our way, a group of Kandha[1] youth appeared in front of the van. Holding long sticks in their hands, they stood in the van's path until it came to a halt. Beating the roof and windows with their hands, they shouted, "Open up!"

As the driver rolled down a window, a young man shouted, "Give us money, come on, give it to us! We want to buy some *pudiya* [chewing tobacco]."

The driver asked, "Why should we give you money?"

The young man retorted, "You think you are so smart. We know who is paying for this car. All of you say you are doing work for adibasis.[2] That is why you get money. This is our money, not yours!" Though there was no exchange of cash in this encounter, it appeared important to these Kandha youth that they perform ownership over economic resources flowing through networks of Adivasi development projects in the region, resources they interpreted and marked as rightfully "theirs."

During my time in Kandhamal, Kandhas, especially those belonging to younger generations, insisted that development officials and caste Hindus repeatedly duped them and, they said, "took money in our name" (*aama na re paisa nauchanti*) because of Kandha "simplicity." These oft-repeated tropes of simplicity—a shorthand for their perceived inability to master money as a system of material and social exchange—were part of a vocabulary of indigenous entitlement through which they insisted they had been cheated by upper castes, state officials, and researchers like me who appeared to be "swallowing up" money (*paisa gili jauchanti*) while claiming that their work would benefit Adivasis. These young Kandhas warned that this would no longer be the case; they possessed a new awareness, and no one could "hide the truth" from them.

That these young men eventually allowed me to leave without my having to hand over cash for their tobacco made it clear that securing money was not their sole objective. Rather, they had sought to perform their understanding of the "value" of their indigenous positioning in the local development economy. Employing a language of ownership, Kandhas asserted their claims over capital, which circulated both through the formal bureaucratic processes of state development and through the informal economy that was its shadow—the pockets of state and development officials, NGO workers like the driver, and even unaffiliated researchers like me, who inquired after Kandhas' problems but did little to change their circumstances.

Although, at the time, Kandhas were vehemently asserting that their indigenous distinction uniquely entitled them to indigenous recognition in Kandhamal and thus denying Pana claims for reclassification as Adivasi, no straightforward narrative of indigenous privilege could explain Kandhas' assertion of proprietary ownership over the capital that coursed through local development. In Kandhamal, as in other parts of India, state-led development of Adivasis is routinely framed pejoratively, pegging them as anachronisms; they are considered the raison d'être for development initiatives yet are also characterized as "impossible to develop" using "modern" strategies.

In fact, Kandha assertions about development precisely responded to state officials' and caste Hindus' pejorative characterizations of them. State officials and caste Hindus insisted that although the Kandhas' status as Adivasis accorded them political power as well as proprietary ownership of land in the local socioeconomic hierarchy, they were neither able to successfully receive the development state's patronage nor to capitalize on the political potential of their indigenous status because of their fundamental inability to become "worldly" by mastering money and exhibiting means-ends rationality. Kandhas' claims about development showed that they were now using these pejorative characterizations to assertively renegotiate indigeneity in the wake of indigenous recognition, which had secured political ascendency for them yet failed to ensure them economic redistribution.

Kandhas' continued racialization as indigenes with no understanding of the material world, as we saw in the previous chapter, lingered in their interactions with the development-state officials and caste Hindus around them. It repeatedly appeared in conversations about money, value, and indigeneity, in which Kandhas were continually pegged as unable to understand how money works in market exchange to index the "true" value of things. Characterizations of Kandhas as simple and, thus, fundamentally out of sync with and unable to progress within a modern economy were used as exclusionary resources by development-state officials and caste Hindus to naturalize Kandhas' economic "backwardness." State officials, development workers, and caste Hindus insisted that Adivasis were incapable of mastering traits connected to economic exchange and value—canniness in commerce, a means-ends rationality, and the ability to understand and exchange true value.

In what follows, by attending to discussions of money, indigeneity, and value, I show how Kandhas appropriate a language of their own racialized simplicity to display their understanding of the shifting contours of indigeneity and indigenous recognition as a set of entitlements from the development state. From demanding their economic dues from caste Hindus to accepting bribes themselves, Kandhas aggressively attempted to counter assumptions that they do not understand money's workings and the broader sociocultural processes it indexes[3] in the local development economy, in order to signal their shifting understandings and occupations of indigeneity. As Nikhil Pal Singh has said, if land, labor, and money are fictitious commodities that compose the foundations of capitalism, they also constitute what Patrick Wolfe calls the elementary structures of race.[4]

Rather than engaging race in terms of ascriptive fixity and aligning racial differentiation with static notions of precapitalist particularity, Pal Singh urges "an attention to the modern, uniquely fabricated quality of racial distinctions as domains for the elaboration of institutionalized coercion and extraction that persistently shadow normative processes of value within contemporary capitalist societies."[5] Taking this exhortation seriously, I show how invocations of money and value as racialized scripts of Adivasi indigeneity serve as fictions crafted by state officials, caste Hindus, and development workers to precisely naturalize the accrual of capital by caste Hindus, historically and within the workings of the contemporary neoliberal development state, as well as the inability of Adivasis to achieve economic progress.

These fabricated tropes of racialized simplicity demonstrate the collusions between the development state and neoliberal logics that entrench Adivasi economic disenfranchisement in India, as well as elide contradictions within the "modern" Indian state. Strikingly, Adivasis appropriate these very fictions using a language of rights and entitlements ushered in by recognition to stake their claims to the entitlements of their proprietary indigeneity anew. Kandhas' uneven deployments of their own racialization, however, make clear the extent to which indigenous recognition does not counter, but rather encapsulates, the logics of the market, as Kandhas describe their disillusionment with these failures of recognition in highly charged and emotive ways. But before we engage with these Kandhas claims in the present day, first a brief history of money and indigeneity in Kandha as Adivasi history.

Money and Indigeneity

In India, British colonial administrators created the very category of "tribal" as distinct from caste-based Hindu society by transporting an Enlightenment framework of primitivity to the subcontinent. While the framework set up a suite of judgments and expectations that framed the tribal as Other in India, British colonists explicitly engaged themes of money and primitivity to create a temporality of modernity. In doing so, they deployed tropes about indigenous lack of knowledge of money, private property, and inability to comprehend true value, as documented in many cases of indigenous groups across settler-colonial contexts.[6]

Prathama Banerjee notes that in colonial Bengal, colonial administrators, such as Augustus Cleveland, were inspired by the Scottish Enlightenment to insist on money's civilizing impact on primitives. Cleveland insisted that a "tribal" group of Paharias preferred to "plunder" instead of trade and work, seizing what they immediately wanted rather than engaging in the impersonal and regulated exchange of money, which evidenced a need for the immediate satisfaction of desires rather than their rational deferral. Supposedly lacking a sense of temporal deferral, the "primitive" tribal was surmised to have no grasp over mediatory entities like money, machinery, and the state. Colonists insisted that tribals existed in a condition of unpremeditated and immediate subsistence acts and were always already outside the money form. At the same time, they emphasized that money could serve as a civilizational force for tribals, including the taming of their "natural" violent proclivities.[7]

Once the mastery of money was linked to the mastery over temporality and corporeality,[8] money also became instrumental in crafting the figure of the sensuous, bodily, archetypal primitive.[9] Kaushik Ghosh's discussion of his Munda tribal interlocutors and their reflections on money[10] echoes these motifs about how the "primitive" is seen to conceptualize money as a thing in itself rather than as a means to an object in the future. If pure abstract exchange was "investment" for a deferred and more productive future, money used to satiate immediate needs and desires—such as alcohol and drunkenness—was seen as the "primitive" form of money or, in effect, the absence of a true understanding of money. Colonists then linked the inability to master money to indigenes' proclivity to succumb to sensuous, embodied immediate desires and thus demonstrate a lack of understanding of futurity itself.[11]

The British discovery, collection, and codification of information about Indian society contributed to colonial cultural hegemony and political control,[12] while the law became the instrument through which peculiarly British notions about how to regulate a colonial society made up of Others was institutionally activated.[13] Both British ethnographers and colonial administrators asserted that the primitivity of tribals required them to be separated from caste Hindu society into what Michel-Rolph Trouillot terms a "savage slot."[14] The figuration of the primitive tribal was carried over from colonial times to the formation of the modern Indian state and was then firmly encoded in the epistemological and legal categories of state recognition. This separation became the enduring basis of social classification in Indian society as, and juridical classification in, liberal recognition, through the juridical category Scheduled Tribe, which rendered tribals the Other of Indian liberalism.[15]

With the inception of the modern Indian state, the paradigm of development has structured the Indian state's paternalistic governance of its tribal citizens, consolidated by the formal adoption of the Indian Constitution in 1950, which juridically classified Indian tribes as Scheduled Tribes and assured tribal communities state-mandated affirmative action. In its earliest Nehruvian iteration from 1947 onward, the modern Indian state was wedded to an aspirational secular, aggressively developmentalist form. Verrier Elwin, the architect of Nehru's tribal policy, insisted, however, that an industrialization-focused, aggressively developmentalist paradigm was unsuitable for Adivasis. Advocating gradualism and streamlined simplicity in the governance of Adivasi communities, he insisted that their life be gauged by the development of "human character" rather than by the metric of economic advancement.[16] Elwin was emphatic that the economic exploitation of tribals by caste Hindu society was a forceful argument against the mainstreaming of Adivasis, emphasizing that tribal history could essentially be narrated as "a story of economic exploitation and cultural destruction by caste society."[17]

These differing modalities of development and associated temporalities of modernity carried forward the colonial temporal lag between the primitive and the civilized into the modern Indian development state. Aiming at noninterference and gradualism, the nonassimilationist paradigm for tribal development transitioned to other forms of governmentality that were instrumental in the proliferation of state and nonstate agencies, reinforcing the imperative of indigenous development as well as the circulation of contemporary discourses of transnational indigeneity within Indian tribal communities.[18] In 1991, India transitioned to a free-market economy with a substantial reduction in state control of the economy. Although neoliberal reforms have been thought to erode the welfare state, India remained an interventionist and developmentalist state, even as it transitioned from its earlier socialist form. The neoliberal character of tribal development is then counterintuitively characterized by the dominant and expansive presence of the state in minority development and welfare alongside the incorporation of free-market ideals within state development.

Through these transitions in state-tribal governmentality, the figure of the Adivasi who is unable to grasp money continued to serve as the basis of colonial paternalist protections, and it lingers on in the Indian nation-state's governance. For instance, citing the example of a 1998 Supreme Court of India ruling mandating that all development projects that threaten to displace tribals must work with a land-for-land rehabilitation plan as opposed to rehabilitation through monetary compensation, Ghosh[19] emphasizes that tribal governance continues to rely on an understanding of indigenes as unable to understand and transact with money. Unlike in some contexts in settler-colonial North America, Adivasis have not had access to capital that unsettles their position at the lowest rung in the socioeconomic order.[20] Yet, it would be a mistake to equate the relative material absence of money with a conceptual and symbolic absence of money as an organizing discourse of indigeneity. While ethnographic and policy accounts are rife with references to the economic exploitation of Adivasis, these accounts rarely theorize discourses of money and indigeneity that undergird commerce and market exchange. They also uncritically reproduce the colonial view of tribals as untainted by the worldly ways of depraved market exchange and therefore naturally perennially exploited by those savvier in commerce, including Panas and moneylenders under colonialism as well as landlords in the modern Indian state.[21]

Adding to recent anthropological investigations by scholars such as Jessica Cattelino who have engaged discourses of money to show how contemporary indigeneity is both challenged and claimed by indigenous communities,[22] I now turn to how these historical discourses of money and indigeneity inform contemporary Adivasi claims to capital. These claims are enabled by a language of rights and entitlements secured by indigenous recognition and the extent to which indigenous recognition acts within, rather than against, the logics of the market that economically disenfranchise Adivasis. Crucially, these developments argue for the clear disarticulation of political and economic empowerment within Adivasi communities, leading to, in the words of Nancy Fraser, recognition without economic redistribution.

The Kandhas in Market Society

British colonists linked tribals' grasp of materiality to an embodied violent primitivity, which they saw to be most evident in Kandhas' practice of meriah human sacrifice. The Kandhas relied on Panas for economic liaison between the Kandhas and an "outside" world of colonial moneylenders, caste Hindu traders, and landowners,[23] which resulted in Kandhas' delayed introduction into market exchange. Painted with the brushstrokes of romantic primitivism as noble savages, Kandhas were subjected to pacification and censure of their violent proclivities, with the colonial institution of the Meriah Agency to stop the "barbaric savagery" of meriah sacrifice.[24] At the same time, colonists cast them as honest and laborious but not "clever enough" to handle the marketing of the products of their agrarian toil,[25] their encounters with commerce always mediated through exploitative and canny others, most prominently Panas.

While Kandhas were considered to lack a grasp of the material world, Panas were understood as materially canny in dangerous ways, tainted by the cunning of commerce. The unequal yet symbiotic relationship between Kandhas and Panas that had begun to sour with the colonial ban on meriah human sacrifice appeared to have become more fraught when Panas were more readily able to enter the modern market economy, aided by greater knowledge of centers and material practices of commerce, than Kandhas, who had long relied on Panas as economic liaisons.[26] This differential readiness for the market economy fundamentally disrupted Kandha social relations with Panas, who were no longer dependent upon Kandhas for their livelihood and were able to take up a number of vocations, while the economic power of Kandhas was increasingly limited by their attempts to engage in state-enforced settled agriculture.

Until the early nineteenth century, Kandhas transacted business chiefly through barter,[27] with money largely used only for ornamentation. By the end of the nineteenth century, the money economy had entirely replaced the barter system, and Kandhas sold their commodities for and made purchases with money. Their precapitalist characterization, however, lingered through the transition from colonial rule into the modern Indian state. Colonial constructions of Kandhas' inability to grasp materiality and transact in the marketplace were layered with caste Hindus and state officials' insistence that Kandhas were unable to exchange commensurable value and, more broadly, unable to transact with money.

As tribal areas opened up to caste Hindu "outsiders" who wished to acquire land to maximize production, Kandhas parted with their lands for sums far below their market value. As a result, it appeared that Kandhas were unable to understand that the terms of land mortgages were unfavorable to them and resulted in the seizure of their lands, turning them into a landless proletariat.[28] Local feudal chiefs, rajas, and even local government officials exploited tribal labor under the *bethi* system of feudal servitude, engaging Kandhas in clearing jungle and building roads for little to no sums of money. This feudal system naturalized, even for Kandhas themselves, the idea that their labor ought to be free for those with authority over them, who were consequently owed customary services.[29]

Kandhas traditionally practiced slash-and-burn shifting cultivation, or poddu chaasa, a practice banned by colonial forest-use acts. Fearing environmental imbalances and consequent impact on the state economy if this ban was lifted, the modern Indian state continued it.[30] This required Kandhas to start using more rooted agrarian practices and increasingly limited them to state-enforced settled agriculture, which was never entirely successful in meeting the community's needs. Although the ban had been lifted the year before my arrival in Kandhamal with the institution of the landmark Forest Rights Act in 2006,[31] when I was there colonial signage with details of the ban was still visible in the surrounding forests, and Kandhas expressed surprise on being informed that the ban had been lifted, reporting no knowledge of the legislation that had secured their rights. In the decades during the ban, Kandhas were subsistence farmers, mostly of kandula legumes and rice for their own consumption, which they supplemented by gathering forest produce like honey, roots, and berries for their own consumption and for sale in weekly haatas (markets).

These haatas served as crucial nodes of commercial exchange, where Kandhas sold produce, forest products, timber, and firewood. They also bought everyday objects from vendors—brightly colored plastic vessels, dried fish, and vegetables transported from other districts. In so doing, they engaged in sophisticated economic transactions that connected the local economy to state and national commercial networks. Moreover, haatas were integral to Kandha sociality. At the weekly haata, Kandhas bantered festively and interacted with people from other villages and districts, making it clear that economic exchange bolstered rather than eroded sociality within indigenous communities, as colonists feared.[32] As I chatted with Kandhas going about their trade in haatas, it became clear to me that they were sophisticated participants within market society despite the challenges they faced because of restrictive lifestyle shifts under colonial and modern Indian legislation.

Even so, the tenacious representational economy that suffused the socio-economic fabric of Kandhamal hinged on Kandhas' racialized figuration as lacking a grasp of money and materiality. Their supposed inability to understand money and, consequently, true value and rational means-end calculation was considered a sign of their slothful recalcitrance. Oftentimes, in the same breath, they were lauded as being "simple yet honest" by state officials and caste Odias, including local ethnonationalist workers, who valorized their incorruptibility by capital in a context in which development had reduced minority residents to being "beggars ready for the next handout," as ethnonationalists would say in order to explain how they had become easy prey for missions.

The Kandhas and the Indian Development State

Since the formation of the modern Indian state in 1947, tribal development has transitioned from the Nehruvian ideal of noninterference and gradualism[33] to a form of governmentality[34] reinforced by multiple stakeholders: state agencies, NGOs, transnational development organizations, and faith-based organizations.[35] In Kandhamal, these included national agencies like the Integrated Tribal Development Agency, regional institutions like the Orissa Tribal Empowerment and Livelihood Program, transnational organizations like the World Bank and United Nations, and faith-based organizations like World Vision. While the multitude of development agencies implies a recession in the welfare functions of the state and a consequent decline in state-led patronage of minority citizens' development, the state continued to loom large as the chief patron of tribal development in Kandhamal. Several Kandhas used the English word "develop," usually in the refrain "How will we develop/get developed?" (*Aame kemiti* develop *hebu?*), directly indicting the *sarkaar* (government) as their chief benefactor, who could do "everything" but was choosing to "do nothing" (*sarkaar aama pain sabu kari paribe kentu aama pain kicchi karu nahanti*) to secure their economic advancement.

At the state-run Kutia Kandha Development Agency in Belghar, I inquired about the agency's work in the region. An official shrugged and said, "It may not seem like much to you but the fact that we have been able to make adibasis wash themselves and wear clothes is itself a very big thing. They are just too ignorant and simple-minded." State officials often resorted to plainspoken, racialized characterizations of Kandhas as "simple adibasis," who impeded the successful implementation of state-run schemes because their superstitious primitivity made them recalcitrant to rational logics of development. Cynically bemoaning their inability to do work of value in state-led tribal development,[36] local officials pointed to the futility of Adivasi development through their continuing state of socioeconomic underdevelopment.

State officials used this shorthand of simplicity to stand in for the supposed ignorance and irrationality of Adivasis, locating the failure of state development in their inability to receive schemes targeted toward their welfare. Adivasis occupied a primitive temporality distinct from mainstream Indian society, they insisted, and were governed by primitive cosmologies irreconcilable with the workings of modern development institutions and governance. As a block development officer explained to me, "Look, madam, there is only so much you can explain [to them]. Take, for example, the matter of cultivation. Every year we conduct agricultural practices training for these people: how to practice irrigation, how not to let your livestock wander around so they do not graze on your fields, how to pick vegetables that can be grown with less water. But after that, they go right back to doing what they were doing. Teaching them new things is useless. They cannot understand these things, so it is difficult to make them change."

He added that Kandhas were so simple that they were easily conned. "They sign over their land for a bottle of liquor. How can you make such a person understand anything?" The officer used the Kandhas' seemingly glaring misapprehension of value in failing to see the incommensurability between a piece of land and a bottle of liquor. In so doing, he emphasized that the ideal subject of the development state was able to grasp exchange and value in modern market society and that the failure to do so was a failure to benefit from development.

Noting repeated references to "simplicity" and "failed" economic transactions, I pressed state officials and development workers about how they understood this simplicity of Adivasis. They supplied a cluster of traits around economic exchange and value: an inability to become canny in commerce, a lack of means-ends rationality that made them unsuccessful in their farming labor, and an inability to understand true value. They cited transactions in which Kandhas failed to exchange commensurate value, such as selling land for a bottle of liquor, gold for grains, and forest produce for a pittance of its market value. Here, state officials were invoking modern money not as a literal currency form but rather as a semiotic system of market society, believing development to mandate the mastery of the modern economy, which Kandhas were seemingly unable to exhibit.

As Taylor Nelms and Bill Maurer point out, the mastery of money is a process of psychological transformation, the inculcation of a disposition of readiness for the market economy, including "the imposition of impersonal, rational, instrumental, calculative modes of thought and comparison; the detachment of human beings from the world of things; and the 'hollowing out' and weakening of social relations and promotion of individualism."[37] Drawing on Georg Simmel's[38] characterization of money as "transform[ing] the world into an arithmetic problem," they remind us that, in market society, the mastery of modern money is synonymous with the inculcation of mental dispositions oriented toward quantitative means-ends calculation of self-interest. Most state officials used Adivasis' perceived failure to engage in successful self-interested exchange as a marker of their inability to develop the necessary psychocultural traits to benefit from the development state's interventions. Most surmised that Adivasi simplicity was essentially an inability to become "worldly," which made them honest, gullible, and incorruptible by capital and, thus, unable to become worthy recipients of state patronage that would enable them to flourish in contemporary market society.

State officials said little, however, about the state's paternalistic protection of Adivasis against exploitation. State literature purports that the purpose of tribal development, and the institution of bodies such as the Integrated Tribal Development Agencies, includes the protection of Adivasis against exploitation, echoing the ideals of Nehruvian protectionism. In Kandhamal, however, there appeared to be little emphasis on the role of the state as paternalistic protector. Instead, state and nonstate development officials emphasized that development demanded the successful navigation of the market economy and the commensurate exchange of value. For instance, several NGOs in the region had instituted a microcredit model, giving small sums of money as loans for "livelihood generation," most frequently to groups of women who used them to buy sewing machines or livestock. Microcredit was a widely prevalent model of development thought to encourage entrepreneurship, fiscal responsibility, and financial ownership.

Kandhas, however, were often excluded from microcredit schemes. NGO officials explained the particular challenges of "doing development work" among Kandhas through the Kandhas' supposed inability to handle money. Insisting that the enterprise of indigenous development could not rely on Kandhas' understanding of money, NGO workers spoke of the need to engage Kandhas on terms that recognized the distinction of their heritage as prideful Adivasis rooted in their land but ultimately not well versed in worldly matters of commerce. Like state officials, they described Kandhas as difficult to engage through contemporary development models.

Kandha and Caste Hindu Economic Relations

If the weekly haata was a time of joyous social and economic exchange for Kandha tribals, then the town *bajaar* (marketplace) was the setting for the reinscription of tribals as primitives who were intoxicated and unproductive, incapable of mastering true value, and, therefore, misfits in contemporary market society. In Kandhamal, while tribal individuals had primary ownership over land, commercial businesses and trade continued to be controlled by caste Hindus—Brahmins, Sahus, Karanas—from outside the district. These businesses included the trading of kandula legumes and *siali* leaf plates made by Kandhas and forest produce, such as leaves, roots, honey, and, prominently, *mahuli* liquor. Odia caste Hindu shopkeepers also ran the smattering of shops close to village squares that constituted the bajaar: grocery stores with rice, lentils, and dry goods; a few housewares stores; and meals-ready places where travelers could eat. These shops mostly catered to caste Hindus, passing traders, and administrative officials.

Few Adivasis could afford goods from these shops; instead, they usually waited for the weekly haata to make their few purchases. The bajaar, however, was where some Kandha men bought the popular mahuli liquor, now brewed more strongly with the addition of cheap "spirit"—a too readily available chemical-based alcohol that catalyzed fermentation and produced a state of deeper intoxication than the traditional brews. Staggering home from the bajaar, some Kandha men would wander into the town square, shout insults and endearments at one another, and occasionally break into song. On such occasions, one could often find them requesting food at a tea stall and being rudely shoved away by the shopkeeper. Caste Hindus would often say, "These Kandhas—tell me how can they improve. They just drink and lie around, they do not know how to do, how will they develop, you tell me." At these moments, Adivasis' drunken inebriation, which colonial officials deemed the definitional "primitive" condition of excess and irrationality,[39] was a "statist symbol of savagery."[40] Caste Hindu onlookers repeated laments about how indigenous peoples were "useless" and unskilled at construing value—of money, time, property—and therefore "wasteful."[41]

One hot afternoon, seated at a meals-ready canteen in the Baliguda bajaar, I watched a Kandha man stagger in and demand a meal. With a look of annoyance, the Odia proprietor asked him to be quiet, commenting that his improper conduct would get him thrown out rather than seated at a table. Almost immediately, the Kandha man responded to the accusations of incivility and impropriety by invoking money. "What do you mean? I have money!" he shouted. "*Ei brahmuna*, why are you not listening to me? I have money. Give me meat! Give me meat, fish, and rice. Give me all that you have!" The proprietor asked him how much money he had. When the Kandha man announced that he had five rupees, the proprietor scoffed, saying that the Kandha would be lucky to get a morsel of plain rice for that sum. At that point, the Kandha man turned to all those present with a laugh at once self-mocking and cynical and said to them, "See, you can all see, the Brahmin will take every penny I have but still will not give me anything."

At face value, this encounter seemed like any other between a shopkeeper and an inebriated and potentially disruptive customer who could not afford the merchandise. But this interaction contained valences shaped by a long-standing history of caste Hindu and tribe relations structured by inequities in economic exchange and development. The caste Hindu proprietor disparaged the Kandha man as not only impoverished and lacking funds but also lacking a grasp of the value of goods in the marketplace, while drawing attention to man's drunken figure as irrational and unproductive. At the same time, the inebriated Kandha quite lucidly invoked a history in which the caste Hindu would extract all his funds from him but never reciprocate the exchange in commensurate value.

Economic exploitation had come to be an organizing discourse for caste-tribe relations in Kandhamal in a deeply visceral way for the Kandha community, even though there have existed modes of patronage and exchange between Kandha and caste Odia groups that exceed narratives of exploitation, including political patronage by Hindu kingship as well as cultural and religious exchange.[42] Kandhas often reiterated that their simplicity and naivete had led them to be repeatedly exploited by caste Hindus in commercial forest-produce transactions and the wrongful seizing of lands. Insisting that "nothing much has changed," they characterized their current state of underdevelopment as a direct outcome of this long history of socioeconomic oppression.

Contemporary development in Kandhamal, as in other parts of India, ordered caste Hindus and tribes using a teleological link between civilization and economic development, in which Kandhas were primitives needing to be civilized and developed, while caste Hindus were already civilized and, therefore, "developed." Development officials actively fused these teleological colonial, casteist, and developmentalist understandings to fix Adivasis as both natural prey for caste Hindu exploitation and failed recipients of the development state. As other scholars have observed, the Indian development state is complicit in the continuation of class-based frameworks in which feudal systems get converted into privileged relationships between elites and the state, institutionalizing class and caste privilege to the detriment of Adivasis.[43]

This caste-state nexus is the very engine that motors continuities from the state as the site of primitive accumulation to an accomplice of Indian neoliberal capitalism. Gopal Pradhan, a Brahmin from coastal Orissa, ran a jewelry store in the Baliguda bajaar, while being frequently delinquent in his role as a local government schoolteacher. He candidly explained to me that he did not really need the income from the teacher position but had taken it because of the pension benefits. Pradhan manned his shop all day and only sporadically went into the school, perhaps once a week, when he knew there might be inspections or visitors. "What do the children do all day?" I inquired. He explained that the school was a safe place for the Kandha villagers to leave their young children while they worked in the fields or went into the forest to gather produce. The school provided rice and lentils for a midday meal, cooked by the children themselves. This, he said, was enough to ensure the children's attendance.

Pradhan opined that the Kandha were "very simple" and prone to getting conned by merchants: "They have very little understanding of money, what the actual value of things are." He gave the example of Kandha villagers pawning their gold or silver jewelry to him for a bottle of mahuli liquor or money to buy grains. Like so many state officials, Pradhan pointed to the seemingly absurd incommensurability of value in that exchange. Not only did he pejoratively and erroneously characterize Kandhas' acceptance of terms of unfavorable exchange due to economic deprivation as a failure to grasp true value, he also seemed oblivious to the fact that his own economic success was predicated on Kandhas' continued economic exploitation. By his own admission, most Kandhas left gold and silver items at his shop for a few rupees, never reclaiming their pawned items until Pradhan sold them as "antiques" for a substantial profit to the occasional foreigner.

Pradhan, like other caste Hindus, believed that Kandhamal's underdeveloped condition could be squarely blamed on the Kandhas because of their inability to understand and benefit from governance and economic policies. Pradhan described Kandhas as having become, in some sense, rulers of Kandhamal—rajas. In his view, the renaming of Kandhamal not only gave Kandhas proprietary land rights but also refocused attention on the primacy of Kandha claims to more than land and territory. Pradhan quickly returned to lamenting that Kandhas were unable to prosper despite their recognition: "They are the main people here, they are not learning, they are not prospering, how will Kandhamal as a whole prosper? But now they own everything, the government has made them *raja* [king] and us *praja* [the ruled/the public]. But how will making them *raja* help, when they do not understand the world?"

Caste Hindus like Pradhan frequently glossed over Kandhas' insistence that caste Hindus' continuing economic exploitation of them was a major reason for Kandhas' current economic standing. Instead, they echoed state officials and located the underdevelopment of the district in the Kandhas' inability to become worldly subjects, neglecting issues of administrative failure as well as lack of local infrastructure and industrial growth. Through such statements, caste Hindus fixed Kandhas not only as the reason for their own underdevelopment but also as scapegoats for Kandhamal's lack of economic progress.

In Baliguda, a single road snaked its way through the *chakka* (square) into town, carrying life through and past its dusty landscape. In the shanty and concrete shops that flanked this narrow road, the unexplainable authority and precariousness of money was visible. Some shops sold containers and kitchenware, from the plastic water carriers that mimicked traditional earthenware to aluminum vessels. Among these items were emptied plastic mineral-water bottles, some dangling by a string and priced at two rupees, while others had been cut in half to form tumblers and were priced at fifty paise. These were objects that could be, and perhaps were, scavenged from the piles of plastic refuse that testified to the arrival of modern material culture and consumption in Kandhamal. Yet, a price had been placed on them in this shanty shop, showing how other forms of value were created in response to Kandhas' perceived failure to master capitalist value—a clear sign of how capital's disproportionate accrual continued to thrive by engaging indigeneity as capitalist lack.

A shopkeeper explained, "The Kandhas like these. They think it is useful to carry water." He ended with an entrepreneurial wink as he said, "And if there is a market, I will supply," thus showcasing his homegrown version of a demand-and-supply relationship on which all commerce hinged. The shopkeeper's assertion that this seemingly valueless, scavenged item had value for Kandhas was synchronous with other statements about Kandhas' perceived miscomprehension of the value of material objects and resultant monetary transactions, which served as the very means of successful commerce, as in the case of the shopkeeper's plastic bottles. Yet, caste Hindus employed this poor understanding of money and material exchange to naturalize narratives of economic exploitation of Kandhas by Hindu upper castes as well as to explain the Kandhas' current state of economic underdevelopment.

Pradhan also gestured to shifting relations between caste Odias and Kandhas as a result of the strengthening of Adivasi identity and the political import of indigenous citizenship in the area. Although the indigeneity of Kandhas was a discourse dating back to colonial governance,[44] the renaming of Phulbani district as Kandhamal in 1992 ensured the primacy of Kandha land rights, giving Kandhas' state-backed status as rightful landowners. The renaming of the district under the Biju Patnaik–led state administration was itself a culmination of a long-brewing indigenous assertion by the Kandhas. While this renaming was not seen as a development of consequence for the Odisha state, it was a watershed moment for local indigenous politics and identity, in which indigeneity was specifically invoked to achieve political ends and deployed as a distinct identity category from which other minorities, most significantly Panas, should be excluded in order to protect Adivasi proprietary claims to autochthony. These shifts reflected the extent to which Kandhas were drawing from pan-national Adivasi politics to shape the discursive terrain in Kandhamal in order to impose limits on who could or could not claim adivasi status. Their maneuvers demonstrated their understanding of indigeneity as a position of sociopolitical privilege even with its attendant pejorative connotations.

Although seemingly inconsequential for national politics, the changes were part of a nationwide surge in the strengthening of indigenous identity with developments such the carving out of new states around adivasi identity,[45] proliferating claims to juridical recognition via the Scheduled Tribe category,[46] and increasing provisions through quotas in state schools and jobs.[47] These developments gestured to significant upheavals in Adivasi politics linked to India's economic liberalization, particularly in terms of the material and symbolic connections between political and economic rights.

Even as the renaming affirmed the land rights of Kandhas and a consequent strengthening of indigenous identity and politics, it did not necessarily translate into greater economic rights or mobility for Kandhas. Local residents insisted, however, that the renaming of Kandhamal was symbolically and materially significant because it effectively positioned upper castes as an ethnic minority, leading them to newly realize that Kandhas' indigenous claims might unsettle their dominance and make them "lower" than Kandhas—a disruption of great significance. Caste Hindu locals voiced feelings of instability, mindful that they occupied land "belonging" to Kandhas and were in some ways subject to their "rule." Although Dalit politics, too, had progressed, its growth had been stymied, as Panas were derecognized as Scheduled Castes upon conversion to Christianity. This loss of recognition and the resultant near absence of discourses of political ascendency and uplift, many Panas reported, had enervated Dalit politics and identity.

Along with state officials, caste Hindus had now come to commonsensically proclaim the primacy of Kandha land rights as paramount. Kandhas' claims to land and their acceptance even by exploitative caste Hindus sharply contrasted with the situation of the landless Panas, who were perennially slotted as outsiders and squatters on Kandha land. Recalling stories that their elders had told them, Kandhas spoke of their long history of economic exploitation by caste Hindu landlords and traders who had tricked them out of their lands, even as these transactions were explained away by caste Hindus who insisted that Kandhas had handed over their lands for a sack of rice or, worse, a bottle of liquor without coercion.

While caste Hindu acknowledgment of Kandha land rights was an important shift both symbolically and economically, it did not evenly secure Kandhas' economic empowerment. Kandhas continued to be characterized as incapable of comprehending true value, including that of their "rightfully owned" land. As Ghosh notes, indigenous sovereignty in India is understood, or rather undermined, both by the paternalistic state and by upper castes with recourse to the formulation that "[A]divasis know how to live on land but are incapable of handling money."[48] Despite their acknowledgment of Adivasi property rights and grudging acceptance of Kandhas as rightful owners, even as "kings" of local lands, caste Hindus viewed Kandhas as unable to fully capitalize on their powerful indigenous status because of their inability to master money. This simple characterization of Kandhas constantly eclipsed the mandates of indigenous identity and its new political iconicity.

While state officials and caste Hindus invoked the simplicity of Kandhas to naturalize their disenfranchised position within the local economy, Kandhas believed that their community had been exploited because of their inability to be wily, a trait they saw as essential for success in economic transactions in the marketplace and for accumulation of profit. Older Kandhas claimed that they really had been simple in the past, because their ancestors lacked the knowledge to judge the fair price for their land or their produce due to their delayed transition to commercial transactions from a barter economy.[49] Some others asserted that they were aware of the true value of their possessions all along and the extent to which they were being cheated but were too oppressed and intimidated to ask for their due.

Older Kandhas insisted that the younger generation was challenging the social order in which they had become slotted as perennially exploited. Sura, a sixty-year-old man, reported a distinct shift: "Earlier, we never complained, we were okay being who we are. We had ordinary needs. Maybe that is why there were fewer problems. But now, everyone knows more, wants more." His young grandson, Biju, added, "We were forgotten in the world out there. This is why we are like frogs in a well, no one knows about us. Only we know what we should have, what is rightfully due to us, no one else does."

Sura often issued statements that were veiled criticisms of the increasing discontent among Kandha youth, lamenting that despite Kandhas' exploitation, they had been happier in the past and more content with their life outside circuits of commerce and capital. Despite more education and awareness, he said, he could only see young Kandhas using an incendiary language to express dissatisfaction with their economic circumstances. It was such dissatisfaction that led Biju to draw on the folk icon of the *kupamanduka*, from an Odia parable, to describe Kandhas as trapped in the dark well of Kandhamal. In the parable, the kupamanduka lives his life largely in the falsely secure confines of his world, thinking himself and his life to be complete. As the tale goes, the kupamanduka is deluded and ignorant, for he is not king of all that he surveys. He is, in fact, trapped in a world of darkness, unaware of the better life that lies beyond his myopic surveying. Biju referred to Kandhas as "kupamandukas," indicating that younger Kandhas were acutely aware that their elders' contentment was a myopic happiness that had been replaced by their more "realistic" assessment of their world as it was seen by others—darkened by deprivation.

These differing generational perceptions demonstrated just how different younger Kandhas' understanding and deployment of indigeneity were from those of previous generations. Older Kandhas commonsensically understood their Adivasi status as indigenous but did not claim it using the same vocabulary of entitlements younger Kandhas did, nor did they see their patronage from the state as necessarily tied to their ability to participate in the market economy. While older generations often declared themselves resigned to the economic exploitation that seemed fated for the community (*aamara bhagya*), younger Kandhas marshaled an incendiary language of rights and ownership to both criticize their exploitation in market exchange and claim capital circulating through circuits of development.

Both older and younger Kandhas insisted that their community's "simplicity" was a marker of their moral superiority that distinguished them from exploitative caste Hindus and valorized their own incorruptibility by capital. At the same time, Kandha youth voiced anger about being denied their economic due to stake their claims anew. They described instances in which they were acutely aware that their land was being "stolen" for a fraction of its worth or that a caste Hindu moneylender was imposing disproportionately high terms of interest for a loan but were forced to agree to the exchange because of immediate financial need.

For younger Kandhas, clearly, the assertion of economic claims in market exchange and entitlements as indigenous citizens reinforced one another. They insisted that they were well aware not only of their ownership of land and its value but also that adibasis should not and could not be easily intimidated by caste Hindus; they would assert their fair due. Nor would they allow Panas to encroach upon their Scheduled Tribe status and gain the same entitlements as them. As Biju said, "After years of exploitation, we are slowly beginning to get our due. And now Panas want it too? They worked for us but they exploited us. Now they are saying their suffering is the same as us? How can it be the same? They have a different history. They do not belong to the land and the land does not belong to them. These lands are ours. Ask anyone, they will tell you. Panas are not Adivasis. They never have been, their land was not stolen from them, they always worked for money, for material gain. We never worked for money, we worked for our land."

Sitting around the Baliguda square one day, I was listening to alcohol-fueled, angry shouting of slogans as several Kandha men vociferously pointed out how state officials had denied them their due as adibasis. In the midst of their heated statements, a shift took place, and some Kandha men began describing how upper-caste Hindus had economically exploited them for years. One man, Galaa, alternated between the roles of Hindu upper-caste trader and duped Adivasi peasant in a highly emotive performance. Alternately shouting as the trader and cowering as the peasant, he enacted how an Odia trader would buy *kendu* leaves and forest produce for a few paise by intimidating the Kandha, who could not claim his rightful due.

Puffing up to embody authority as the trader, Galaa barked at an imaginary figure on the ground, *"Ei* Kandha, give me those leaves for two rupees." Shifting to the ground, he cowered with exaggerated fear as the Kandha and said, "Take it, *mai-baap*."[50] Galaa spoke of humble leaf plates selling for "thousands," conjuring up a dark fantasy of an insurmountable impasse between Kandhas' grasp of money and the canny ways of the "modern" market economy. He shouted, "Now look what has happened—the trader made his money selling our goods for thousands and thousands of rupees and look where we are! Just because we are simple and trusting! Look how we live!" Galaa's performance clearly showed that, for Kandhas, their denial of mastery of money and a desire for capital had begun to bleed into each other. His enactment vividly demonstrated how the struggle over indigenous recognition between the Kandhas and the Panas had revitalized long-simmering discontents in the Kandha community about their continuing economic marginalization.

As Kandhas drew attention to the modalities and perpetrators of their exploitation, they forcefully contrasted their simplicity with the immoral and cunning ways of caste Hindus and Panas who had exploited them. Kandhas themselves invoked their simplicity to insist that they did not have monetary greed and thus did not know how to cheat people for monetary profit. They had not been, and could not be, tainted by capital, they said, valorizing their own morality and uncritically reproducing tropes about the socially and morally corrosive effects of money. At the same time, they voiced resentment about the exclusion of Kandhas from networks of capital, asserting that they were being denied the development that was "rightfully theirs." Speaking of "their money" taken away by moneylenders, petty traders, Panas, and now state officials, they used a language of ownership that signaled a distinct shift in how Kandhas positioned themselves in a local socioeconomic hierarchy: from simple people who could not be faulted for their inability to understand economic transactions, to indigenes who were aware of their entitlements both in the marketplace and from the state and who would no longer be kept outside circulations of capital. It was in these claims that Kandhas' leaning into recognition and capitalism became most visible, making clear the extent to which recognition carried the force of the market within it.

These generational differences were not without ambivalence, and regardless of the sophisticated shifts in their understanding of money's pragmatics in the local economy,[51] Kandhas continued to express ambivalence about money's meaning. For older Kandhas, discussions about a seemingly growing materialism among the young became occasions to discuss the decline of youth interest in community practices. Parents spoke of their children hankering for cycles and radios, for city riches, which could only be slaked with money, and linked it to growing disinterest in Kandha traditions.

In a clear, bell-like voice, Sura sang a Kui song about the hills (*dongaras*) that surrounded Kandha villages. Sighing as bittersweet nostalgia overcame him, he said, "Who wants to learn this song anymore? Young people today want transistors and cycles; they do not want what we wanted. We try to teach them, but their mind is somewhere else. They are already elsewhere." Often these conversations ended with older Kandhas emphasizing the need to preserve practices, such as youth dormitories and ritualized song and dance. Kandha elders insisted that interest in these practices had waned among their youth, who seemed too preoccupied with rejecting a Kandha past marked by economic exploitation to take pride in those aspects of their heritage that could never be grasped through money and commerce, which, as one man said, was where their real sanskruti (civilization/culture) resided.

This economic exploitation continued also to color their interactions with Panas, as Kandhas insisted that the Pana bids for indigenous recognition were merely another tactic of Kandha exploitation, which threatened to usurp their proprietary indigeneity and, thus, their rightful due. In our conversations, Panas acknowledged the continuation of economic inequities that favored caste Hindu economic dominance, but only in halting and hushed tones in settings where neither Kandhas nor caste Hindus were present. Santosh Digal, my journalist friend who had attempted to convey just how Pana identity functioned as an interminable and inescapable scourge, was careful to point out that, unlike Kandhas, Panas lacked the political power with which to assert their dissatisfaction with these inequities.

Panas denied the charges of exploiting Kandhas by insisting that they, too, were struggling economically and desirous of development. They had tried to help, rather than swindle, Kandhas by being their emissaries when "they did not have knowledge of an outside world." Their close proximity to, and oftentimes inextricability from, Kandha life and livelihood meant that they too continued to endure economic hardships and suffered alongside them. Yet, when Panas tried to speak up against caste Hindus, their alleged history of cunning chicanery was invariably invoked to foreground their role as economic liaisons between Kandhas and upper castes and as instrumental in the economic exploitation of Kandhas.

Pana reluctance to discuss the past was clear. It was only after several months had passed that I could press my Pana interlocutors about their relative silence compared to Kandhas' volatile and voluble assertions about caste Hindu economic dominance. They tepidly acknowledged persisting inequalities but returned to the unspeakability of their past, which enervated their political claims. To furnish defenses against their characterization by Kandhas and caste Hindus as economically exploitative and materialistic, Panas would have to dredge up a "dangerous" history in which they emerged only as wily, treacherous, and exploitative. It was such an unspeakability of the past for Panas, Santosh Digal often lamented, that had resulted in indigenous politics far outpacing Dalit self-determination. Kandhas deployed a politicized language as Adivasis, reaching deep into their historical exploitation to articulate their claims with force, as Panas became ever more vigilant about the dangers of history, forced to stay silent about the continued economic hegemony of caste Hindus.

Often my discussions with my Kandha and Pana interlocutors became too heavily weighed down by these differing, contentious claims. At those times, I would attempt to reorient myself by seeking a perspective that was neither Kandha nor Pana, by consulting with Bijoy Behera, a journalist who belonged to the barber (*nai*) caste, whose juridical classification was Other Backward Caste. Behera became a vital interlocutor and facilitator for me, as he allowed me to shadow him on his travels to remote highland villages to conduct what he ambiguously referred to as "press work." Though Behera's own caste classification as an Other Backward Class acknowledged socioeconomic underdevelopment and ensured provisions for affirmative action, he rued that his recognition did not come with the powerful political iconicity of the Adivasi as indigene.

Behera complained that he and others like him were truly disenfranchised. They were neither wealthy and exploitative like upper castes nor able to claim the political visibility and land entitlements that came with indigenous recognition. He issued a caveat for times to come, when the tyranny of caste Hindus and state officials would come to an end: "The Kandha, he was once blind, now he is no longer blind/he is no longer that blind (*Kandha kebe thila andha, au nahin sei andha*)." Behera insisted that Kandhas had been "blind" to the circulation of capital in the district because of their simplicity.

Now as Kandhas plainly "saw" the inequities in the distribution of capital, their feelings of being left behind, of never being able to access development and material uplift even when it was "right in front of their eyes," had brought them to the brink of "something big." Behera did not deny Panas' dilemma but affirmed that it was necessary for Kandhas to demand and safeguard their entitlements, despite their incendiary nature. The Panas, he said, had managed to progress through conversion to Christianity, a phenomenon I detail in the next chapter, accessing education, capital, and a better future for their children through missions. Yet Kandhas had gone "nowhere." Unable to materially advance through mission services and state development, Kandhas lagged behind economically despite the great momentum gained by Adivasi politics in the wake of indigenous recognition. Like an overwhelming number of locals, Behera, then, upheld Kandha economic claims over those of Panas.

"Why do you think they are reacting so angrily to Panas right now?" he asked. "Adivasis are no longer the stupid simpletons everyone thinks they are, they know what is going on and they are not going to take it anymore. These Panas, these caste Hindus, they think they can take something from the Kandhas? No more!"

Recognition Without Redistribution

Nancy Fraser famously asserted the bivalent nature of both gender and race as collectivities, encompassing both political-economic dimensions and cultural-valuational dimensions and, thus, implicating both redistribution and recognition.[52] Although Fraser aimed to be critical of economic as well as cultural reductionism, her approach was soundly critiqued for subordinating the politics of culture and identity to economic concerns.[53] It became evident in Kandhamal that the political-economic and cultural dimensions of race were inseparable in consolidating the disenfranchisement of Kandhas. Fraser's separation of these valences, however, allows us to see how processes of recognition may *appear* to secure political empowerment for subjects of recognition, while failing to ameliorate and instead even furthering economic disenfranchisement. These uneven effects of recognition for Adivasis attest to the toothlessness, and even the seductive dangers, of recognition in securing attachments among its subjects even while hardening racial authenticity and failing to ensure economic commensuration.

These false promises of recognition in securing economic redistribution are hardly contradictory if we understand indigenous recognition to be fully implicated within the logic of capitalism and, thus, serving only to further the destructive effects of capital, as argued by Glen Coulthard.[54] And yet, though recognition was unable to dismantle a racialized Adivasiness as a condition of political-economic disenfranchisement, Kandhas clung to the language of recognition and proprietary indigeneity. Indeed, recognition's failures only seemed to make Kandhas again turn to it for commensuration and justice.[55] Their racialized figuration as lacking a mastery of money circulated despite their indigenous recognition, providing new scripts for novel forms of state and market coercion and extraction.

Moreover, Kandhas' patronage by a withholding development state that increasingly engaged market logics was also consolidated by recognition, suggesting that Kandhas occupy a neoliberal indigeneity to receive the state's development. Sharply contrasting the paradigmatic neoliberal retreat of a thinning state[56] and minorities' definitive turn away from the state toward the market, recognition and the imperative of indigenous development seemingly catalyzed Kandhas' political visibility as indigenes while making them turn toward, rather than away from, the neoliberal state and the market.

For Kandhas, recognition's failure to effect economic redistribution and its seeming potential for securing their political ascendency uneasily coexisted in an uneven terrain of neoliberal multiculturalism "without guarantees."[57] This terrain was coming to have unforeseen and counterintuitive consequences, both for Kandhas themselves as well as for Panas, whose politics were being steadily outpaced by the unstable progression of indigenous politics.

CHAPTER 3

Duplicitous Dalits

While Kandhas as Scheduled Tribes received tribal recognition regardless of their religious identification, Panas inquired as to why they could not access recognition as converts to Christianity. Panas hesitantly acknowledged that their social marginality continued to mark them within their Christian faith. Yet residents of Kandhamal widely invoked Pana converts' derecognition to assert that conversion must be dramatically improving Dalits' economic status, thus, and be the reason the state had "decided" that it was no longer necessary to provide for them.

The derecognition of Dalit converts has impacted Panas since the adoption of the Indian Constitution and the 1950 Presidential Order that made recognition through the Scheduled Caste status dependent on Dalits needing to profess to be Hindu, excluding Muslim and Christian converts. According to local state officials, who were able to provide only approximate figures, almost 60 percent of Panas were Christians even prior to the formation of the modern Indian nation-state, another 20 percent had converted to denominations of Christianity over the years, and the rest were undeclared. A number of these recent Pana converts continued to use their Scheduled Caste status, but an overwhelming majority of Panas had never availed themselves of formal recognition through the Scheduled Caste category. Several Panas insisted that legal derecognition had secured a false perception of Christian converts as advancing economically through conversion, while stymying the adoption of a politicized Dalit identity.

Webb Keane argues that religions produce semiotic forms that are crucial to understanding religious proselytizing as a globalizing force.[1] The globalization of Protestant Christianity has been facilitated by the development of certain semiotic forms and ideologies, several of them inseparable from purportedly secular narratives of modernity. Keane details one such ideology as the creed form, characterized by the idea of having mastery over one's thoughts and the impetus to purify, which Bruno Latour asserts to be an impulse characteristic of modernity.[2] Drawing on Latour, Keane argues that the drive to purify the world of impure hybrid forms is best understood against the background of the religious themes; purification never succeeds and instead produces results that seem to be inherently unstable. Such failure and the inescapable materiality that semiotic form introduces into even the most transcendentalizing projects are acutely visible in conversion. This tension between materiality and transcendence is particularly significant for Dalits appear unable to inhabit a pure Christian modernity, characterized by solitary reflection and interiorized spiritual belief. Rather, their inability to put aside community interests and material suffering provides a space for a relentless project of failed Christian purification, a purification also sought by the law.

This chapter shows how this desire for purification traverses two distinct legal provisions: constitutional mandates securing the derecognition of Dalits and anti-conversion laws. Although these aspects of the law are not often put in dialogue with each other, these legal vectors intersect and cross-pollinate in their social circulation to reinforce an inalienable materialism of Dalits. As a paradigmatic figure embodying Dalit materialism, the derecognized Pana Christian becomes a flashpoint for the articulation of Christian and Hindu fears about Dalits as spurious converts with suspect motivations for conversion. This analysis, then, emphasizes the chimeric doubleness of the Dalit convert position within India. As both spurious Christian and national subjects, Dalits are constantly interrogated and doubted within the law, doubts that come to be mirrored within Hindu ethnonationalism.

Dalit Derecognition

My journalist friend Santosh Digal often fretted that Panas struggled to express pride in their culture, their heritage. Their heritage was inextricably intertwined with that of Kandhas but only through an insistence of Panas' canny, even criminal, materialism. A legacy of pariah-like untouchability had rendered Panas unable to articulate the positive dimensions of their identity and culture. Panas were gaining more exposure to an explicitly politicized rhetoric through nascent Ambedkarite politics—a growing awareness that Dalits needed to articulate an assertive politics based on self-respect, encouraged by the leadership and philosophy of Dalit icon Dr. B. R. Ambedkar.

Ambedkar's statues, busts, and teachings were increasingly revered in several Pana houses, signaling a growing adoption of Ambedkarite notions of Dalit political emancipation and self-assertion. This burgeoning politicization of Panas as Dalits was also informed by newly explicit dialogue between Christianity and Dalit identity that offered a vernacular liberation theology. This dialogue afforded Panas some understanding of their political rights as Dalits and a contextualization of their ritual untouchability as a product of systemic oppression in caste society.

Yet Santosh Digal grimly suggested that being oppressed could hardly be a source of pride in one's heritage. Panas, he insisted, struggled with an ability to stand up as a community, in many ways claiming loyalty to caste hierarchy before they could claim loyalty and kinship to one another. He continued, "Now young Panas are understanding that they are Dalits, they are getting a little knowledge about Ambedkar and his teachings, and the fact that as Dalits, they have rights. But if you think about it really, how can one be Pana and have pride in themselves when you are constantly reminded of how low you are, how bad you are, how immoral your ways are. Is it a surprise that Panas are fleeing from their past? Every day, I want to flee from it too."

Santosh Digal and other relatively socioeconomically mobile Panas spoke of how the Panas' distinctive identity stymied their politicization as Dalits and continued to be a source of casteist humiliation and discrimination. With the advent of Ambedkarite identity politics, a younger generation of Panas stressed the importance of being reclassified to attain economic uplift; to do so, they drew attention to the impossibility of political visibility for Panas as Dalits if they remained legally invisible. Through legal recognition through the tribal category and attendant entitlements to land, they would not only achieve economic uplift but also finally shrug off their continual xenophobic characterization as outsiders in Kandhamal. A number of Panas spoke about how conversion to Christianity had, in fact, all but erased Dalitness from their identity through their derecognition through the Scheduled Caste category, which made it difficult to establish a distinct Dalit platform for self-determination.

"Everyone knows us as Christians and Panas," they said to me. "Panas are now Christians but are we Dalits? We are only now understanding what it means to be Dalit because the law has stopped calling us Scheduled Caste. What are we? We are not Adivasi, we are not Dalit. We have lived alongside Kandhas, we have suffered as they have suffered, even now we live in the economic circumstances of Kandhamal just like they do. But we cannot say that we also need something."

Panas emphasized a central conundrum engaging Christian conversion, legal identity, and political visibility in Kandhamal that extended beyond the local particulars of the Pana identification. Even as they are understood to be outside the fourfold varna caste hierarchy, Dalits within the Indian state are marked as de facto Hindus, and their recognition through the Scheduled Caste category is contingent on this assumed Hindu position.[3] Conversion to other religions such as Islam and Christianity renders Dalits ineligible for recognition as Scheduled Castes and, indeed, positions them only as religious minorities rather than caste *and* religious minorities within the Indian nation-state. This legal disqualification was motivating Pana Dalits to understand recognition through the Scheduled Tribe category as a minority position of privilege allowing access to recognition regardless of their religious affiliation and also as original settlers, rather than outsiders, on the lands of Kandhamal.

Pana derecognition made them ineligible for quotas to receive jobs as cleaners, teachers' assistants, and peons. Moreover, derecognition disarticulated their Dalit identity from their Christian identity. Panas pointed out that there was no way of saying "Dalit Christian" or "Scheduled Caste Christian" using legal terms. The derecognition of Dalits upon conversion stymied their economic uplift, but it also disarticulated Dalit and Christian identities to render the chimeric Dalit Christian a figure that could not be named legally, and therefore, to be all the more distrusted socially. As Santosh Digal despaired, Panas were already distrusted as cunning mercenaries but were also visibly vulnerable as subjects of exclusion by the law, which compounded the social mistrust surrounding them.

To remedy their exclusion, Panas were seeking tribal rather than Scheduled Caste recognition. Panas were circulating petitions featuring thousands of signatures and thumb prints, and attempting to meet with officials in Phulbani and Bhubaneswar. These petitions were oftentimes circulated by local Pana pastors in their church, who had taken it upon themselves to get involved because they wished to address the abjection of their parishioners. When asked what motivated these bids, several Panas from Christian families who had converted before 1950 insisted that their grandparents and parents had questioned their exclusion from the tribal category from the very inception of Kandha recognition by returning again and again to the inextricability of the Pana from the Kandha condition. Over the years, educated Panas, including a prominent high-ranking officer in the Indian Administrative Service, had returned to the district to explain that it was unlikely that local

Panas' modest efforts at circulating paper petitions and approaching state officials in Phulbani would change constitutional criteria for the recognition and derecognition of Scheduled Castes.

After years of such discussions, Christian Panas understood their recognition through the Scheduled Caste status to be all but unattainable through due legal process. But from the very beginning of their exclusion from Scheduled Caste recognition and Kandhas' recognition, Panas wondered if their shared history with Kandhas might make them eligible for tribal recognition. Increasingly, younger Panas discussed tribal recognition with recourse not just to the freedom to practice their religion without derecognition but also to land rights. An overwhelming majority of Panas did not have official land titles. Though some Panas had built houses, the land on which they had built was not officially theirs. In fact, several were approaching local authorities and the block development officer to argue that their ownership of the houses indicated that they had settled on these lands and, thus, should be able to register formal land titles. But this was proving difficult for Panas to secure; Kandhamal's lands were seen as belonging to Kandhas, on which Panas were considered to be informal and illegal squatters.

Following the renaming of Kandhamal in 1992, Kandhas had steadily begun to seek land titles for the sites of their homes and small land holdings. This was a difficult and drawn out bureaucratic process, and not without significant difficulties for Kandhas who struggled to assert their claims with casteist local officials. With a growing and highly visible politics of indigeneity since the district's renaming, however, this slow process of formalization of ownership of land was aided by an understanding of Kandhas as rightful owners and original settlers on land in Kandhamal. Though land holdings were extremely modest, and often included rocky and mountainous land unsuitable for settled agriculture, a large number of Kandhas were dependent on agriculture as their primary livelihood, and grew turmeric and Kandula legumes, in addition to relying on forest foraging. Over 70 percent of all cultivable land in Kandhamal is owned by Kandhas. In the district, a long history of dispossession and economic exploitation by caste Hindus had begun to fray in discourse if not in practice with an increasingly prevalent notion in the district that caste Hindus could no longer maintain their caste dominance through ownership of shops and houses in town centers like Baliguda and felt unsettled as they now understood themselves as occupying Kandha lands. Contrasting this naturalization of, and now iconicity of Kandha indigenous rights to land, only 9 percent of the district's cultivable land is owned by Panas. While Kandhas were intimately identified with land, the Pana condition was one of chronic landlessness. With no naturalized claims to land, Panas infrequently sharecropped and rented land from Kandhas, and a small number worked the fields of their landowning Kandha neighbors. However, largely, Pana landlessness had only further driven them away from agriculture toward employment in municipal offices, local schools, and mission institutions, which ironically in some ways, provided upward mobility that was difficult to secure through Kandhas' difficult agrarian toil but also was unable to resolve Pana lack of land as both property and home.

Tribal recognition promised the accordance of land rights that would provide economic stability as well as reprieve from the xenophobic characterization of Panas as outsiders. Panas also saw it as securing freedom from caste stigma. More recent Pana converts who still used their Scheduled Caste status remarked that the Scheduled Tribe category did not carry the stigma of untouchability and extreme marginality in caste society, which the Scheduled Caste category had been unable to resolve and had, indeed, even reinscribed for Dalits. Bijoy Digal, a young Pana man, had just returned from the capital city of New Delhi, where he had been chosen from his parish to attend a pan-Indian congress of Christian youth. Bijoy stressed that while Christian faith leaders were now trying to speak of the Dalit condition as one with distinct political power and entitlements, Dalit youth could hardly take pride in their recognition as members of a Scheduled Caste. In fact, he pointed out that several young Dalits rejected the legal term "Scheduled Caste" itself in favor of the more explicitly political self-referent "Dalit." He said, "When you say Dalit, you use the term to show that everyone has tried to break you in Hindu society, but you have emerged as powerful, you have drawn strength from all that has been done to you. But when you say Scheduled Caste, you are to be pitied, you need help because you are so far behind in society. And yet, people around us, they begrudge us even this pity. People do not want us to gain benefits through the Scheduled Caste category even when they know how behind we are."

Regimes of recognition appear to be motivated by an imperative to redress historical injustices and contemporary social inequalities. Political categories, however, can acquire a life of their own—escaping their intended purposes as they are deployed in novel and surprising ways.[4] Panas clearly articulated the different casteist valences that these categories of legal recognition carried within them, showing how social and cultural valences of caste and race are critical to recognition's import and impact for minorities. "Scheduled Caste" continued to carry the stigma of their Dalit identification. This was not so with the Scheduled Tribe classification; the tribal category secured the distinction of their cultural heritage and land rights through tropes of romanticized savagery but also appeared to grant Adivasis respect as indigenes with a distinct heritage. The Scheduled Caste category, on the other hand, was unable to secure respect for Dalits in the same way while being unable to resolve their chronic landlessness. As Kandhas insisted that recognition through the tribal category was rightfully only theirs because of their distinct Adivasi heritage, Panas came to understand tribal recognition as affording a suite of entangled economic and cultural-political privileges that recognition through the Scheduled Caste category did not afford for Dalits.[5]

Christian Conversion as Dalit Materialism

In Kandhamal, a history of fraught relations between the two groups had become increasingly used to indict Panas as canny, materialistic economic exploiters of Kandhas. While these motifs of Pana materialism could be attributed to a distinct local history in which Panas had become configured as Kandhas' Others, the extent to which they are echoed in the case of other groups that would claim Dalit status within the modern Indian state can be seen in accounts such as that of the Pariahs in now Tamil Nadu. As Rupa Viswanath details, missions seemed confounded by the Dalit desire to convert in groups, throwing into disarray Christian assumptions about the conversion of an individual soul and also about the separation of pure religious belief from material-political desires.[6] Missionaries despaired that they could never fully assess whether Dalits' motives for conversion were influenced by poverty or a desire to escape their abjection in a caste hierarchy in which they were reviled as polluting.

Viswanath highlights how the mass conversion of Dalits challenged missionary expectations of the singular, pure belief in a self-motivated authentic conversion. Pariah conversions were distinctive in the vast numbers who converted; missionaries were approached, and baptism demanded, by groups or representatives of groups rather than single individuals. Conversions were initiated by Pariahs themselves, even as missionaries continue to be indicted as coercing and luring Dalits to converts. Viswanath emphasizes that it was not simply the social, as opposed to individual, nature of these acts of conversion that rendered them deviations from the proper form. Rather it was the

impossibility of separating Dalits' material motivations from the purely spiritual. Missionaries insisted that Pariah poverty made it impossible for conversion to occur for reasons of conscience alone. In the Pariah—and indeed
the Dalit—condition, bodily and spiritual misery were so closely connected
that they could scarcely be separated, challenging the dichotomous analysis
of the world into spirit and matter, to become the very paradigm of inauthen-
tic conversion.[7]

As both David Mosse and Viswanath observe, Hindu nationalist rhetoric
captures anxieties about Dalit conversion originating in mission panics. The
epithet "rice Christian" and the corruption of pure religious belief it signi-
fies are common features of the rhetoric of high-caste Hindu anti-conversion
activists; indeed, the term originated among missionaries as a term of abuse
directed at rival missions. And yet while critiquing and lamenting a materialism that oftentimes became the very marker of the distinct demands of caste
public and Hindu society within India itself, Viswanath notes that missions
saw such interests as virtually ineliminable, and missionaries felt compelled
to attend this intractable problem of Dalit materialism, resulting in a proliferation of discourse on the dualism between spirit and matter.

Dalits, including Panas, were not usually the original targets of evange-
lism. Missions began their activities in areas that later became Kandhamal
in pursuit of Kandhas as special subjects of their proselytization. Missions
cast Kandhas as noble primitives who were difficult to persuade to convert
and whose reluctance only lent them more value in the eyes of missions, who
strove harder to woo them. Pursuing Kandhas, missions articulated their
concern that churches established for the Kandhas were overwhelmingly
attracting Panas. Historian Barbara Boal details in *The Konds* the "sense of
shock" missionaries experienced upon realizing that the church established
in in the Kandha hills in 1908 was not Kandha at all but rather "overwhelmingly" a Pana movement.

By 1927, mission accounts described Kandha converts as few and hard
won, issuing statements to their supervisors that the "Kond Hope" should be
abandoned. Not only were Kandhas reluctant to adopt Christianity because
it required them to relinquish their own cosmologies and practices, they also
hesitated to discard their own observation of purity and pollution taboos
against Panas. Boal notes that Kandhas frequently turned away from the
church or refused to formally convert when they discovered that they would
be required to eat alongside Panas and to abandon the pollution taboos they
observed against them. Kandhas' desire to continue to mark distinction from

Panas as servile, impure, and lower than them in caste hierarchy then was consequential even in their adoption of a purportedly egalitarian Christianity.

These historical accounts show how Christianity cemented the authenticity of Kandhas as Adivasi indigenes who were sought after and highly regarded precisely because of their reluctance to relinquish their own cosmologies. Boal notes that the account of Dr. Donald McGavran, an early mission worker, likened the Panas to "Israelites who are waiting staff in hand, loins girded to leave the land of bondage," while contrasting them with Kandhas as the "Egyptian aristocracy and landowners who would not also be persuaded to join the march to Canaan."[8] In contrast to the highly regarded and difficult-to-lure Kandhas, missions rued Panas' eagerness to convert, always doubting if their conversion was motivated by a true understanding of religious doctrine and sincere faith rather than their disenfranchisement within caste Hindu society. Dalits' zeal to convert was interpreted as a sign of their inalienable materialism, which made them less than desirable converts, as their motivations could never be located in pure spiritual belief. Kandhas engaged with Christianity polyontologically, holding disparate beliefs without contradiction, partaking of different religious beliefs at different points and believing in disparate cosmologies with their own distinct mystical potency that could be tapped or appealed to by the same person.[9] Panas, on the other hand, were more likely to adopt Christian practices in more steadfast ways, even with the threat of public censure.

Legal Doubt and Ethnonationalist Criticism

Missionaries and Christian workers emphasized that religious conversion through material allurements was never a goal for them. Rather, these material provisions and discussions of economic uplift during community outreach were part of the nurturance of long-term relationships between missions and their congregants, embodying a Christian ethos of care. There were distinct variations in style among various denominations. Newer evangelicals were prone to engaging the material suffering of the sick and ailing bodies through what they called healing prayers, missionaries and evangelists across denominations emphasized the material suffering of their congregants, lamenting their crushing poverty and suffering, and emphasizing their desire to work for the poorest and neediest.

In Rutungia gram Panchayat, I spoke with Father John, a Tamil Jesuit priest who had worked among Adivasis in Jharkhand before coming to

Odisha. As John walked me through the compound of St. Xavier's School, a residential school largely catering to Adivasi and Dalit children, he described the pains he had taken to become fluent not just in Odia but also in Kui to engage both Kandhas and Panas. Although he readily admitted that the school focused on instruction in Odia and English and discouraged the use of Kui beyond the school and home, several missions invested in the preservation of Kui as a language and the cultural distinction of Kandhas as Adivasis, and also had begun to employ a vernacular liberation theology to engage Panas as Dalits. Pastor Digal, who frequently sought me out to discuss Christianity's importance for Pana uplift, was proud that he was a local Pana who had risen in the ranks of mission work to do pastoral work within his own community. Like him, a growing number of Dalit missionaries were able to precisely address the Dalit condition by describing how Christianity could lend them strength and pride to claim their Dalit identity. Pastor Digal and some young Pana faith leaders spoke quite emphatically about their desire to see Panas "develop" and materially advance. Yet they found themselves quite helpless when it came to addressing the question of Panas' landlessness. They encouraged Panas to embrace a sense of Dalit identity as a platform for political consciousness, but they knew that Dalit politics would not be able to secure Pana access to land, given the strength of Kandha indigeneity and the history of Kandha-Pana hostilities locally.

As they pointed out the limits to missions' reach in securing enduring institutional and legal change for Panas, John and Pastor Digal attributed the success of mission institutions to mission workers' ability to put aside the taboos of caste hierarchy to approach Adivasi and Dalit communities with compassion and commitment. They belabored the salience of selfless service while doing the work of God in uplifting the poorest and neediest. This ethos of service was reflected in missionaries' willingness to enter the homes of local Kandhas and Panas and to eat, sit, and share the most intimate aspects of their daily existence with them. Despite the role that Christian conversion had played in the perception of inalienable Dalit materialism, missionaries stressed their desire to engage in an intimate, everyday presentation with their parishioners to unravel casteism's everyday, embodied aspects.

John declared himself to be avowedly apolitical, refusing to discuss the advent of Hindutva or the rise of violence against Christians in Odisha. He was reluctant to discuss any active religious pedagogy and denied that Adivasi and Dalit children were being instructed in Christianity in his school, though I would find out from others that catechism classes were part of the curriculum. While he was willing to speak at length about the socioeconomic needs of Adivasi and Dalit communities, he insisted that he never allowed himself to harbor even the slightest thought of conversion, lest it contaminate his work.

The unwillingness of missionaries like John to discuss conversion, their preoccupation with denying the coercive possibilities of mission outreach, and their emphasis on nurturing pastoral care stemmed in large part from the vigorous circulation of discourses of forced minority conversion both within the law and ethnonationalist rhetoric, in which material allurements were cast as particularly deceptive and malicious ploys to secure spurious conversions. The circulation of anti-conversion laws constructs all missionaries as potentially always engaging in illegally luring minority subjects by offering them services, such as education and health care, that directly engaged their material circumstances. More fundamentally, a vexing questioning continues within Christianity to ascertain the sincerity and authenticity of converts. Such questioning persistently seeks to determine if converts are motivated to convert because of pure spiritual belief, or if their beliefs are contaminated by material desires.

Anxieties about the separation between pure religious belief and materialism originating in the history of Christian proselytization are encoded within statutes aiming to *curb* such proselytization in India. Caste Hindus and ethnonationalists directly invoked anti-conversion laws to speak of the material benefits of Christian conversion and argue for the continuation of the ineligibility of Pana converts for recognition. The Orissa Freedom of Religion Act of 1962 is one of six state-level statutes informally known as "anti-conversion" laws seeking to regulate religious conversions.[10] The first of these laws to come into effect, the Orissa Act, purports to institute a system of administrative controls, including filing returns on every conversion, to prevent conversions by force, fraud, or inducement/allurement. Although the Indian Penal Code (IPC) clearly defines "force," "fraud," and "inducement," the Orissa Act deviates substantially from these established definitions, such that the act specifically targets Christian proselytizing as a criminal offense. "Force" includes the threat of divine displeasure or social excommunication; "inducement" includes the offer of any gift or gratification, in cash or kind, including the granting of any benefit, pecuniary or otherwise; and "fraud" is defined to include misrepresentation or any other fraudulent contrivance.

Webb Keane[11] argues that Christianity's sheer complexity is produced through a recurrent conflict between purifying projects of transcendence and countermovements toward materialization, each provoking the other. Seeing Christian conversion as a process of transformation to modernity, and its particular implications for Dalits who favor community over solitary spiritual contemplation, showcases precisely how missions' relentless purification of conversion only provokes its counter-materialization. As Christianity engaged with the Dalit condition and its material abjection, a constant dialectic between purification and materialization was visible not only in Christianity's rhetoric but also in the everyday practices of missionaries like John who sought to purify converts' motives as well as their own, even while trying to address the material uplift of potential converts. A significant number of Panas discussed benefits they received from churches—education for their children, roofs for their houses—but hastened to add that their conversion was motivated only by true love and respect for Christ and his teachings. Some other Panas read the Bible, said prayers with their families, and celebrated Christmas. Yet, they hesitated to call themselves Christians and disavowed their material motivations for conversion, articulating existential doubts about their position within Christianity. Expressing such uncertainties, they wondered if their conversion was, in fact, "genuine"—if it would be recognized in the afterlife.

Shadowing an evangelical pastor, I met an erudite old Pana man, Binoo, who repeatedly declined the pastor's overtures to formally convert to Christianity. His entire family had converted and was imploring him to as well, particularly as his health declined, so that he would find a place in a Christian heaven. His sons, educated in mission schools, had secured respectable jobs as high school teachers in the district capital, Phulbani. His wife, grateful for the support their family had received from their parish over the years, converted as a gesture of gratitude and loyalty to the faith that had nurtured them. Binoo understood her motivations, he said. "After all, it is only when one's stomach is full that one can think of higher thoughts and values." He read the Bible daily and loved to retell its stories to his grandchildren. He did not, however, wish to formally convert to Christianity. As a Pana, he insisted he was born a Hindu, even when caste Hindus did not acknowledge him as such, and he wished to die as one. "I see these converts around me, and I feel they have one foot in one boat and another foot in another boat. They are not able to go anywhere at all, they are stuck in the middle."

Binoo acknowledged that he felt guilty for not showing his gratitude toward Christianity by converting, but he remained plagued by the thought that converting was a sin. His older brother had converted to Christianity and died suddenly soon after. He could not help but think that his brother had been punished for the sin of abandoning his dharma. If he converted in his old age, he might not attain a place in either Christian heaven or Hindu heaven. Instead, he worried that he would be condemned to have no spiritual home and to simply wander in the afterlife. Binoo's words were moving reminders that Panas had internalized a damaging and fraught understanding of their own status as spurious converts within Christianity, while also marking themselves as "betraying" Hindu dharma if they converted.

When I first reached out to members of the Vanvasi Kalyan Ashram in New Delhi and subsequently in Bhubaneswar, Odisha's capital, every conversation started with the Hindu nationalist rhetoric of needing to save minorities from coercive religious conversion. In these conversations, Christian missions, faith-based nongovernmental organizations, and development agencies were spoken of as being hand in glove in reducing minority groups to beggars, who had become accustomed to selling their dharma (religion) and *desa* (nation) for material gain. While elsewhere in India xenophobic characterizations of Islam and Christianity as bearer of values alien to Hindus and coercive proselytizers circulated with equal force, in Odisha, Christianity's force and influence emphasized the extent to which conversion to Christianity was a particularly charged node at which to see ethnonationalists grapple with conversion and its imagined ties to transnational capital and material gain, which threatened to unsettle minority positions in the lowest rungs of caste capitalism. Even as minority groups hardly transcended their disenfranchised social and economic position through conversion, there were pathways—such as access to mission education in English and to health care, and modest support from missions like materials for building houses—that offered minorities some economic opportunities in a context of state neglect.

Vanvasi Kayan Ashram officials were able to further nuance differing implications of caste identity in the conversion of minorities as they juxtaposed Adivasis and Dalits as two contrasting kinds of converts. Kandhas were reluctant and partial converts wedded to their own cosmologies, remaining on the fringes of Christian identity and practice in the district even while missions fundamentally sought them as their primary targets of proselytization and prized converts. When Hindu ethnonationalism accelerated its efforts in the district from the 1980s onward, an overwhelming number of Kandhas, like other Adivasi communities elsewhere in India, "returned" to Hinduism. The ethnonationalist notion of Adivasi "return" to Hinduism rhetorically constructed Adivasis as always already Hindu while unevenly acknowledging their distinct cosmologies.

Dalits such as Panas, on the other hand, were not only excluded from the Hindi rhetoric of affinity and regard; a deep history of caste ostracization and pejoration also continued with them to Christianity. Panas struggled with their construction as spurious and unwanted converts to Christianity, yet they spoke of finding peace and regard within it, as one young Pana woman described it, "a stillness within, a coolness in the heart." For Panas, Christian conversion promised greater acceptance and egalitarianism than did caste Hindu hierarchy. Local caste Hindus and fewer Kandhas described Panas disparagingly as "naturally" attracted to Christianity because of their inalienable materialism. Yet my Pana informants stressed the love, care, and regard that they had found in their Christian faith, even as their social marginalization remained far from resolved.

Ethnonationalists sometimes invoked Islam in xenophobic conversations about conversion, but they particularly indicted Christianity as a bearer of Western and un-Indian values. They lay charges about the pernicious effects of materialism, consumerism, and economic greed on minorities being promoted by the activities of missions and transnational aid agencies, denigrating the service work of missions and faith-based NGOs. Using the catchphrase "lady, paddy, hen, pen," Hindu ethnonationalists insisted that Christians engaged a fourfold strategy for conversion: they engaged women as sexual lures; mission workers gave sustenance by providing rice and grain; they plied potential converts with substances that were illicit and polluting within Hinduism, like animal meat and alcohol; and finally, education in mission schools gave minorities fluency in the English language, which opened them up for the adoption of Western values. And yet while Hindu ethnonationalists accused missions of encouraging pathological economic dependence and materialism among the minority residents of Kandhamal, they attempted to emulate and compete with mission schools and health centers, engaging in a mimesis of Christian service provision.

When I observed Vanvasi Kalyan Ashram's projects in the region such as schools and health clinics, however, they appeared to be struggling and unsuccessful fledgling enterprises. Ethnonationalists acknowledged the complexity of running long-term service-providing centers in the remote geography of Kandhamal, where funding and staffing had proven difficult. Pointing out that mission schools and clinics received funding from other parts of India and support from their headquarters abroad, ethnonationalists insisted that Hindu service provision could never compete with such disproportionate access to transnational capital. Misra babu, a Vanvasi Kalyan Ashram official acknowledged the difficulties he and his colleagues faced in trying to grow Hindu ethnonationalist service organizations.

Misra babu would later grudgingly admit that, unlike mission workers, ethnonationalist workers were not able to overlook caste affiliation in order to approach minority residents in a way that dismantled purity and pollution taboos, and "caste feeling." He acknowledged mission workers' success embodying intimate care and regard for Kandhas and Panas in ways that were difficult to mimic. "Our workers," he said, "still think about things like untouchability, whose house to enter or not enter, whether we should accept water from the people who we visit. These missionaries, they go everywhere, they learn the language, they sit with you, eat with you. They make you feel like family." But this Christian ethos of embodying regard for those lowest in the caste hierarchy was not pure or innocent of ulterior motive, as he hastened to add. "You think they are so good, their heart is good, they do not think about who is higher and who is lower but this is actually their weapon. They do not do this out of the goodness of their heart, it is all a well thought-out plan to make adopt their dharma (religion) and leave ours (Hinduism). Today, if someone comes to you and shows such false love, says soft words to you, you will be duped too."

In late October 2007, Vanvasi Kalyan Ashram's Misra babu asked me to accompany him to survey a few ethnonationalist service institutions. Misra babu had become an important interlocutor after I spent a few months shadowing his work. During this time, I became friendly with his wife and two young daughters and frequently visited their home. He opened up to me on a few occasions about the toll his work in Kandhamal's remote, difficult terrain had taken on his family. His wife, a teacher in the local Hindu-ethnonationalist school, Saraswati Sishu Mandir, worked long hours as she took on additional tutoring work to make ends meet. Both his young daughters frequently fell ill with malaria that was now endemic to the region. At other times, he would extol the virtues of his work in order to recruit me as a Hindu nationalist worker. As on other days, he was making visits to community projects operating in close partnership with Vanvasi Kalyan Ashram, including an orphanage for Adivasi children, a health clinic, and a livelihood training center. These operations were scattered over long distances in Kandhamal, spanning three administrative blocks. Each of these fledgling outfits spoke to the struggles of ethnonationalist service provision. While attempting to mimic the very strategies of Christian service that they critiqued as materialistic bribery, ethnonationalists in Kandhamal struggled with lack of funding and the inability to retain workers in Kandhamal's remote geography.

During our visits that day, other workers emphasized their inability to secure steady funds for their projects and their decreasing staff. Misra babu appeared fatigued and disheartened. On our way back to Baliguda, we discussed the relative success of Christian development and service provision. Emboldened by my relationship with Misra babu, I suggested that Christians were providing critical services in a climate of extreme neglect and in a geography where outreach efforts were so difficult.

My statements provoked Misra babu and he thundered, "Do you think we Hindus will stand by and watch when our Gaumata is slaughtered? When the waters of our holy rivers are filled with cow blood? When our temples are burnt down and replaced by hospitals? When our Hindu civilization is annihilated and replaced by foreign people with foreign values all in the name of economic prosperity and development for the poor? You ask what is wrong with Christians developing these people? What is wrong is that this country will no longer be ours! It will be filled with money and people from outside, it will no longer be Hindustan. The way things are going in this country, soon for hospitals and NGOs to be built—you will see the Ganga red with blood— red with the flesh and blood of our holy cows, red with the blood of Hindus themselves."

In Misra babu's fiery depiction, Christian capital corroded the social and moral fabric of the Hindu nation and threatened the bodily safety of Hindus. Hindu ethnonationalism unevenly struggled to at once mimic and denounce Christian service provision, while continually characterizing Christian capital as un-Indian; to do so, it decried materialism in order to valorize a kind of ascetic self-denial among minority groups even in the face of economic hardship. This ascetic self-denial alluded to the Brahminical ideological undergirdings of caste capitalism, which vilified Christianity as enabling an un-Indian materialism among minorities.

The most successful ethnonationalist institutions in the region were Vedic schools located in Chakkapada and Jalespata run by the Vishwa Hindu Parishad, an ethnonationalist organization devoted to the pedagogy and dissemination of Hindu ritual and practices, which aimed to recruit and educate Kandha children. I visited the school at Jalespata, where the students were all local Kandha girls who had a grueling and austere regime as they learned to recite religious verses, conduct upper-caste religious rituals, and engage with Hindu texts. While they were also exposed to a standard school curriculum, they were primarily being trained to become religious leaders who would renounce the life of householders in order to devote themselves to the service of the Hindu nation. Misra babu, and other ethnonationalist interlocutors, acknowledged that these schools aimed at transforming the habitus and comportment of Kandha children so that they would be seen with new respect in caste hierarchy. As ethnonationalist workers hastened to add, this respect for minorities was not dependent on material acquisitions, unlike in the case of Christianity, but rather on embodying upper-caste purity in terms of aesthetics and sensibilities. Such a holistic transformation, essentially a targeted ethnonationalist program of conversion, had predominantly recruited Kandhas while Panas as Dalits were conspicuous in their exclusion.

Hindu ethnonationalist rhetoric showcased what both David Mosse[12] and Nathaniel Roberts[13] have argued to be a "pervasive elite consensus" about being born Hindu as a kind of divinely mandated ethnic heritage, which forecloses possibilities of discussing conversion to Hinduism. Such a consensus renders the Hinduization of minority groups as "reintegration" into the nation, construed by Hindu nationalists as *ghar wapsi*, or "homecoming." Relatedly, when the Hindu religion is treated as foundational to social life, conversion to Islam or Christianity, especially by Dalits, is seen as rupturing social relations and threatening public order, suggesting external coercion and force, which necessarily needs to be regulated by the law.

KumKum Sangari observes just how Hindu ethnonationalist attacks on conversion functions as a strategy for the mobilization, minority baiting, and fixing of Hindus as victims of historical wrongs.[14] Clear parallels can be seen between the crystallization of personal laws, debates on a uniform civil code and the Hindu right's positions on conversion and reconversion; in their capacity to alter the very terms of the discourse, they rest, unsurprisingly, on similar ideological presuppositions. These disparate legal debates have discrete as well as intersecting legal and political histories with significant shifts between the 1920s and 1990s; yet they are often intertwined into a single issue within Hindu ethnonationalism.

As Sangari suggests, resonances between liberal law and discursive diatribes by the Hindu right have turned conversion into a "national" issue. Doubts about Dalit converts within Christian proselytization and conversion, crystallized within anti-conversion law and reinforced Dalits' loss of patronage through derecognition, are mirrored within ethnonationalist rhetoric. Anti-conversion laws and their legal-bureaucratic requirements render an idealized conversion imagined as a private act of one's volition into a public act[15], shaping and perpetuating discourse about conversion and converts with symbolic and practical consequences. Conversion laws construct women, Adivasis, and

Dalits as victims and converts as passive dupes of converters' machinations and material bribes. Paternalistic protectionism dominates discussions of conversion within Adivasi communities, even when the issue at hand is the perpetration of ethnonationalist violence against missionaries. In the aftermath of the 1999 murder of Christian missionary Graham Staines and his sons, attributed to the ethnonationalist group Bajrang Dal, the nationally appointed Justice D. P. Wadhwa Commission of Inquiry expressed concern for minorities as duped converts rather than alarm over ethnonationalist violence against Christian missionaries.[16] Not all subjects of protectionist paternalism, however, are similarly implicated by anti-conversion laws. Anti-conversion laws have distinct implications for female converts,[17] so too for Dalits. In Kandhamal, this complementarity in ethnonationalist rhetoric and the paternalistic language of the law dovetail on debates about Dalit materialism. Christianity and Hinduism converge on the figure of the materialistic Dalit convert, which exemplifies just how anti-Christian ethnonationalist rhetoric often captures anxieties and issues internal to Christianity itself.

Duplicitous Dalits

Writing about the social effects of legal recognition of Dalits, anthropologist Clarinda Still[18] astutely notes that in a contemporary context in which overt discrimination on the basis of caste is delegitimized,[19] alternative terms are used to justify avoidance of Dalits. Recognition and reservations represent the protection, favor, and benevolence of the state, attesting to the importance of the state for Dalits' aspiration and mobility.[20] Yet, the recognition of Dalits through the Scheduled Caste category and its mandates for reservations become a critical flash point at which upper-caste Hindus articulate their casteist superiority, often engaging a seemingly elliptical language of the habits, morality, and degree of cleanliness of Dalits to explain why they are unworthy recipients of the state's patronage. In Kandhamal, despite the absence of recognition, local Hindus described Dalitness engaging casteist language in terms of a cluster of immutable traits of dishonesty, duplicity and doubleness to justify the derecognition of Dalits as only natural and "fair." Rather than protesting the patronage of Dalits by the state, caste Hindus and ethnonationalists asserted that the derecognition of Christian converts and the withdrawal of the state's patronage meant that Pana Christians were materially benefiting from conversion by tapping into an imagined excess of

Christian capital and thus no longer needed the state's patronage. Both recognition, and its withholding for Dalit converts, function to reprovoke casteism in insidious ways. Yet Dalits find themselves unable to refuse recognition as their derecognition results only in the sociolegal erasure of their political identity and economic claims.

As Pana Christians made a case for their minimal economic advancement given their landless condition, caste Hindus dismissed their claims as signs of their greedy materialism that led them to want to "grab money from everyone." As Gopal Pradhan, a schoolteacher at a local school for Scheduled Caste and Scheduled Tribe children, insisted, "They are already getting wealth from their religion, their leaders are already providing for them. Now they say they want benefits as Scheduled Castes also. Forget that, they are now even claiming tribal status. They want to now claim that they are the same as Adibasis. Is that not a sign of their dishonesty, their unchecked greed?" Caste Hindus criticized Pana bids for tribal status decrying them as dangerously duplicitous, citing their alarming willingness to move between Christian and Hindu, Pana and Kandha, and Scheduled Caste and Scheduled Tribe identities, with scant regard for fidelity toward faith, ethnic heritage, and legal identity. Caste Hindus suggested that if Panas wanted recognition, they ought to renounce their Christian faith rather than engage in a doubleness that led them to continue to affiliate with Christianity while demanding access to recognition. Doing so, caste Hindus demonstrated how the figuration of Dalit materialism traversed sociolegal vectors in Kandhamal to compel a vernacular articulation of how the patronage of Dalits through recognition was seen as permissible only if Dalits marked themselves as Hindu within a Hindu state.

Kandhas did not similarly argue that Panas deserved no economic uplift. They were, however, emphatic that Panas should only access it through their own distinct recognition through the Scheduled Caste category rather than claim a shared heritage with Kandhas by citing their use of Kui language to claim an inseparability of Pana practices from Kandha. Several Kandhas pointed out that Pana use of Kui was merely imitative. It was not a language that originated in their community; rather, they had learned it simply as employees of Kandhas in order to liaise between them and caste Hindus.

Kandhas asserted their independence as indigenes who were capable of sustaining themselves without needing to convert to other faiths, even when they had been continually dispossessed of their land, forbidden by colonial legislation to access forests, and swindled by caste Hindus. They marked their own self-sufficiency in distinction to their disparagement of Panas as culturally and

economically dependent, imitative, and even parasitic, both in their dependence on Christian capital as well as on Kandha identity. They forcefully argued
that Kandhas never needed Panas for their survival, denying their ritual roles as
integral to Kandha economic life. They insisted, however, that Panas could sur-
vive only by taking what they could from Kandhas and that Pana bids for tribal
recognition were just one more attempt by Panas to live off Kandhas. Badiri
Majhi, a local panchayat leader who claimed to be an unbiased peacemaker,
suggested that so long as Panas did not encroach upon Kandha heritage and
their Adivasi distinction, no one in the Kandha community would begrudge
them their economic dues or speak ill of their past.

In their proclamations about the falsehoods animating Pana claims on
tribal classification, Kandhas and Hindus made it clear that tribal recognition
had secured and ossified Adivasi distinction and naturalized Adivasi authenticity, while Dalit recognition remained disputed and vexed with conversion
abetting these perceptions. As they insisted that Panas no longer needed
uplift after conversion, Hindus imagined Pana converts to be tapping into a
network of Christian capital through mission and transnational aid agencies.
Kandhas unevenly affirmed Pana need for uplift but were emphatic that it
could not be secured by encroaching on their entitlements; sometimes they
noted that Panas' conversion had unsettled a local hierarchy of relations and
now Panas were no longer employees, even servants, of Kandhas and "lower"
than them. Rather, they were a competing marginalized group which had
become relatively more "advanced" or "forward" after being routed into different pathways of education, employment, and, consequently, capital through
Christian conversion.

With the intensification of ethnonationalist scrutiny of Christian conversion and the continued legal impossibility of Pana recognition through the
Scheduled Caste category, several Panas felt compelled to hide their Christian
identity publicly. Some procured caste certificates from the local municipal-
ity by greasing the palms of clerks who attested to their Hindu status so that
they could gain jobs through the Scheduled Caste category. Panas reluctantly
accepted their manipulation of legal categories and bureaucratic evidence to
be necessary evils motivated by economic desperation. But ethnonationalists furnished these manipulations as evidence of Dalit duplicity, confirming
the chimeric doubleness of the Dalit convert as both spurious Christian and
failed national subject.

Refrains about the legitimacy of conversions in legal and nationalist
imaginaries, then, became productive of two foils around racialized casteist

alterity—Adivasi authenticity and Dalit duplicity—both within Christianity and within ethnonationalist politics. As Hindu ethnonationalists insisted that material lures and promises of economic uplift and development are used by missions to secure Christian conversion, doubts about Dalit materialism in fact mirrored long-standing Christian panics about conversion and Dalits. Conversion's inability to separate spirit from matter to ascertain purity of motive, solidified distinction between minorities, demanding different burdens of proof from Adivasis and Dalits both within faith and within the law.

CHAPTER 4

Adivasi as Hindu

I had been led to Kandhamal by the All India Vanvasi Kalyan Ashram, which marked it as a site where I would witness the palpable vitality of the Adivasi embrace of ethnonationalism. Two decades after ethnonationalists' first forays into Kandhamal, Hindutva, the political-religious ideology of Hindu ethnonationalism, had matured and settled among Kandhas but also quickly became charged with renewed fervor as Kandha and Pana struggles over recognition came to a head. Kandhas' relationship with Hindutva, I was told by the Odisha leadership of the Vanvasi Kalyan Ashram and Vishwa Hindu Parishad, had been secured through the propagation of religious practices that had laid the foundation for more explicitly politicized conversations about the need for Adivasis to support the project of consolidating a Hindu nation.

As Kandhas were taught and participated in forms of community prayer known as *satsangas* and associated lifestyle practices that aimed at securing ritual purity, they had come to articulate a sensuous, embodied relationship with Hindutva. Through their engagement with Hindutva religious pedagogy, they had begun to serve as officials in the local operations of Vanvasi Kalyan Ashram and Vishwa Hindu Parishad. They had also begun sending their children to study in residential schools run by the Vishwa Hindu Parishad in the area to be trained as religious leaders who would renounce domesticity and family life to devote themselves to the service of a Hindu nation.[1]

Adivasi groups such as the Kandhas have increasingly formed a key constituency for Hindu ethnonationalism, despite the continuing socioeconomic and political marginalization of Adivasis within caste Hindu society. This remarkable and dramatic mobilization of Adivasis into aggressive and conservative ethnonationalism, alongside the disputed and constructed nature of indigeneity in India[2] reflected in the Indian state's withholding of formal indigenous status to Adivasis,[3] have led to indigeneity in postcolonial South

Asia being discussed as distinct from other settler colonial settings at the vanguard of contemporary theorizations of indigeneity.[4] In these accounts, the Adivasi embrace of Hindutva is marked as a rare perversion of indigeneity.[5]

As I shadowed ethnonationalist workers, sat alongside Kandhas in the ritual settings of satsangas, and probed how they understood their encounters with and incorporation into ethnonationalism, rather than being an aberration, Adivasi participation crucially relied on an indigenous authenticity as an embodied religiosity Other to secular modernity. Contemporaneous to distinctly secular, modern invocations of indigeneity, however, both ethnonationalists and Kandhas invoked a precolonial past to assert the inextricability of Adivasi and Hindu, drawing attention to Hindu-adivasi relations of intimacy and patronage.

In what follows, we see the conditions of possibility within which a Hindutva indigeneity emerges as a complex, historically unruly product of colonial categorization, precolonial history, and indigenous assertions after recognition in the postcolonial state. Adivasi participation in Hindu ethnonationalism makes clear the ontological and temporal unruliness of contemporary Adivasi indigeneity and indigenous politics, as well as how this complexity precisely lays the foundation for an aggressive indigeneity articulated within ethnonationalism. Although ethnonationalism has been narrated as doing violence to Adivasi communities by casting Adivasi practices as simply uncivilized, *jangli* (from the jungle) precursors of Hinduism,[6] such critical readings of Hindutva flatten contradictions in the making of Adivasi indigeneity in the Indian postcolonial state and thus its uneven resonances with Hindutva, by failing to consider the contradictions and tensions within Adivasi indigeneity *itself* as a political formation.

Adivasi as Kin Other

Months before my first visit to Kandhamal, I met Swain babu, then the secretary of the Vanvasi Kalyan Ashram, at the state headquarters in Bhubaneswar. Swain babu took some paper and a pencil to draw an informal map of what he called the "most successful belt" of Hindu ethnonationalism in Odisha. Spanning the neighboring Gajapati district to a large part of Kandhamal, he scrawled lines connecting health centers, Saraswati Sishu Mandir schools, Vanvasi Kalyan Ashram offices, and residential schools for tribal children. Run by different outfits of the Sangh Parivar, these institutions cooperated

through a division of labor[7] that engaged education, public health, and livelihood training in a strategy that is mimetic of Christian missions.[8]

After some hesitation, Swain babu began layering the map with a few
other markers, indicating what he referred to as *satsanga gharas* (community
prayer houses) and *yagna bhoomis* (ritual grounds), not among the service-
providing institutions listed by the Vanvasi Kalyan Ashram. As he did so, he
struggled to find the right words.

"These people, the Adibasis," he said, "they have this *dharmic katarta*
[religious fanaticism], once you teach them some religious thing, they really
believe in it, they really do it. In this area, in the beginning, we thought how
do we get them to come to us, how do we get them to listen? Someone would
start telling a story from the Ramayana [ancient Hindu mythological epic],
and they would start gathering around. First one would come, then several
would gather around and listen for hours to stories from the Ramayana.
We started teaching them prayers and hymns, urging them to participate in
satsangas, and now they do it every week. If you go there on a Thursday,
sometimes you will see thousands of Adibasis praying and singing. No one
needs to tell them anything, they have so much *bhakti* [devotion]. They are
really attached to their rituals. They do it better than you and me."

In his initial hesitation to reveal the extent to which the dissemination
of Hindu piety had been critical to the mobilization of Adivasis, Swain babu
revealed ethnonationalists' awareness that their strategies were not unlike the
conversion of Adivasis to Christianity, which they so vociferously critiqued
as an instrumental "misuse" of minorities that was ultimately a violence to
the Hindu nation.[9] In marked distinction to Christians, however, a common refrain in Kandhamal was that Hindus did not offer material "bribes"
to engage Kandhas and instead offered them little to no services, capital, and
other forms of material advancement. And yet Kandha embrace of ethnonationalism had been so vociferous as to defy the expectations of ethnonationalists themselves.

Hindutva understood Adivasi religiosity in a way that secured their indigenous distinction in ways that were not dissimilar from those of Christian
missions, who lauded Kandhas for their refusal to abandon their cosmologies, which only served to heighten their allure as reluctant and prized converts. In contrast with their reluctance to convert to and steep themselves
in Christianity,[10] Kandhas not only embraced Hindutva with enthusiasm but
also described their engagements with Hindutva as affirming their own distinct Adivasi ways of channeling divinity; they asserted that Kandhas had

been Hindu for "all time." As Swain babu and other ethnonationalists detailed the powerful adoption of Hindutva by Kandhas, ethnonationalist workers emphasized the fidelity to both dharma (religion) and *rashtra* (nation) they had secured among the Kandha community through the propagation of community prayer known as satsangas, the ritual purification practices such as vegetarianism and abstinence from alcohol, and the circulation of mythological narratives.

As I spoke to my Kandha interlocutors about their participation, however, a puzzling paradox began to appear. Hindu ethnonationalism understood Adivasi attraction to religion in distinctly racialized terms, in which Adivasi cosmologies were governed by an immutable embodied religiosity from which their politics were inseparable.[11] To precisely engage this embodied religiosity, ethnonationalist workers propagated satsanga as well as associated lifestyle practices as sensuous forms of community piety. These practices drew on early nineteenth-century reform movements that puzzled over a need to modernize and adapt Hinduism, which was perceived as weakened and unable to counter the perceived aggression of conversion by proselytizing religions.[12]

These earlier movements, including most notably Dayanand Sarswati's Arya Samaj movement, reclaimed minority communities from proselytizing religions through ritualized bodily purity intended to civilize and clean them. Thus, in using bodily practices of ritual piety in order to secure Adivasi belonging to an imagined Hindu nation, Hindutva was hardly novel as a form of aggressive "reconversion" or reclamation of Kandhas from Christian missions, the movement known as ghar wapsi. My Kandha informants affirmed this by detailing their previous exchanges with a multiplicity of Hindu reformist sects, including the older presence of Dayanand Saraswati's Arya Samaj in the district and newer influences such as the Brahma Kumaris, who disseminated and popularized Hindu ritual practices, prior to and continuing alongside Hindutva. Yet my Kandha interlocutors celebrated these ritual practices as affirming their own indigenous heritage. They recalled a long history of Kandha veneration of Hindu practices, ritual, and political exchange as well as synergies between Kandhas and Hindus in their regard for aspects of nature, including, most crucially, land.

This chapter disentangles this paradox by showing how a long history of Hindu and Adivasi religious exchange resulted in blurred lines between Adivasi and Hindu cosmologies, informing symbolic agreements and exchanges between Hindus and Adivasis. These resulting fusions created conditions of possibility for the privileged recognition of Adivasi indigenes within Hindi ethnonationalism as kin Others— through, what Donna Haraway might describe as, a project of kin-making as Othering.[13] Plains-dwelling Adivasis such as the Kandhas occupied a distinct, racialized savage slot in their embodied, vital attachment to religion. Yet, they were also seen as in kinship with, and inextricable from, Hindus in their shared beliefs.

The very category "Hindu" emerged out of the colonial encounter,[14] as did the category "tribal." Precolonial forest polities point to prior ritual worlds that predate the colonial separation of people and practices into "Hindu" and "tribal."[15] Through colonial, state, and ethnographic knowledge creation and enumeration, the categories "Hindu" and "tribal" became increasingly disarticulated from each other. This epistemic disarticulation was further consolidated when tribal groups adopted the self-referent "Adivasi" in the 1930s, to mark these groups' prior claims to indigeneity as a platform for identity politics. Differences between Hindus and Adivasis deepened through Adivasis' lived experiences of rebellions and protests distinct from nationalist struggles, which have been documented and theorized within Subaltern Studies as subaltern political resistance.

The indigenous peasant served as a paradigmatic figure within Subaltern Studies from which Ranajit Guha and others aimed to counter Eric Hobsbawm's characterization of a peasant consciousness "not quite having come to terms with the secular-institutional logic of the political."[16] As Dipesh Chakrabarty elaborates, Guha argued against this characterization by detailing how a "peasant-but-modern political sphere was not bereft of the agency of gods, spirits, and other supernatural beings."[17] Advancing a more expansive understanding of Adivasi indigenous politics as modern politics that challenged secular social-scientific assumptions, this influential legacy also led to an insistently narrow interpretation of tribal political agency to be read as forms of resistance. Thus while Subaltern Studies emphasized that tribal peasant consciousness is not prepolitical, it also inspired a legacy in which tribal politics became dominantly understood in terms of resistance to hegemonic politics.[18]

In the wake of this legacy, the participation of Adivasis in an aggressive and violent form of conservative politics has presented a crisis both analytically and politically in South Asia.[19] Until recently, Hindu ethnonationalism has been understood to be uncomfortable with indigeneity as "fundamentally the condition of 'before,' of cultural, philosophical, and political life."[20] Hindutva's attempt to recast the Adivasi (original dweller) as the *vanvasi* (forest dweller) denotes a struggle over notions of authentic Indian identity and lineage as rooted in the Indian soil.[21] This reframing as semantic aggression[22] reveals the disputed nature of primary claims to nation between Hindus and Adivasis, in which ethnonationalists doctrinally reject the Aryan-invasion theory, which posits Adivasis as original settlers and Aryan Hindus as outsiders.

Adivasi political identity has been largely thought to be undermined within the movement[23] as well as in national politics. Yet my conversations with Kandhas and the many exchanges I witnessed between Kandhas and ethnonationalist workers—the term I use to aggregate the Vanvasi Kalyan Ashram, Vishwa Hindu Parishad, and Bajrang Dal officials who engaged Kandhas through visits to villages, panchayat meetings, and religious pedagogy on the ground—betrayed an active, though uneven, deployment of indigeneity rather than its unequivocal dissolution.

The encounters I witnessed among Kandhas and ethnonationalist workers from this triad of Sangh Parivar organizations undeniably demonstrated an ambivalence around indigeneity, tacking back and forth between claims that "Adivasis have always been Hindu" to reextractions and repurifications of an indigenous authenticity articulated in terms of religious fundamentalism (*dharmic katarta*) and sacred regard for land. Ethnonationalists' sometimes consistent, at other times contradictory invocations came together to produce an indigenous distinction, which seemed at once to rely on the momentum gained by indigeneity as a political discourse through state recognition, as well as on a fundamentally racialized Othering of Adivasis as indigenes whose politics were bodily and sensual and who needed to be engaged through religious rather than secular political appeals.

What resulted was an uneven valorization and reification of a distinct racialized indigeneity within Hindutva, evidenced in ethnonationalist workers' recursive return to motifs of Adivasi religiosity and ties to land devoid of material motivations. Both ethnonationalist workers and Kandhas cast Adivasis as always already Hindu, pointing to shared cosmological beliefs to dissolve distinctions between Adivasis and Hindus. Caste Hindus, however, also insisted on Kandhas with their indigenous distinction as particular kinds of politico-religious agents whose embodied religiosity was distinct from that of Hindu moderns and whose devotion to the sacred soil of the Hindu nation made them vital to the continuation of the movement. Kandhas received these assertions, though not without pejoration, as affirmations of their own indigenous history, which relied not on secular homogenous time but rather on time mapped and narrated using gods, spirits, and nature-culture figures as well as Hindu spiritual figures and politico-religious frames.

Kandhas' engagements vividly underscored the need to engage indigeneity as temporally and ontologically unruly, as Lucas Bessire and David Bond
assert, responding to recent anthropological efforts to present a purified radical alterity as a panacea for forms of modern politics. I, then, depart from
South Asian readings of Adivasi as subaltern to attend to the shifting meanings of Adivasi indigeneity colonial and neocolonial imaginaries to illustrate
the indeterminate unruliness of Adivasi indigeneity as a potent political substrate for Hindutva.

Indigeneity as Embodied Religiosity

In Baliguda town, I was urged by locals to visit a village not far away that
had become renowned for its *shraddha* (devotion). So devout were its residents that Swami Laxmananda Saraswati, widely hailed for his patronage and
for what some described to be his paternalistic protection of Kandhas, had
renamed the village Sri Rampur, after the Ram, an important symbolic *Über-
mensch* in Hindu ethnonationalist imaginary, in recognition of its residents'
unfailing participation in Hindutva piety.

Upon my arrival, I found the villagers sitting at the entrances of their huts,
engaging in banter as they anticipated the beginning of satsanga. Women oiled
and neatly combed their hair; their saris were clean and colorful. Because it
was the day of the satsanga, men went without their usual pudiya (chewing
tobacco), which they used to stave off hunger pangs and give them energy. A
few string cots had been placed near a hut that was to serve as the venue for
the satsanga. As the single-roomed mud hut became increasingly crammed
with attendees, and it became harder to accommodate them inside the limited
confines of the satsanga ghara, the gathering moved outside.

The clouds burst. It started pouring. Quickly, the gathering moved back
inside the satsanga ghara, a small mud hut with a thatched roof, lit only by
a dim oil lamp placed in the front of several colorful pictures of Hindu gods
and goddesses. The *satsangis*—men, women, and children—sat next to each
other, cross-legged on the concrete floor, their bodies in close proximity.
Bright-gold marigold garlands, strung by hand by the women, adorned the
photos, and the smell of incense wafted in the air.

The Kandha men sat in front, each assigned a ritual task. One young man
was responsible for playing the drumbeat that provided the foundation for
the prayers and chants; another was tasked with playing the accompanying

brass cymbals. A third led the gathering in prayer with a strong, clear voice; the prayer was then repeated by the assembled men and women. A few men sitting closer to the front of the room carried thin, worn texts filled with devotional songs (*prarthana*) and hymns (*shloka*) that served as guides. The women sitting behind them did not have these hymnals; most unable to read, they were always required to repeat but never to lead rituals.

The men began chanting, "Hare Rama Hare Krishna Hare," their voices swelling higher after every repetition. Eyes closed in prayer, the men and women clapped their hands in unison, keeping time with the beat, drowning out the sounds of thunder and rain.

After the satsanga that day, as I sat with some of my Kandha friends, I asked if they had asked God for something, since Kandha religious ritual has been traditionally held to be a reciprocal relationship of giving and receiving from divinity. An older man, Muttha, said, "Now what will we ask for? We ask for nothing, we just remind ourselves of his presence, just remember him. If we do not remember God, how will he remember us? That he sees us praying to him is enough." For Muttha and his friends, as they prayed in the satsanga, God saw the Kandhas' seeking him and remembered them.

It was implied that Muttha felt as if God had, in fact, forgotten the Kandhas' existence and, in the space of the satsanga, came to see them and remember their presence under his care. Muttha's wife added, "Satsanga is just a way of remembering God. After all, what differentiates animals and humans? Only that human beings remember God." Kandhas' invocations in the satsanga appeared to appeal a divinity for whom they could only become visible by performing the correct ritual, itself a trace of an ongoing colonial encounter and one that dramatically contrasted with anthropological accounts that detail the relationships of Kandhas with spirit gods, understood to be relationships of deep intimacy and reciprocity.[24]

These distinctions in the experience of divinity were accompanied with shifts in community practices. On the night before the satsanga, Kandha men and women washed themselves and bathed their children. Most Kandha villagers who participated in satsangas had converted to vegetarianism and did not eat any meat. Households saved money to buy ghee, an expensive clarified butter, with which to cook their food. Women were restricted from leading ritual and from participating when they were, as some female satsangis reported, "menstruating and unclean."[25] Kandha men were encouraged by ethnonationalists to give up the consumption of alcohol, once part of their daily ritual upon returning from working in the fields, in order to retain ritual purity. Participants swept out their mud houses and wiped down their facades with cow dung, a ritual purifier and disinfectant in Hindu practices, one of five products of the Holy Cow.

They took pleasure in planning additions to their villages, usually a small shrine housing a patron god or goddess in the village square with a saffron flag that fluttered at the apex of the shrine's triangular roof or a carefully tended Holy tulasi (basil) plant. Villagers described these additions as enhancing the aesthetic beauty of the village. Kela, a young Kandha who was now himself an ethnonationalist worker, tried to convey just why his fellow village council members were trying to persuade villagers to save some money to build their own shrine: "Imagine, sister, how beautiful our village will look with our own shrine, how beautiful."

Satsanga participants emphasized satsanga and the adoption of upper-caste Hindu values as "cleaning up" the community by encouraging productivity and industry. Sushila, a devoted satsangi who often attended satsangas cradling her three children, extolled the virtues of these practices, saying, "We are much cleaner now, we do not eat meat or any polluting foods. The village is cleaner. The entire atmosphere of the village has become better. Men do not drink as much and create trouble at home or in the bajaar [market-place]. They go to the field to work regularly. Are these not good things? No one wanted to come to our village because they thought we dirty. Is it not better that we learn to improve ourselves?"

In her description of the rewards of these practices, Sushila employed a discourse of hygiene and cleanliness that indexes several complex, nested concerns. Mary Douglas has asserted that in Hinduism the unclean and the unholy are closely tied together.[26] Ethnonationalists disseminated ideas about cleanliness that portrayed Kandhas as needing to become cleaner in order to access the experience of God. Kandhas were placed in a lower status and, thus, as aspirants to a higher status in a caste hierarchy that fundamentally rested on notions of rightful access to Hindu divinity. As Douglas empha-sizes, however, concerns about pollution and cleanliness are not merely func-tional but also bear symbolic valences, serving as analogies for a social order.

Kandhas emphasized their cleanliness in order to distance themselves from colonial tropes of primitivity and savagery, as well as Hindu nation-alist rhetoric that depicted "clean," ritually pure Hindus as the only rightful residents of the nation. They conveyed their understanding of the politics of belonging to a cleansed Hindu nation (rashtra) whose social fabric was both constituted by racialized caste identities seen to be carrying the bodily stigma

of vocations regarded as polluting by upper castes and increasingly imagined as cleansed of "foreign" figures, such as Muslims and Christians, who
nationalist workers insisted were "matter out of place." Satsangis belabored
their cleanliness to show that they understood the metonymic relationship
between the personal-social body and the body politic, in which bodily per-
fection symbolized an ideal theocracy, willing their rightful belonging and
visibility within an idealized Hindu nation.

Amid a waning of pleasure in agrarian toil and seemingly in Kandha heritage, Kandhas, notably a large number of the young, were taking pleasure
in participating in satsangas popularized by the Vishwa Hindu Parishad,
extolling their aesthetic pleasures in Kandha lives of toil cast by state officials and aid workers as deficient and unproductive, as labor "without fruit"
(*bina phala*). While Kandhas continued to speak of their labor as affirming
their rooted belonging to their land, state officials and aid workers often denigrated Kandhas' labor as yielding little to no economic advancement for them.
Kandha youth increasingly sought work outside the district and Odisha State,
turning to migrant construction labor in states as far away as Gujarat, rather
than toiling in their ancestral fields. This turning away from the land appeared
to Kandha elders to be a sign of youth turning away from community, crystal-
lizing concerns that they were no longer taking pleasure in Kandha traditions
and livelihood.

Weighed down by their daily struggles, Kandhas expressed an existential
fatigue, a degradation of their labor and themselves. The transcendent experiences within satsangas, they said, provided reprieve from their harsh realities,
granting them the pleasure of forging a relationship with divinity through
their bodies and senses.

For Kandhas, these aesthetic experiences provided, as Lauren Berlant
puts it, "a different pacing than the working life, donating to the worker the
privilege of slowness, of time to have a thought/experience whose productivity is subjective, connecting the sensorium to something that felt nonin-
strumental, absorbing, and self-affirming."[27] Such reprieves from labor that
offer sensory pathways to religious experience do not appeal only to indigenous subjects.[28] These aesthetic experiences were induced, managed, and governed within satsanga ritual, developing a distinct, novel "pious sensorium"[29]
among participating satsangis. These satsangis emphasized their cleanliness,
such as my friend Mohan, who insisted that I should never hesitate to come
to his house to play with his children and share meals. He explained that his
family was now vegetarian and his household immaculate, showing that he

had clearly internalized upper-caste preoccupations with bodily and ritual purity through fasting, vegetarianism, abstinence from alcohol, and community cleansing and beautification.

And yet despite the clear novelty of the sensorium, Kandhas described satsangas as connecting them anew with their Adibasi sanskruti at a time when their young were turning away from their traditions. Recalling a long Kandha history of using sensuous forms to access divinity, including through possession and shamanic rituals conducted with the village *jani* (priest) and *bejunis* (shamans), they described their immersive satsanga experiences as lingering, sometimes calming, and at other times excitatory and invigorating. They always invoked divinity using dance and music, insisting that summoning divinity through their senses and bodies was part of a long Kandha tradition in which God could be "felt" in participants' bodies.

Where once bejunis were appointed to invoke divine forces through bodily possession on behalf of the village, Kandhas described the satsanga as enabling access to the divine through the senses, much like their ancestors' experiences of divinity. Raju, a young man, emphasized the sensory aspects of satsanga experiences: "First, I came because the villagers wanted me to play the drums. But then, I really enjoyed it. The whole satsanga ghara would be full of sound. My eardrums were filled with the chanting and the drumbeats. I felt my heart pounding in time to the drum. I felt so energized, like the *prana* [spirit/life] had come back into my body."

Kandhas described how sensory and aesthetic pleasures forged an intimate relationship with a higher presence, insisting that sensuous invocations of divinity affirmed their embodied indigenous religiosity. Sonu, a young satsangi, said, "I first started going to satsangas because I liked playing music. I was tired of working in the fields and wanted to forget my worries for a while. But I don't think I knew how to experience God. Now it is different. I think that when I hear the music, I hear God. When I play the drums, I play for God. This is how my ancestors also were. Our rituals are always about invoking God, experiencing God like this through singing and hearing songs."

In their conversations with me, ethnonationalist workers repeatedly drew attention to tribal embodied attraction to religion as well as attachment to musical and dance forms. In so doing, they engaged an enduring figuration of indigenous groups as primitive unmoderns by drawing on secular liberal assumptions of an undeniably settler-colonial Hinduism. These recursive framings of Adivasis also echoed ethnonationalists like Swain babu's assertions that once taught the "right ways," tribals engaged in piety "better" than upper-caste Hindu moderns, illustrating Michael Taussig's observation that indigenous groups are thought to replicate the culture of colonizers in a "purely sensory" way, bypassing processes of intellectual intentionality.[30]

This racialized characterization of tribal communities persuaded, or rather governed by, "nonrational," sensate appeals provided a register of embodied difference, which allowed ethnonationalism to hail Adivasis as valuable because of their inalienable religiosity. And yet the insistence that these satsanga experiences were in keeping with how Adivasis had always communed with divinity suggested that Kandhas were experiencing these practices not merely through their racialized difference from Hindus but also as vital continuities between Adivasi and Hindu ontologies. In many ways, my own reading of these practices as imitative of Hindu ritual, even as Kandhas claimed them as their own, exemplifies what Taussig criticizes to be a tendency of anthropologists to reduce indigenous lifeworlds, defending the independence of lived culture from anthropological reductionism. It was with this admonishment in mind that I set out to understand how and why Hindu and Adivasi practices appeared to have become so blurred in Kandha lived experience as to resist any easy separation between Hindu or Kandha, not merely in terms of practices but also in terms of ontologies.

Adivasi as Hindu

State officials, NGO workers, and anthropologists described Desia Kandhas as Adivasi who had lost some of their Adivasi-ness through Hinduization as a result of contact with plains-dwelling Hindus. Desia Kandhas spoke of their own Adibasi identity with assumed matter-of-factness. Equally matter-of-factly, they described a neighboring Kandha group—the Kutia Kandhas, described by the Odisha State as related to Desias but developing differently over time because of their relative isolation—as "ek nambariya Kandhas" (literally, "number one Kandhas"), reflecting the extent to which Kandhas had internalized a discourse of ontological purity around Adivasi cosmologies.

The Adivasi incorporation of Hindu practices resulting in what appears to be an assimilative Hinduization, as in the case of the Desia Kandhas, has often been simplistically discussed as the "Sanskritization of Adivasis," which relies on M. N. Srinivas's notion of religious-moral aspiration as "Sanskritization," or "the process by which a 'low' Hindu caste or tribal group, changes its customs, ritual, ideology, and way of life in the direction of a high, and frequently 'twice-born' caste."[31] Sanskritization also undergirds state knowledge production that designates plains-dwelling Adivasis such as the Desia Kandha as animists who have become Hinduized through an accidental yet inevitable process of the erosion of Adivasi cosmologies through contact with Hindus. By using Sanskritization to understand Adivasis' embrace of Hindutva, the success of Hindu ethnonationalism among plains-dwelling Adivasis already Hinduized would appear to be the result of a process in which a long history of Adivasi assimilation had already secured the foundation for a Hindu ethnonationalist mobilization.

Kandhas, however, did not describe their engagements with Hindutva piety in terms of unidirectional osmosis and exchange in which they aspired to become twice-born upper castes to achieve socioreligious ascendency in caste society. Notions of Sanskritization erroneously characterize tribals' attraction to Hindu practice as merely imitative practice rather than acknowledge overlapping modes of religious life.[32] It was these overlapping modes of exchange and intersection between Adivasi and Hindu lifeworlds that Kandhas described as affirming their Adivasi heritage, aided by a history of blurred lines between Adivasi and Hindu beliefs and practices as well as a shifting register of indigenous political assertion.

Anthropologists describe Desia Kandhas as animists with a highly organized and stratified religious system. Within this system, *janis* (priests/diviners) and *bejuns* and *bejunis* (male and female shamans) are assigned roles in leading religious rituals, which are connected to healing of bodies and communities and are seen as acts of reciprocity with divinity to ensure material well-being.[33] My Kandha interlocutors claimed that these practices were integral to Kandha cosmology, while also discussing affinities between Hinduism and Kandha practices to emphasize "we have been Hindu for all time (*aame sabu bele Hindu thilu*)."

When Kandhas spoke of how they had come to embrace Hinduism, they invoked intimate, embodied associations with Hindu practice, privileging deep sensual, embodied attachments to ritual practice: the smell of incense at prayer ceremonies, the chimes of prayer bells in the hands of priests, and the resounding vocalizations of priests. They linked these experiences to a highly visible and public Hinduism that surrounded them in the form of festivals (*parba-parbani*) and public processions (*jatra*), describing their attraction and incorporation of Hinduism in ways that were at once intimate and public.

Gala, a sixty-year-old man, told me he could not remember a time when Hinduism had not been a part of their lives. Reaching back into the

open-ended nostalgia of their childhood, Gala and his compatriots described
how Kandha men would take their young children from villages to see the
Durga Puja jatra (procession) in Baliguda. He recalled vivid memories of
sitting on his father's shoulders as a small child to see the statue of Durga
past the milling crowd: "I remember the sun was on my face and I was tired.
But I saw the statue and forgot everything. The decorations were so bright
and shiny, her face so beautiful. I still cannot forget the sweet I ate there."
Gala sighed, remembering his childhood, and continued, "We Kandhas have
always celebrated Hindu festivals. We give offerings to Maa Paatakhanda, we
take part in all her jatras [public religious processions], Adibasi *mane* Hindu
[Adibasis are Hindu/Adibasi means Hindu]."

His compatriots enthusiastically echoed him. To ask when Hinduism
had first come to Adibasis, they insisted, was to ask when the world had first
started or if someone had marked the beginning of time. Emphasizing the
timelessness of Adivasi as Hindu, and even the ontological inseparability of
Adivasi from Hindu, Desia Kandhas marked themselves as always already
Hindu rather than as imitating and absorbing Hindu practices, as is commonsensical in sociological understandings that undergird state knowledge
practices. Gala not only recalled the magnetic and public presence of Hindu
goddesses such as Durga but also linked them to local village deities, such as
Maa Patakhanada, described as an incarnation of Durga and, thus, absorbed
into the local Hindu pantheon, illustrating that a process of "historical cultural osmosis occurred between shakta traditions and Adivasi religiosity"[34]
in which local goddesses had become inextricably linked to goddesses in the
Hindu pantheon.[35]

By invoking goddesses and rituals that had undergone a process of osmosis
resulting in a blurring of boundaries between Adivasi and Hindu lifeworlds,
both nationalists and Kandhas undid any clear-cut distinctions asserted
by colonial and postcolonial anthropologists that cordoned off tribal from
Hindu. Understood in this historical sense, nationalist workers and Kandhas claimed affinities that ostensibly undid ontological separations between
Hindu and Adivasi cosmologies, by hearkening back to long-standing histories of ritual and social interaction and overlaps, attempting to remediate the
disarticulation of Adivasi from Hindu advanced by colonial classificatory and
ethnographic practices.

These dissolutions, however, were performed alongside both ethnonationalists' and Kandhas' subscription to the modern Hindu nation's encap-
sulation of the Adivasi as indigene, a categorical understanding clearly

discontinuous with the precolonial past in which neither Hindu nor Adivasi existed. Kandhas moved between these temporalities without contradiction, employing an unruly historicism at the service of emergent politics. The fact that they endorsed precolonial understandings of Adivasis while continuing to uphold their Adivasi indigeneity made it clear that Kandha political articulations within Hindutva could not be understood by merely engaging temporally bound categories of the precolonial and modern. Bessire and Bond remind us to resist a narration of contemporary indigeneity that flattens its inherent temporal unruliness[36], and this caveat particularly resonates for Adivasi indigeneity.

Kandhas also invoked shared beliefs in social hierarchy as an important convergence in Hindu and Kandha cosmologies. While Kandhas were considered ritually polluting within the caste Hindu hierarchy, they asserted their own hierarchical superiority over the Pana Dalits, who were seen as "lower" and against whom Kandhas practiced taboos to preserve their own ritual purity. By insisting that they continued to never eat alongside Panas or to admit them past the thresholds of their dwellings and that they restricted Pana access to Hindu temples,[37] Kandhas asserted that they were socially higher than them and, in that sense, more proximal to Hindus.

Gala said, "When a Pana came to our house for some work, my father would remind him, you cannot cross my threshold [*pinda*], you must sit outside, away from the entrance to the house. We Kandhas still do not accept water from Panas. They did our work for us, and we employed them because we had to but we never accepted water from them, we would not eat alongside them—that is our tradition." While this relationship may appear to be particularly pronounced between Kandhas and Panas because of Kandha characterizations of Panas as their employees or even servants, practices of ritual purity and untouchability by Adivasis against Dalits are not restricted to Kandhas and have been reported among other Adivasi communities.[38]

By detailing their practice of ritual taboos against Panas as a reminder of critical differences between the two groups, Kandhas emphasized that the affinities between Kandhas' view and Hindus' view of social relations fundamentally hinged on socioreligious hierarchy. Sonu said, "You see, we are not all the same. Kandhas and Panas are not the same. They are trying to say they are the same as us but they have never been. They have a different history, different beliefs. So we cannot be equal. And the Hindu brothers also understand that everyone is not equal, they are different with their own practices, and everyone cannot just eat together, be together. These differences between us are important, and the Hindu brothers have also always believed that. They also do not accept water from Panas, they do not see them as Hindu."

Kandhas, then, were eager to point to their own "higher" position in a social hierarchy in which they saw themselves as equal and thus more proximal to Hindus. Sonu continued, "We have always been close to Hindus, we were actually equal to them but then we lost our position because we lost political power, the Hindu kings ruled us and Hindus became stronger. We were equal to Hindus before, Hindu kings used to fear us. They know that. That is why they are coming to us, they know that we are similar to them, though now our position has become lower, we were equal to them in power."[39]

Kandhas also regularly brought up polysemic practices that resisted categorizations of Adivasi and Hindu. One such practice was that of wearing sacred threads, or *paitas*. Kandhas insisted they were known to wear sacred threads as a high-status Kshatriya warrior group "long ago" at a time when they were "equal" to Hindu Odias.[40] Others noted that religious movements, including the Tarini cult and Dayanand Saraswati's Arya Samaj movement, introduced thread wearing as a marker of abolition of caste and gender hierarchies.

These contestations reinforced how Kandhas, like Adivasis elsewhere in India,[41] were subjects of a long succession of reformist movements, starting in the late nineteenth century, that sought to modernize a Hinduism perceived as under siege by proselytizing religions like Christianity.[42] These movements' goal was to achieve *shuddhi*, a transformative, purifying "reconversion" of minority communities from Christian conversion, in order to secure homecoming, or ghar wapsi, of these communities into Hinduism.[43] The wearing of threads could, however, also be traced back to an earlier history before the Kandha subjection to reconversion, within which a number of peasant Adivasis, including Kandhas and Gonds, understood themselves to be high-status warriors and actively sought to claim this status as members of the Kshatriya caste. They took on practices, such as the wearing of sacred threads thought to be worn only by Brahmins, as a strategy of countering agrarian interventions made under colonial rule that reallocated land and thus threatened Adivasi peasant control of land.[44]

Even as Hindu ethnonationalism's "reconversion" of Adivasis drew on this long succession of reform movements in India as well as Adivasis' agentive manipulations of caste as social hierarchy, they layered new valences onto the long-standing "reconversions." Addressing these multivocal contestations over the wearing of paitas among Kandhas, nationalist workers insisted that Kandhas were empowered to display their paitas without fear and shame and that the efforts of the Vishwa Hindu Parishad since the 1980s had ushered in a new era of democratization of upper-caste religious piety and ritual aesthetics. Nationalist worker Das babu often remarked that Hindutva had ushered in respect for Kandhas by acknowledging that their piety made them equal to Brahmins: "They take pride in wearing paita. We tell them—anyone who prays, carries out rituals with shraddha [devotion], they are Brahmunas. You follow every ritual, you show so much devotion so why shouldn't you wear these sacred threads. In fact, we say you are better than some brahmunas. Your devotion, your bhakti is your ultimate service to the nation."

Although the Kandha community had themselves actively manipulated caste as socioreligious hierarchy as well as continually been subjected to "civilizing" socioreligious pedagogy by a succession of reformist Hindu sects, nationalists lent new symbolic meaning to these accelerated engagements with piety via Hindutva over the two decades preceding my fieldwork. They cast Kandhas as empowered indigenes reasserting equality with upper-caste Hindu Odias, as workers such as Misra babu, Sahu babu, and Das babu provided a language of ascendancy that figured Kandha engagements through an embodied transformation, akin to conversion,[45] yet claimed ethnonationalism's affinity and regard for a reified, immutable authentic indigeneity. Ethnonationalists were coming to suggest that Kandha ascendancy was not merely an aspirational elevation in a local caste hierarchy but also a process through which Kandhas were becoming Hindu. In fact, Kandha as Hindu was a long-circulating, ambivalent script. Ethnonationalists reframed this ambivalent history at the service of renewed assertions of Kandha indigenous identity.

Sonu, now an ethnonationalist worker engaged in community outreach for the Vanvasi Kalyan Ashram, explained, "You see. They are telling us—we honor those who wear paitas, we see them as the highest among us. They understand that these paitas are ours. It is not as if we are wearing them to imitate someone. Kandhas are known to wear paitas much longer than we even knew that there are Hindus around us. See my wife. You see her, she is wearing a paita. Do Hindu women wear paita? No, only Hindu men wear paita. But see my wife—she is wearing one. Yes, she has gone to the Arya Samajis, but that is not why she is wearing paita, she is wearing it because her Kandha forefathers (puruba-purusa) used to wear it, because it is a Kandha practice to wear paitas. These Hindu brothers say they honor and respect our paita wearing, they respect our Kandhas. People say you are imitating Hindus. No, this is ours."

As Sonu indicated, Kandhas had long believed paitas both to signal their deeper engagement with Hindu piety and to be a marker of their purified, Kshatriya warrior status, but they now insisted on it as an assertion of their own Kandha heritage. The plurality of forces acting upon Kandhas made clear the futility of attempting to recoup a purified radical Kandha alterity outside Hinduism. It was such recurrent incursions of Hinduism upon Kandhas and their agentive manipulations of caste alongside that had led to the seeming unthinkability of Adivasiness as ever being outside Hinduism, long before the arrival of Hindutva in Kandhamal.

During the course of my fieldwork, I had several conversations with Laxmananda Saraswati, whose stewardship of Kandhas had led him to be hailed as a father figure (*bapa*) in the community. After an initial distrust of my motives and following a thorough interrogation of my provenance, he assumed that my own Odia upper-caste origins made me sympathetic to the nationalist reclamation of Kandhas. This assumed sympathy to nationalist politics, my ongoing relationships with other workers and Kandhas, and, as I was told, my unwillingness to leave the district despite the threat of violence secured my access to Laxmananda. My presumed sympathy to the deployment of upper-caste practices as an ongoing project of Hindu hegemonic mainstreaming of Adivasis motivated my own discomfort at being identified by so many of my Kandha informants as an upper-caste Hindu for whom they had to maintain ritual purity and perform their pious Hindutva identity, as they invited me to share vegetarian meals, participate in satsangas, and witness Kandha rituals. It was precisely this perceived status, however, that secured my relationship with Kandhas.

Laxmananda invited me to eat with the young women he was training at the Kanyashram in Jalespata so that I might observe their training, and he impressed upon me the urgency of "reclaiming" Kandhas from missions. Laxmananda was emphatic that the Vishwa Hindu Parishad's dissemination of religious piety had secured a newfound empowerment and regard for Kandhas. Kandhas were treated poorly not just by caste Hindus, he insisted, but also by state officials and missions as irrational, filthy savages. Ground down as they were by their pejorative characterizations, he insisted that their participation in Hindutva had gained newfound respectability and sociopolitical ascendency.

"People used to say Kandha! Chee!" Laxmananda said, as he simulated blowing his nose on the ground as a sign of disgust. "Now go see these

thousands of Kandhas reciting shlokas [religious verses] in pure Sanskrit! Go
see! Did anyone ever imagine this! We have put them in touch with their self-
respect, their power. Over the years, they lost this self-respect. We brought it
back to them. We don't give them paisa [money], unlike the Christians. We
do not bribe them. You tell me—what material benefit do they get from us?
Then why do they embrace us, listen to us, call us brothers? It is because our
shared history, a history in which we Hindus always respected Adibasis, their
devotion to Hindu dharma and to the rashtra."

Laxmananda hailed the Vishwa Hindu Parishad's dissemination of Hinduism as democratizing ritual piety while also affirming Kandha pride in
their indigeneity. He drew attention to the dispersal of a language of democratization secured by multicultural recognition into ethnonationalist rhetoric. He celebrated Hindutva's securing of such a strong relationship with the
Kandha community that they now wanted their children to become formally
trained to conduct Hindu rituals. Laxmananda ran residential Vedic schools
in Chakkapada and Jalespata, in which Kandha boys and girls underwent a
grueling and austere regime as they trained to recite religious verses, conduct
religious rituals such as *yagnas* (holy fire ceremonies), and learn Sanskrit to
study religious doctrine.

During visits to the Kanya Ashram in Jalespata, I met young Kandha girls
training to become religious leaders (*sadhvis*) who would renounce the life of
householders (*gruhastha jeebana*).[46] They impressed upon me their desire to
devote themselves to the service of the Hindu nation. It was important, they
said, for young Adivasis to represent their communities in national politics
but to do so in the highest religious ranks to signal Adivasi ascendency within
Hindu samaj. In so doing, the girls engaged notions about the democratic
equality of indigenous difference consolidated through recognition. A young
woman, Radha, had spent five years away from her family at the ashram. I
asked her what motivated her commitment to her training and her endur-
ance of such a difficult separation from her family. She responded, "Now in
the villages, the *pracharaks* that go around talking to people, they are still
Brahmunas and Karanas. Soon, there will be people like us who can go to
our own communities, talk to our own people." For these youths who had
left their homes to undergo this demanding training, their participation in
ethnonationalism was motivated by their desire to assert indigenous sovereignty—the ability of Adivasis to represent and govern themselves even as
they participated in majoritarian politics.

A History of Ambivalence

While Kandhas emphasized their deep affinities with Hindus, they regularly returned to the social and ritual exclusion of Kandhas by caste Hindus, uneasy reminders that caste Hindu and Adivasi relations could not be revised by ethnonationalists to become neatly encapsulated within ethnonationalist scripts of affinity and regard. Recasting caste Hindu ostracization as a failure to recognize Adivasis as true Hindus, Kandhas returned often to their exploitation by caste Hindu landlords and moneylenders as well as to their abjection—a state of being "forgotten," cast off and neglected by Hindus until they "returned" to them.

One day, as I sat with Gala and other elders, after a discussion of the changes that had come about in the community, Gala turned to me to clarify his position. "These Hindu brothers," he said, "they are coming to us now. But for a long time, no one cared. They had forgotten us. Now they are saying we respect you as Hindus. But it is true that earlier no one even asked—are you Hindu? They treated us poorly, like we were dirty animals. They had forgotten our power, now they remember. Even the Hindu kings used to be afraid of our forefathers. They knew that they could not just suppress us. They had to win us over by respecting us."

Like Kanu Majhi earlier, older and younger Kandhas were careful to point out their ongoing marginalization and neglect by Hindus, and that ethnonationalists' regard for them did not change that history, even though they were now being asked to proclaim their Hindu identity in highly visible ways. As Kanu and others grumbled, indeed protested, against a seamless reframing of Hindu-Adivasi affinity, I sought to clarify the abjection articulated by Kandhas in terms of being forgotten by their Hindu "brothers" until they had "returned" to them.

Despite being subjects of vigorous mission activity and Hindu reformist sects during a period of state-mandated "noninterference" and gradualism in the early days of postcolonial nation building, it appeared that Kandhas had understood the arrival and intensification of Hindu ethnonationalism in the area as a "return" of Hindu political engagement of Kandhas. In contrast to mission and other Hindu-reformist engagements in the community, this ethnonationalism explicitly engaged Kandhas through modalities that did not separate their religious and political engagements in ways that recalled histories of Kandha subjection under and patronage of Hindu kingship. As Felix

Padel notes, and as some of my informants detailed, Kandhas had a strong collective memory of being recipients of Hindu kingly patronage, a relationship of a political subjection that involved a particular intimacy between Hindu kings as ruler and ruled. Hindu kings served as patrons for Kandha chiefs and clans (*mutthas*) in preindependence India.[47] Biswamoy Pati details this intimacy by drawing on colonial accounts that describe Kandha leaders or *pat majhis'* presence at coronation ceremonies of Hindu rajas, dressed in ceremonial cloth, on which the raja was then seated.[48]

It is this intimacy that Veena Das emphasizes in her foreword to Padel's book, teasing out how Kandha subjection under Hindu kingship needs to be complicated in order to engage the importance of the relationship between Hindu rajas and tribal subjects. Although the British colonial administration conceived of rajas being rulers and as "controlling" tribal subjects, the relationship between the Hindu rajas and the tribals was intimate rather than hierarchical, and it was often articulated through a language of reciprocity. While religious texts on statecraft provided the parameters of the relationship between the king and his control over tribal subjects, Kandha chiefs did not consider Hindu rajas to be rulers as much as patrons who could serve their needs, receiving their cooperation in turn.[49]

At the time of my conversations with Kandhas, more than 170 years after the Ghumsur Wars of 1836–1837, which saw colonists taking control over Kandha populations and disrupting Hindu kingship and patronage of Kandhas,[50] and sixty years after the formation of the postcolonial Indian state, Kandhas continued to invoke a history in which they played important ritual and political roles that consolidated Hindu rajas' rule. They insisted that Hindu political leadership had always relied on the support of Kandhas to consolidate their role and power and that Kandhas were kingmakers who had the ability to appoint or dismiss a Hindu raja.

This Kandha intimacy with Hindu kingship distinctly informed Kandhas' engagement with Hindu ethnonationalism; they narrated their participation not as an imposition of politics from the top down but as a resumption of intimacy between Kandhas and Hindus in consolidating Hindu political rule. Through this intimacy, tribal chiefs felt as though they "tasted the outside world" through rajas.[51] This relationship of intimate patronage also reappeared in Kandhas' statements about how they were making forays beyond the district through Hindutva and seeing the world (*duniya dekhuchu*), including trips in which some Kandhas described being seated en masse in trains to go "far away" to serve as religious workers (*kar sevaks*)[52] that aided the demolition of the Babri Masjid trips to sites such as Ayodhya, purported birthplace of Ram and a site of Hindu-Muslim contestation.

F. G. Bailey famously reported Kandha ambivalence toward Hindus, in which Kandhas reported subjection, equality, patronage, and oppression in equal measure by caste Odias.[53] Speaking with Kandhas, this ambivalence could be parsed as a coexistence of a Kandha cosmological affinity with Hinduism and an intimacy with Hindu political rule concomitant to a racialized Othering of Kandhas by upper-caste Hindus. To resolve contradictions presented by their own endorsements of Adivasi and Hindu affinity, Kandhas often explained that a "misunderstanding" (bhool bhujabana)—indeed, a misrecognition—caused by lack of spatial proximity had fundamentally led to what Kandhas saw to be a failure of reciprocal intelligibility: Kandhas' failure to truly "recognize" (chinhiba) Hindu regard for Kandhas and caste Hindus' failure to understand the extent to which Kandhas had regard for Hindu beliefs and "the fact that Kandhas were really Hindu."

Kandhas' statements mirrored an essentially Hegelian recognition in which Kandhas asserted that their self-consciousness as autonomous agents—their knowledge of themselves as Kandhas—had come about only by interacting with Hindus as autonomous subjects. This relationship of mutuality was famously extended by Frantz Fanon as he insisted that race and violence (indeed, race as violence) within colonialism exacerbates the need for recognition,[54] even though such recognition, feminists point out, keeps subjects locked into an embodied identity.[55] Although these ideological functions of recognition were undeniably true of Hindu and Hindutva recognition of Kandhas, Kandhas seemed only to emphasize it as a process of mutuality, wherein Hindus became Hindu by being recognized by Kandhas, and Kandhas, in turn, realized themselves as such by being recognized by Hindus.

At moments when Kandha ambivalence toward Hindus peeked through, nationalists played up the larger visibility of Adivasis in caste Hindu traditions in Odisha. Hinduism in Odisha is characterized by the integration of "little" and "big" traditions[56] and the "elevation" of tribal gods into caste Hindu practice, most notably Odisha's patron deity, Jagannath. To revise the vexed history of social relations between tribals and Hindus, nationalists pointed to local goddesses such as Maa Patakhanda, who had been absorbed into the Hindu pantheon and had become highly regarded by Hindus. They did not suggest a seamless assimilation or incorporation of her into a shakta tradition but rather marked her as distinctly venerated by Kandhas as well as "equally" treated by Hindus, who worshipped her in local shrines alongside goddesses such as Durga.

They turned to Hindu epics, reiterating the valuable presence of jungle dwellers in the epic Ramayana, which narrates the struggle of prince Rama to rescue his wife, Sita, from the demon king, Ravana. They hailed these forest dwellers such as the Vanar Sena, an army of forest dwellers they insisted were Adivasis, who had come to the aid of Lord Ram. Even as colonial tropes of Adivasi animality[57] seemed to be only consolidated in the figuration of Adivasis as half-monkey, half-human, Kandhas discussed their presence in mythology as proof of their indigeneity—what they described as "their existence for all time" as well as their roles in supporting Hindu kingship in scripture.

Negotiating this uneven give-and-take over deities and religious mythological narrative and practices,[58] ethnonationalists invented traditions through the use of Hindu texts, symbols, and rituals to lend a sense of belonging to a nation, a process also observed by Kalyani Devaki Menon in the mobilization of women into Hindu ethnonationalism. Nationalists referred to Kandha men as *bhaimaane* (brothers) and women as *maamane* (mothers), fraternal and maternal kin who came to the aid of Hindu kings and, thus, whose service had always been vital to the Hindu nation. This language of kinship coexisted alongside nationalists' subscription to a necessary distinction between Hindus as secular moderns and Kandhas as religious indigenes. Despite their doctrinal denial of indigeneity as "prior,"[59] nationalists valorized Kandha adivasi indigeneity in terms at once allochronistic yet affinal.[60]

Although Desia Kandhas had embraced Hindutva rhetoric about Adivasis as always already Hindu, there was not always unanimous agreement among my interlocutors about the overlaps between being Adivasi and Hindu. Alongside a language of rights and entitlements deployed by Kandha youth that older Kandhas flagged as novel and distinct from their own "contented" ways, the generational shift in Kandhas' occupation of their indigenous positioning reared its head within Hindu ethnonationalism too. While older Kandhas were less exuberant about the ethnonationalist rhetoric of seamless continuity between Kandha and Hindu beliefs and practices, younger Kandhas were eager to claim affinities with Hindutva. Older Kandhas acknowledged that they had a long history of exchange and patronage with Hindus but disagreed that there were no ontological distinctions between Adivasi and Hindu.

Drawing attention to shifts in Adivasi cosmologies under ethnonationalist influence, an eighty-year-old Kandha man, Kanu, attempted to explain how Hindu piety had replaced traditional figures such as the Mountain God and

Sickness Goddess with personified gods and goddesses from the Hindu pantheon. "We never worshipped a photo or an idol," he said. "We worshipped what surrounds us. The mountain, the sun. They have spirit but they are not a *murti* [statue or idol]. Now they are saying it is the same thing. But who will argue [*kentu kiye jukti kariba*]?"

Kanu continued, "It is not like we did not know what it is to be Hindu, that we did not believe in Hindu dharma, that we do not regard Durga mata, but I would not say we were exactly like them. We have always had our own practices. Now my son and others are pointing out that we are the same but that we just never realized it earlier. Yes, but if we were always the same, it is also true that no one came to us, asking what we were or what we really believed. If no one comes to you asking if you are Hindu, why would you think of it, you would just do what you are doing. The Brahmunas and Karanas did not mix with us, they did not ask us if we are Hindu earlier, they did not come to us as they are coming to us now."

Kanu's words, once again, appeared as a powerful vernacular articulation of Hegelian recognition. Kanu and some other older men did attend satsangas, though they acknowledged their participation to be sporadic. "It is fun [*maja*]," Kanu said. "It is pleasurable, we sing, we remember God through music, why would we not go? It is like a festival day [parba-parbani]. This is not something alien to us, we have engaged song and music to access god for all time [*sabu bele*]." At this point, Kela intervened, "See my bapa [father] says we were different, but can he remember a time when our community, when we did not revere Hindu dharma? Our elders agree that what we are doing is not outside our Adibasi beliefs, it is not something that has never been part of us, part of our life."

Younger satsangis described an older generation as "Hindu in their hearts [*hrudaya*] and minds [*mana*], but still wedded to older practices." In subsequent discussions, Kela acknowledged the looseness of satsanga practice among older Desia Kandhas: "They are old, you cannot make them change their ways. But in their heart, if you ask them, you will realize they have never been outside Hindu dharma. Even now they believe in Hindu dharma, but they are too old to change everything about their life, they will do what they have been doing. It is their true feeling, their closeness to Hindu dharma. Their regard for Hindu beliefs is what matters."

Kanu acknowledged his sluggish participation when Kela was absent. "I go to satsanga," he said, "and I enjoy it. But some of us, we do not do the other things that the younger people attending satsangas are doing. They are

saying they are not changing anything; my son is also saying that. But you
see we Adibasis have always used alcohol, we sometimes even use alcohol in
our religious rituals. But these Hindu bhaimaane, they are stopping us from
drinking. I am so old, my friends and I have a drop in the evening when we
return from the fields, that is what I have always done. Now in my old age,
how will I change?"

At this point, Kela, his son who had become a prominent satsanga leader
and Vanvasi Kalyan Ashram worker, interrupted him to insist that Kandhas
had always been Hindu but did not have "proper" or "good" (*bhala*) knowledge of ritual practice and thus did not do satsanga or *pooja* as they do now.
Instead, they often congregated around Hindu temples, even when they were
not allowed in. He explained to his father, "Don't we think our land is sacred?
So do Hindus. Don't we also think the sun is an important force? Hindus worship it as Surjya debata. So how are we so different? We just didn't know that
we believed in the same things as much earlier and now we do." To emphasize
his point, Kela turned to me and asked, "Who says we can't be Adibasi and
Hindu at the same time?"

Younger Kandhas drew attention to distinctions between belief and practice—and also between ontology and identity—to explain older Kandhas' disruptions of the rhetoric of seamless continuity between Adivasi and Hindu.
Older Kandhas, they said, were Hindu in belief if not always in practice; their
hrudaya-mana (hearts and minds) were Hindu, even if they hadn't always
known to call themselves Hindu. In conversations away from his father, Kela
sensed my doubts about Kandha claims about their always-Hindu status in
my quest for an originary Kandha radical alterity. He asked me to ask older
Kandhas and his own father if they could deny that their heart-minds[61] were
never outside Hindu dharma. When I returned to Kanu Majhi another day,
he affirmed this to be true; he could not deny that he could not recall a time
when he and his purba-purusa (forefathers) had not venerated Hindu dharma
or had seen it to be external to their ritual piety.

The intimacies Kela expressed could be read as merely aspirational
performance or effects of Hindu-nationalist brainwashing of Kandhas, as
asserted by so many secular accounts of Hindu nationalism. These readings
fundamentally deny religious cosmology as a site of Adivasi deployments of
politics of indigeneity. Through their separation of belief from practice and of
ontology from identity, a newer cadre of Kandhas, like Kela, smoothed over
inconsistencies and dissonance about the seamless reframing of Kandha cosmological agreements and affinities with Hindus by ethnonationalists.

Such generational differences suggest that Kandha engagements with religious politics—drawing at once on precolonial affinities, colonial ruptures, and an ongoing and seemingly interminable settler colonial Hinduization—were being renegotiated at a time when asserting ethnonationalist claims was inextricable from deepening indigenous politics in the Indian state. Kandhas did not merely draw attention to their distinction by pointing to incommensurable differences between their cosmologies and those of Hindus. Rather, by emphasizing intimacies between indigenous and Hindu cosmologies, they remade their indigenous distinction in order to make political claims through participation in ethnonationalism, as Kela said, as "Adibasi and Hindu."

Indigenous Ascension

Through their participation in satsangas and in Hindutva, my Kandha interlocutors continually relayed their empowerment through their access to high-caste ritual, asserting their control over, rather than subjection through, ritual practice. Forced to witness Hindu ritual from afar despite their shraddha (devotion), Kandhas asserted that now Hindutva had secured their rightful access to Hindu ritual worship, although they continued to control and restrict Pana access to temples. They occasionally hired Brahmin priests to undertake yagnas and rituals and to organize their own village festival celebrations. With the adoption of Hindutva practices in their villages and homes, Kandhas asserted their rightful access to temples and ritual piety, celebrating these practices as revealing and refining their long-standing Hindu positions.

Raju, a young Kandha man who had gained great popularity for his strong, moving vocals during satsanga prayers, crystallized the deeply politically empowering nature of Hindutva as religious politics: "Earlier when we entered a temple, we thought the priest was looking at us and thinking that we were dirty and polluting the temple. We were too poor to buy the right *prasad* [sacred offering]. We did not have two rupees to buy the right coconut, the right flowers. But now we have nothing to fear because we can remember God in our own village. We can pick flowers from our village and offer them, and that is enough for God. We do not have to enter the high- caste temples and worry about being driven out. We can do our satsanga and not fear being shunned and ridiculed."

Raju and his young friends asserted that they were now positioned to subvert caste hierarchy, in which their disenfranchised position overshadowed their piety. Now, away from the forbidding eyes of those higher up in caste and class, they felt free to be Hindu according to their desires and means. These Kandha assertions betrayed how ethnonationalism had elided critiques or challenges to a larger racialized caste hierarchy in which Kandhas continued to be disenfranchised and suffer humiliations by moving practices of community prayer and ritual purity into Kandha villages. As ethnonationalists used the language of indigenous ascendency to affirm Kandhas, they invented traditions[62] that suggested ascendency within a seemingly democratizing socioreligious hierarchy. These fragmented,[63] invented traditions were unstable and ambiguous rather than being explicitly false or spurious, suggesting an indeterminacy of the separation of Adivasi and Hindu rather than crafted traditions where there were none.[64]

As Kandhas reminded me, often contrasting their situation with the Panas' incorporation into Christianity, their own vigorous and pleasurable participation in Hindutva was not aimed at material gain, nor was it motivated by a desire to undo indigenous distinction to simply become Hindu, as suggested by a straightforward narrative of Sanskritization as indigenous assimilation. Rather, Kandhas' recognition had ushered in a language of proprietary indigeneity and democratic ascendency, whose political force Kandhas drew on to understand the affinity and regard of Kandhas as distinct kin Others within Hindu ethnonationalism.

Adivasi Hindutva

Minority participation in Hindu ethnonationalism is understood largely as a national program of social engineering in which all minority traditions are equally and similarly subsumed into Hinduism as a "great" tradition.[65] Dalits too have been incorporated into religious majoritarianism through movements such as the Valmiki movement, in an illustration of religious majoritarianism's continual efforts to incorporate subaltern religion and the consolidation of such efforts by the colonial and postcolonial state.[66] In Kandhamal, with an overwhelming Pana embrace of Christianity, ethnonationalists focused on Kandhas as a privileged kin Other. This focus was not merely tactical but rather revelatory of the enduring purchase of Adivasi authenticity within a Hindu and Hindutva imaginary, mirroring indigenous recognition as a privileged discourse within Indian multiculturalism.

In Kandhamal, the mobilization of Kandhas undeniably demonstrated that Adivasi indigeneity was a privileged "savage slot," outlined by ethnonationalists using a racialized register of Adivasi-embodied religiosity and a veneration of land untainted by material desires. This distinction—or, rather, recognition—of Kandhas, too, hinged on an idiosyncratic authenticity articulated in terms of Hindu-Adivasi intimacies distinct to India, in which the colonial separation of Adivasi from Hindu was remarshaled as a false ontological separation and thus as a potent political substrate on which ethnonationalists consolidated not just an affinity but rather an inseparability of Kandha from Hindu.

At the same time, this Kandha distinction used tropes of authenticity resonant far beyond India, as it hinged on racialized ideas of an inalienable indigenous religiosity and naturalized ties to land.[67] Crucially, while state officials and caste Hindus deployed racialized indigenous authenticity as a lack,[68] a continuing barrier to Adivasis becoming fully realized political and economic agents, who could capitalize the potential of indigenous recognition and receive the benefits of the development state's patronage, the idiosyncratic, ethnonationalist variant of indigenous authenticity was affirmed as a breeding ground for "true attachments," marking Adivasis not merely as foot soldiers[69] but rather as flag bearers for the propagation of Hindutva. Celebrating such an affirming ethnonationalism as a "return" of Hindus to Adivasis that undid an epistemic and social disarticulation of both groups, Kandhas did not see their participation in ethnonationalism as mandating the dilution of their Adivasi identity and, thus, contradictory to indigenous assertion.

What emerged through Kandha Adivasi engagements with Hindutva was a highly ontologically and temporally unruly portrait of indigeneity, demonstrating the recalcitrance of contemporary Adivasi indigeneity, to any straightforward, purifying narrative.[70] Rather, Adivasi participation in Hindutva precisely throws into relief the dizzying pluralities at play in the making of Indian indigeneity and Adivasis' own use of an unruly historicism to articulate intimacies with Hindutva.

As Kandhas insisted on an inseparability of Adivasi from Hindu that resisted any simplistic notion of Sanskritization as indigenous assimilation, they vividly recalled Kandha intimacies with Hindu political rule, remarshaling their role as respected, intimate subjects of Hindu kingship, at once capable of enervating kings' political power or bolstering it by offering their subjection at the service of the consolidation of Hindu political rule. Drawing on a precolonial history of intimacy, they also engaged an understanding of their indigeneity in terms of cultural and political equality and democratic political assertion in the wake of indigenous recognition. Their contemporary, increasingly neoliberal, indigeneity was then built on a heritage not just of Kandha ambivalence and ambiguity toward Hindus but also of an ontological *inseparability* of Adivasi from Hindu.[71]

During my time in Kandhamal, indigeneity's purchase—rather than negation—challenged a long-assumed ethnonationalist discomfort with indigeneity and a disputation of Adivasi claims as prior to those of Hindus within the Indian nation-state. Since then, scholars have shown how territoriality and ethnicity are reworked to consolidate politics of indigeneity to confirm a growing reliance on indigeneity,[72] attributed to a novel capacious flexibility of "neo-Hindutva."[73] The novelty of this capaciousness can be questioned, however, with scholars such as Kalyani Devaki Menon long asserting Hindutva's facility in becoming meaningful in its constituents' lives "by resonating with their constructions of the past, and appealing to their fears in the present," fundamentally through an accommodation of dissonance.[74]

If these reflect this capaciousness of Hindutva that reworks indigeneity despite a doctrinal mistrust of Adivasiness as a condition of prior claims undermining those of Hindus—its ability to "speak in tongues"[75] when confronted by incommensurations within Adivasi lifeworlds—they equally speak of the astonishing and oftentimes confounding temporal and ontological unruliness of Adivasi indigeneity itself. Hindutva as a neocolonial regime of recognition deceptively appeared to secure ascendency for Kandhas. Amid caveats to turn away from such recognition to other forms of self-determination, notably land,[76] we now turn to how Adivasi claims and naturalized ties to land are capable of producing the exclusion of Dalits from an Adivasi-Hindu history of ritual exchange and mutual regard to reproduce Dalits' failure to be seen as rooted to land and nation.

CHAPTER 5

Sacred Land, Sacred Nation

In this chapter, we turn to how Kandhas express intimacies engaging their cosmological view of land as Dharini Pennu, the Earth Goddess, and ethnonationalist regard for the land of the nation as Bharat Mata (Mother Land) to consolidate and privilege Adivasi claims to land as naturalized and proprietary. These Kandha intimacies with ethnonationalism are detrimental to Panas as landless Dalits, as they come to provide the grounds for xenophobic imaginings of landless Dalits as squatters on Adivasi lands marked by both cosmological and economic unbelonging as well as Christian capital as threatening the bodily purity and integrity of a nature-culture figuration of Adivasi land. Ethnonationalists invoked Kandha worship of land as Dharini Pennu as sacred and integral to their cosmology, insisting that the purity of such a nature-culture figure was under siege by Christian capital to reincite hostilities against Dalits. Kandhas experienced these panics about Christian capital and its corrosive effects, not merely in secular economic terms of alienation from land as property, but rather as threatening a bio-moral transmutation at the center of Kandha cosmology, which configures Kandhas as inseparable from their dharma (religion) and their land as a sentient nature-culture figure. Using charged, sensuous terms to insist that their land, their territory, was being sullied by Dalits, Kandhas reinvoked patterned relationships between caste ideology, space, and the marking of bodies and the sensorium by the environment.[1] Adivasi ontologies of land then coalesced cosmological and economic assertions over land, emphasizing how just indigenous ontologies and religious cosmologies can become implicated in upholding majoritarian regimes of capital in which landless Dalits are abjected.

The Muddiness of Indigenous Ontologies

Recent anthropological debates about indigenous ontologies focus on how "indigenous cosmopolitics"[2] sharply challenge conventional notions and divides assumed within Eurocentric divisions between religion and politics, as well as nature and culture. As anthropologist Marisol de la Cadena suggests, indigeneity's engagements with nonhumans as actors in the political arena challenges the separation of nature and culture that underpins the prevalent notion of politics and its according social contract. The emergence of nature-culture beings in mainstream politics is a product of an expansive and simultaneous crisis of colonialism and neoliberalism—and their ecological, economic, and political manifestations. Such nature-culture figures as political actors do not merely represent excessive, residual, or infantile conjurings of indigenous lifeworlds. Rather, they trouble established conceptual orthodoxies within politics, and accordingly their presence may evince a moment of rupture of modern politics and an emergent indigeneity. Here, indigenous forces and practices are seen as possessing the capacity to disrupt prevalent political formations and reshuffle hegemonic antagonisms by rendering illegitimate the exclusion of indigenous practices from nation-state institutions.

Criticisms of the ontological turn have lamented its preoccupation with a hopeful politics-as-they-could-be, rather than politics as they are represented in current modes of resistance, suffering, and governance among indigenous peoples.[3] In what follows, I complicate such an overwhelming focus on the redemptive and hopeful political potential of indigenous ontologies by instead showcasing the dark possibilities of the reabsorption of indigenous ontological claims in political and economic hegemonies. Both Adivasis as indigenous political actors and ethnonationalists used their distinct indigenous veneration of land as a nature-culture figure to claim political intimacies between them and uphold dominant regimes of land and capital, from which landless Dalits are excluded. These ontological intimacies suggest the need to engage indigenous ontologies as unruly, unstable and porous, as well as mark the Eurocentric limits of debates in which indigenous ontologies are framed as challenging and, therefore, expanding conventional understandings of modern politics.

These Kandha-Hindutva reframing of affinities over land expressed in nature-culture relationalities are not devoid of dominant logics of economic and political control. In fact, Kandhas as Adivasis engage land as a nature-culture figure to assert their economic entitlements to land, but not in ways that overtly reject majoritarian control over lands through which they see themselves as dispossessed. Rather, Kandhas' claims on land as a nature-culture figure allowed the rearticulation of intimacies between Adivasi and Hindu cosmologies that reactivate Dalit landlessness as a condition of religious-cultural as well as economic exclusion within Hindu majoritarianism. The uneven ways in which Adivasis were claimed as kin of upper-caste Hindus within Hindutva, secured by temporally unruly fusions that defied linear histories of Adivasi and Hindu. Adivasis were claimed as kin precisely through an Othering, which also became acutely visible while engaging Adivasi distinction vis-à-vis land as a nature-culture figure.

Indeed, the ontological turn has ignored how claims about land as a sentient nature-culture figure can run unevenly alongside indigenous claims to territory and natural resources that might uphold dominant regimes of capital and value, unevenly protesting but also engaging market logics of land.[4] This analysis presents land as a particularly salient site at which to see the *muddiness*, rather than a presumed purity, of indigenous ontologies become visible as land as a sentient being is invoked in ways that collapse distinctions between nature and culture, religion and politics, but also ultimately run unevenly alongside and uphold dominant regimes of land as property. Engaging the muddiness of indigenous ontologies remediates an insistence of indigenous ontologies as a hopeful salve to politics in the present day, gesturing to tensions, aggressions, and contradictions animating them and their implications for politics in contemporary India[5] and elsewhere.[6]

Land as Dharini Pennu

Colonial accounts depict meriah sacrifice to be at the center of a Kandha religious cosmology in which the appeasement of land with human blood was seen as ensuring fertility for a community that sustained itself through agriculture. Humans feed personified aspects of nature through blood sacrifices, which in turn "feed" the community, assuring villagers good health and harvest, and social harmony. If this cyclic relationship breaks and crops fail or disease breaks out, villagers view this to be a sign of Dharini Pennu's displeasure, dissatisfaction, or even anger that can only be assuaged through ritual, accompanied by an appropriate sacrifice prescribed by the jani (village priest). The Kandha relationship with Dharini Pennu, the Earth Goddess, then, does not install a divide between nature and culture; instead, it places humans and nonhuman actors in a cycle of reciprocity and mutual dependence.[7]

With a ban on human blood instituted after the British colonial administration's installation of the Meriah Agency, the harvest festival now centers on the sacrifice of a rather expensive podha (ox) by Desia Kandhas whose blood is offered to Dharini Pennu.[8] Kandhas, however, continue to endorse the belief that Dharini Pennu could only be adequately appeased with human, not ox, blood. It is for that reason that Kandhas would speak of a number of "accidental" nicks and cuts made by the sacrificial knife on the bodies of the gathered crowd such that "enough" human blood would fall to the earth to restore the ritual to what "it ought to be."

Colonial accounts encapsulated meriah sacrifice as motivated by an authentic indigenous cosmology in which an inalienable primitive religiosity, rather than material gain, drove the barbarism of human sacrifice. Colonists' reductive reading of indigenous Kandhas' cosmological beliefs fundamentally misapprehended the Kandhas' engagement with the material world. They characterized Kandha cosmology as clearly engaging a flawed instrumentality that failed to cordon off nature from culture and, therefore, misunderstood the material world by insisting that substances such as blood could appease land. Colonists reconciled Kandhas as barbaric but ultimately guileless primitives to rationalize and, consequently, violently punish their engagement in human sacrifice.

Colonial governance and legal discourse also indicted local Pana Dalits, who procured the human victims of sacrifice for Kandhas for a fee, as overwhelmingly responsible for human sacrifice. Colonists insisted that Panas were motivated only by the canniness of commerce, unlike Kandhas, who were motivated by their pure and guileless religious cosmology. As we have seen, these colonial constructions of Kandhas and Panas lingered in caste society, and they were now commonsensical scripts through which both groups and relations between them continued to be engaged in Kandhamal. Yet Kandhas described their continued reverence for Dharini Pennu as a nature-culture figure by precisely emphasizing their material expectations from Dharini Pennu.

When I asked Kandhas about the significance of Dharini Pennu in Kandha cosmology, they described Dharini Pennu as a mother who nurtured them, "filling our stomachs when we are hungry," by ensuring fertility and a good harvest but who, when angered, punished her children through famine and sickness. Dharini Pennu, as described by Kandhas, is at the center of a

Kandha cosmology that deeply regards the sacred character of all aspects of nature that surrounded them. Kandhas revere water (Paani), hills (Dongara), and the land (Dharini) as sentient, gendered beings, yet they are not seen as assuming human contours. My interlocutors described them as possessing living spirit but never visualized in human form.[9] Kandhas described these figures as governing crucial aspects of Kandha life that ensured material flourishing in which Dharini Pennu was responsible for ensuring agrarian yield and prosperity and bodily sickness and health for the community.

Villages saved money all year for the purchase of oxen for sacrifice and for other aspects of the ritual celebration; Kandhas explained that Dharini Pennu herself demanded to be remembered and nurtured in exchange for caring for them by ensuring their material well-being. A young man, Gopal Majhi, explained the community's reasoning for incurring considerable expenses every year to observe the festival of Dharini Pennu, stressing just how integral she continued to be to Kandha cosmology because of her ability to control every aspect of Kandhas' everyday existence and survival. "I can't explain our feeling for Dharini Pennu in simple words," he said.

> It is not a festival like Durga Pooja, which we observe from afar, which we sometimes celebrate, and sometimes not. Dharini Pennu is important to everything we do. Anything we do—like the crops we grow, how abundant our harvest is and the food we put in our mouth and even the health of our community—it is all because of her. We can go without doing Durga Puja or a temple puja or other small rituals, but we cannot go without remembering and revering Dharini Pennu. Ask the elders. Any time we miss sacrificing an ox, and satiating her with blood, destruction follows almost immediately. Our crops fail, we do not have enough to eat and the children start falling very ill; they get mysterious ailments for which we have no cure. We cannot forget to acknowledge her because even now, if you anger her, she will destroy you. But if you do your duty (*karma*) toward her and do not neglect her, she will not harm you.

Gopal attested to the continued importance of material reciprocity in the relationship between Kandhas and Dharini Pennu. According to Kandhas, Dharini Pennu demanded to be nurtured in return by appearing in dreams or by issuing warnings by way of small accidents, like a bodily injury sustained in the fields. Contrary to the colonial insistence that the Kandha regard for land was motivated by a sacred reverence innocent of material desires,[10] Kandhas fundamentally engaged their relationship with Dharini Pennu in terms of material reciprocity and exchange. Gopal's use of the distinctly Hindu doctrinal term "karma" also showed the dispersal of Hinduism into Kandha cosmologies, underscoring the permeable and porous, rather than static, nature of indigenous cosmologies.

As with Adivasi and Hindu alliances that were articulated through a symbolic give-and-take over religious practices, Hindu kingship historically harnessed Adivasi indigenous regard for land to forge political alliances between Adivasis and Hindus, long before the formation of the modern Indian state and the emergence of the distinct Hindu ethnonationalist movement. Burkhard Schnepel, for instance, has shown that Hindu kings gained the trust and solidarity of their tribal subjects by patronizing powerful local goddesses as well as by worshiping land. This helped Hindu kings secure their legitimacy as rulers by linking them ideologically and ritually to the land of their kingdoms and their Adivasi inhabitants.[11] Using religious iconography and symbolism to cast their shared worship of land as a particularly salient mode of relatedness, Hindu kings secured Adivasi patronage without confrontational oppression and displacement. Their sacred regard for land also secured a discourse of mutual cosmological regard between Hindus and Adivasis.

Aniconic symbols—such as stones, trees, or mounds of earth—were given human form and appearance in the form of personified deities as female goddesses, which paved the way for the worship of personified female deities. Gradual shifts in Adivasi understandings of land's form ensued, which altered the extent to which land and goddesses in the shakta tradition were related. These shifts, however, continued to be couched in a language of continuity of shared beliefs in land's sacred nature, by Hindus and eventually Adivasis alike. Thus, although Hindu and Adivasis did not quite engage land as a nature-culture formation in similar ways, they insisted on their reverence for land in terms of variations within a continuum of relatedness. These gradual shifts over hundreds of years in the veneration of land resulted in more and more movement from nature to culture without marking the personification as a significant rupture in nature-culture imaginaries of reverence and kinship.

Such a history of shifts in Adivasi ontologies of land through manipulations of iconicity, that is, a relationship between a sign and its object in which the form of the sign recapitulates the object in some way, made political rule and economic control of Adivasis possible under Hindu kingship. Bruce Mannheim outlines several key effects of iconicity.[12] Iconicity naturalizes one set of semiotic distinctions by referring it to another that is understood by the speakers to be more basic, essential, outside volitional control, or outside culture. It allows particular linguistic and cultural patterns to be referred to each other, such that they become mutually interpreting. It aligns structural forms across distinct cultural domains to unify cultural patterns. It fits the form of a speech event closely to the specific contours of its setting, making it compelling to the participants and providing cues that they use to interpret it. Finally, by bringing distinct cultural and linguistic structures into structural alignment, it enhances their cognitive retention by individuals. Hindu majoritarian manipulation of the iconicity of land had facilitated a formless veneration of land as a sentient being to a worship of land as a personified deity, such that land and the Hindu goddess form became mutually interpretive of each other in ways that at once recalled the specificity of Adivasi cosmologies of land while also suggesting the interchangeability of land and deity. Crucially, such an alignment between the two now ensured that Kandhas saw such an interchangeability to be essential, undisputed, and only natural within a Hindu-Adivasi cosmological order.

Dharini Pennu as Bharat Mata

As debates over Pana bids for tribal recognition began to roil the district in 2007, ethnonationalist workers from the Vanvasi Kalyan Ashram and Bajrang Dal began to frequent Kandha villages after a brief lull in their outreach. At this time, Panas were circulating petitions for their reclassification as Kandhariya Panas. Leaders of the Kandha identity movement Kui Samaj and other community members remained vehemently opposed to this reclassification. Tensions ran high in the district as ethnonationalists and Kandhas actively conferred on issues of Pana reclassification with dangerous economic implications for Kandhas. At the outset of these visits, Kandhas greeted ethnonationalists with more than a little anger, chiding them for not coming around more often, for once again "forgetting" them, saying "*Aagya mane ta aamaku bhuli jauchanti* [These honorable people are always forgetting us]." Kandhas' sometimes plaintive, other times resigned complaints rearticulated a sense of neglect and abandonment that ethnonationalists found themselves consistently burdened to assuage. Ethnonationalists attempted to placate Kandhas by insisting that they could never forget their Adibasi brothers. They explained that they had been busy with their service to the nation (*rashtra seba*), especially as Christian threats to the nation's security and integrity were not without serious implications for Kandhas themselves. They were here, then, to inform Kandhas about events unfolding around them in order to expose "truths" hidden in plain sight.

In these renewed and charged attempts of right-wing workers to engage Kandhas, ethnonationalists attempted to reconcile contradictions and discontinuities in their positions on Adivasi as Hindu and Adivasi as indigenous but in kinship to Hindus engaging Hindutva and Kandha veneration of land as a nature-culture figure. The singularity of Adivasi-Hindu intimacy was claimed through discursive deployments of land's distinction as a nature-culture figure, which upheld Kandhas' religious and cultural distinction. Kandhas and ethnonationalists emphasized Adivasi and Hindu affinities in terms of a shared devotion to the holy land of the Hindu rashtra. Their attempts to translate and render commensurate their differing engagements of the nature-culture continuum was secured within a much longer history of Hindu control of lands through an iconicity that had made land and the form of the Hindu female goddess mutually suggestive, which was rearticulated in an ethnonationalist veneration of Adivasi land as Bharat Mata. These discursive engagements of Dharini Pennu and Bharat Mata secured the foundation for authentic Adivasi belonging to the Hindu nation while they also acknowledged the Adivasi condition to be prior to that of Hindus, despite Hindutva's doctrinal denial of Adivasi indigeneity as a condition of original settlement and, therefore, political claims preceding those of Hindus.

After a long day of mobilizing Kandhas to agitate against Pana bids at reclassification, sitting at a village square, Misra babu, a Vanvasi Kalyan Ashram worker, conversed with Kandha villagers over a cup of tea. Misra babu fiercely impressed upon the members of his Kandha audience that it was imperative to combat Christianity's morally corrosive influences on the district. He reminded them that Christianity was a foreign influence alien to them, unlike Hinduism, which had always been part of their ancestors' lives. Gesturing to the gathered Kandhas, he implored, "Ask them, have they not always celebrated Durga Puja? Do they not regard Maa Patakhanda? Do they not worship this earth they live on? Do they not regard the soil of Hindustan as their motherland [*matrubhumi*]? They do! So how can people say they are not Hindu?"

The Kandha men sitting around me chimed in, "We are Hindus! We pray to the earth of Hindustan, so we are Hindu!"

Misra babu and other nationalists celebrated Kandhas' worship of Dharini Pennu by remobilizing a historically wrought relationship in which Hindu and

Adivasi cosmologies had over time gradually appeared to converge somewhat seamlessly on the worship of land. In this instance, Misra babu articulated Kandha-Hindu intimacies by, once again, turning to the inseparability of the Hindu goddess Durga and a local folk goddess, Maa Patakhanda, juxtaposing big tradition and little tradition Adivasi goddesses[13] side by side in shakta Hindu worship. At other times, however, he also used these relationships to blur nature-culture distinctions between Kandha veneration of land as Dharini Pennu and Hindutva personification of land of the Hindu nation as Bharat Mata. He would remark that just as Maa Patakhanda was a goddess figure revered in keeping with Hindu shakta tradition, so too was the Kandha veneration of Dharini Pennu as Bharat Mata. He and other ethnonationalist workers sometimes invoked Dharini Pennu as a nature-culture figure to engage another strand especially salient within Hindu ethnonationalism: the worship of the land of the nation as a distinct form of what Chetan Chatt calls geopiety[14]—a symbolic devotion to land at the cornerstone of Hindu ethnonationalism's distinctly territorial form of devotionalism,[15] a worship of the land of the nation as Bharat Mata. Nationalist workers enthusiastically proclaimed that akin to Kandhas, they too revered land as a goddess in a personified female form known as Bharat Mata, the Mother Land, quite literally conjured up as Mother Goddess, which originated in a process rooted in anti-British-rule nationalism predating Hindu ethnonationalism.

Sumathi Ramaswamy reminds us of the mutual implication of nation and gender as a "dangerous liaison"[16] in the reproduction of nation's territory as a deeply gendered, divinized, and affect-laden place.[17] Bharat Mata is the nation recast as "modern yet modest," with her essential difference from a hegemonic West ensured by her rootedness in a selectively appropriated "Indian" tradition that is modeled on upper-caste Hindu and Sanskritic-Aryan norms.[18] Bharat Mata is crafted as a mother figure who presides over the nation as her home, a home that is the last bastion of autonomy and authenticity in a world made over by empire and colonialism. Yet she is not hidden within the domestic realm and is instead a public woman who is seen as "invincible but also vulnerable; as benevolent but also blood thirsty; as comely maiden but also ageless matron."

To Ramaswamy's formulation, historian Charu Gupta adds that this maternal figuration of the nation imbues it with moral fervor by politicizing its religious, cultural, and aesthetic aspects. The figure of the mother can be specifically claimed as the colonized people's "own" while it takes on various attributes, such as a glorious figure of abundance; the powerful mother Kali and Durga, a destructive *shakti*; or an enslaved, all-suffering figure, a tearful victim and a frail widow to serve as a uniting anti-colonial symbol. This work of imagining the nation as mother, Gupta emphasizes, renders the nation a tangible and enduring entity, which may be affectively experienced. The nation as mother invites the devotion of a loyal political citizenry, who gain idealized personhood and identity largely as male Hindu sons of the nation.

While the genealogy of the nation as Bharat Mata seemingly draws on an enshrined shakta tradition in Hinduism to be presented in a "garb of venerable antiquity," Sumathi Ramaswamy reminds us that Bharat Mata is, in fact, a tangled product of charged encounters crafting a fraught and conflicted postcolonial Indian modernity that attempts to resolve contentious debates between authenticity and imitation, tradition and modernity, and religion and science, while emphasizing the essentially Hindu character of the nation. Hindu ethnonationalism's reworking of Bharat Mata aggressively moves away from all pretensions of secularism to embrace a Hindu majoritarian feminized nation against whom religious Others commit violence[19] and whose moral purity is critical for Hindu integrity and, thus, whose protection can trigger and reproduce a performative masculinist nationalism.

We might recall that slaking the thirst of Dharini Pennu through meriah human sacrifice had been critical to the different racialization and casteist construction of Kandhas as authentic if misguided indigenes and Panas as their mercenary Others under colonial rule. In the years after the violent censure of meriah sacrifice and its impact on Kandhas' self-understanding, the worship and veneration of Dharini Pennu had at first been muted but continued through the sacrifice of oxen and, sometimes, cheaper pigs and roosters.[20] These practices sat somewhat awkwardly within Christian practices but had been largely ignored and bracketed by missionaries.

With the advent of Hindutva in the 1980s and onward, Kandhas reported that Dharini Pennu began to be flagged as central to Kandha cosmology and, as such, became more performative and visible as a marker of Kandha identity, even as its central practice of animal sacrifice sat uneasily within the ethos of vegetarianism in ethnonationalism. Marisol de la Cadena observes that the emergence of nature-culture beings in mainstream politics needs to be contextualized with recourse to both colonialism and neoliberalism—and their ecological, economic, and political manifestations. Kandhas were aided by neoliberal turns, including a growing turn toward Adivasiness as a condition of territorial entitlements that resulted in the renaming of the district in 1992 as Kandhamal, as well as the arrival of Hindutva in the area to foreground

Dharini Pennu as central to their cosmology, after British colonialism suppressed and muted Dharini Pennu with censure of human sacrifice. Kandhas insisted that the appeasement of Dharini Pennu was critical to their community's material well-being, as the only way to ensure agrarian fertility and minimal sickness and societal strife. By the 2000s, the veneration of Dharini Pennu was once again highly visible within Hindu ethnonationalism as a singular distinction of Adivasis—a sacred regard for land as venerated person rather than mere possession. Hindu ethnonationalism has weaponized an upper-caste aesthetic infrastructure of a performative militant vegetarianism[21] as a means through which to attack minority religions and low-caste groups who eat meat,[22] which has been critical in the propagation of Hindutva. In Kandhamal, however, eliding the history of human sacrifice linked to Kandhas' worship of Dharini Pennu and the sacrifice of oxen discordant with an upper-caste vegetarian ethos of Hindutva, ethnonationalists invoked the Kandhas' worship of the land as devotion to the motherland.

In Kandhamal, ethnonationalists engaged Bharat Mata to recall a temporally unrestricted invented tradition of a shakti or goddess tradition within Hinduism that absorbed any number of folk female figures. The reconfiguration of Dharini Pennu from a formless nature-culture figure to an alternately punitive or nurturing maternal figure reproduced Kandhas as her devoted protectors and masculinist ethnonationalists. After our return from Srirampur one day, Misra babu explained, "Our Adibasi brothers, they see land like a mother as we do, like Bharat Mata whom we worship. It is not easy to narrate to you in words the high regard they have for their land. This land to them is so pure, so sacred. They will not let anyone destroy it, do anything to it. They are saying that Adivasis are protecting the land, now even the courts are saying that. We are also trying to do that. We are also trying to protect the soil of Bharat Mata from outsiders who are endangering it, who are selling it for their gain. But these Adibasi bhaimaane, they have been doing this protection, this worship, for centuries, long before us. They are not motivated by *aarthik swartha* (material self-interest) in caring for their land. Their feeling for it far exceeds what we can narrate in words." In Misra babu's naturalization of Adivasi stewardship of land, despite extant understandings of indigeneity's negation within Hindu ethnonationalism,[23] there was an acknowledgment of Adivasi indigeneity as a distinct minority formation "prior" to Hinduism as well as echoes of tropes of indigenous natural harmony with lands and environment.

Ethnonationalist workers praised Kandha worship of Dharini Pennu as another form of territorial geopiety while consolidating their Adivasi figuration as naturally tied to the soil of the Hindu motherland. In their veneration of Dharini Pennu, Kandhas aimed to ultimately secure material reciprocity; they spoke of Dharini Pennu as needing to be appeased to ensure material gain through agricultural success and land and health for their community. Ethnonationalists, however, pegged Kandhas' natural and selfless devotion to land as unmotivated by material desires, mirroring a colonial discourse of Kandhas' immaterial, "purely" sacred regard for land devoid of economic interests. They hailed Kandhas' devotion to their land as testament to their devotion to the Hindu nation (rashtra), predating Hindu ethnonationalism's own deification of the land of the Hindu rashtra as Bharat Mata. Ethnonationalists relied on Kandhas' distinct cosmology that pivoted on Dharini Pennu as a nature-culture figure to invoke Adivasi indigeneity as a political formation prior to Hinduism in order to consolidate indigenous authenticity, characterized by an immutable and inalienable religious cosmology that centers on a reverence toward the land of the Hindu rashtra.

Despite ethnonationalists' concerted semiotic efforts at reconciling Dharini Pennu and Bharat Mata as seamlessly interchangeable nature-culture figures, Hindus and Adivasis did not articulate the nature-culture continuum similarly. Older Kandhas particularly stressed that the personified deities were hardly interchangeable with the formless Dharini Pennu and disrupted Kandha ontologies, altering their cosmological worldviews. Gala, as a community elder, often vividly and poetically described feeling Dharini Pennu's reassuring presence around them without assuming that Dharini Pennu looks like Kandhas themselves; she was formless and omnipresent precisely because she did not assume human contours.

On the other hand, ethnonationalists gave Bharat Mata a deified human female form, which was highly visible in Vanvasi Kalyan Ashram, Vishwa Hindu Parishad, and Bharatiya Janata Party publicity materials, including pamphlets and posters that increasingly found their place as decorations on the walls of satsanga houses and the entrances of Kandha homes. The iconic representation of Bharat Mata presented discontinuities that were not unseen by Kandhas, especially by Kandha elders, who repeatedly remarked that murti (idol) worship was alien to the community and that worshipping aspects of nature was different from seeing them as persons in human form. And yet despite these significant disagreements, land's status as a nature-culture figure served as a semiotic reminder of synergies between Hindus and Adivasis, reassuring Kandhas in equal measure of nationalists' *bhala mana* (good intentions, literally "good mind") and *ekabhaliya bichara* (shared

thinking) that assured Kandhas of ethnonationalist devotion to land and signaled their shared desire to protect it, precisely within a context of manipulations of iconicity through land as formless Dharini Pennu and as personified
goddess-nation.

Raju and Sekha were among a group of young men who had begun attending Hindutva satsangas after being assured of mobilizers' good intentions
toward Kandhas because of their shared reverence for land as a mother figure. Sekha said, "These Hindu brothers want the same thing as us, they give
importance to the same things as us. They worship the land—they see her as
a goddess. They are also tied to her, to the soil of the nation. Can Adivasis be
separated from our land, can we allow someone to destroy it? No, it is our
mother, it is our entire existence. we can't describe what it is to you in words,
what is the special feeling we have for our land. You know this. We have told
you so many times. When someone hurts our land, misuses it, abuses it—we
feel the pain in our bodies."

Raju added, "At first, we thought why are these Hindu brothers coming
to us, why are they inviting us to participate in these rituals? What is their
motive, are they here to take something from us, steal something from us?
But then we began to understand that they are coming to us because they
share the same reverence for land as us, they also feel pain in their bodies
when somebody does something wrong against it. They also worship the land
as a mother, they want to protect her and they know we have been doing that
for a long time, even before them."

Raju indicated that Hindu ethnonationalism's attempts to engage Kandhas had been received with trepidation and fear because of a long history of
economic exploitation and extraction from Adivasi communities and social
ostracization. Ethnonationalists had not entirely smoothed over these exploitative histories and, instead, found themselves attempting to reconcile them
with their rhetoric of seamless caste Hindu regard for and fraternity with
Adivasis. It was at these times that ontologies of land as a shared maternal figure within a nature-culture continuum sutured Kandha and Hindu ethnonationalist cosmologies by recalling a longer tradition of political patronage and
subjection through shared ontological beliefs.

Throughout, Hindu ethnonationalist rhetoric insisted on a seamless continuity between Kandha and Hindu beliefs. Eliding the history of human
sacrifice linked to Kandhas' worship of Dharini Pennu and the sacrifice of
oxen discordant with an upper-caste vegetarian ethos of Hindutva, ethnonationalist workers invoked the Kandhas' worship of the land as devotion to

the motherland. This inclusion of land did indeed challenge assumed divides between nature and culture by placing nonhuman actors at the heart of politics but in perverse ways, opening up discussions between ethnonationalists and Adivasis about how indigenous beliefs in the sacred qualities of nature dovetails with ontological beliefs in Hinduism, such as the deification of aspects of nature such as sun and water.

Ontological Affinities as Reterritorialization

Ethnonationalists' reworking of Dharini Pennu as Bharat Mata, then, relied a long history of the manipulation of ontological beliefs about land through iconicity, in which formless land and personified Hindu goddess figures had become mutually referential to secure a gradual indigenous assimilation. Adivasiness as indigenous assimilation has largely been engaged using Sanskritization, which has only implied a hegemonic and apolitical displacement of indigenous ontologies through a passive absorption of hegemonic upper-caste Hindu practices by minorities. As ethnonationalists remobilized a long history of reverence for land to show historical affinities between Hindus and Kandhas, however, Kandhas' uneven but strategic subscription to this rhetoric recentered Adivasis as political-economic agents who rearticulated cosmological affinities within dominant political regimes to retain control over land, showing how indigenous ontologies must be engaged with an eye toward indigenous economic claims.

As anthropologist Piergiorgio Di Giminiani argues, a jural language of property often converts ancestral indigenous territory into quantifiable compensation divorced from topological characteristics, fixing indigenous geographies to neutralize the threat they pose to existing property regimes.[24] He contends that it is vital to observe the agency of both indigenous claimants and state power in land claims, transactions, and translations between place and property as enacting a process of what philosophers Gilles Deleuze and Félix Guattari might describe as reterritorialization. Such a process of reterritorialization elucidates how asymmetric tensions between indigenous transactions and state translations of ancestral territory recode fluid indigenous spatialities that are conceptually antagonistic to state geographies. In this analysis, the accommodations, adaptations, and translations of Adivasi as indigenous ontologies, both under Hindu kingship and within Hindutva, emerge as projects of reterritorialization in which Adivasis' nature-culture articulations of land become accommodated into Hindu-majoritarian political and economic control of land.

In an uneven neoliberal economic terrain on which Adivasis seemed unable to economically progress despite indigenous recognition, landless Dalits had come to appear relatively economically mobile, disrupting the region's local caste and tribe hierarchies. Here, in response, land as a nature-culture figure was used to assert Kandha Adivasi ethnonationalist belonging while also upholding their economic entitlements to land over those of Dalits.

Here too, caste as aesthetic infrastructure at the service of capital secured an anti-Dalit consensus among caste Hindus and Kandhas. Kandha disgust at purported Pana Christian immorality, coalesced through the vitriolic speech of Hindu ethnonationalists, was articulated in terms of the pollution, defilement, and sullying of their sacred land as the land of the Hindu nation. This defilement was cast as sullying a biomoral continuity between Adivasis, land, and dharma that defied secular understandings of land as a property, unevenly engaging the sentience of land and a transubstantial inextricability of Adivasis from their land. As Kandhas flagged their singular veneration of land as the sentient and omniscient Dharini Pennu, with whom they were engaged in a relationship of intimate material reciprocity, they also insisted on land as "rightfully ours," in ways that flagged their economic entitlements to land as property.

Some Kandhas, especially elders, continued to express doubt about the seamless continuities on which ethnonationalists insisted by pointing to the Hindu deification and personification of aspects of nature and to Kandhas' formless regard of land and dongaras (hills). Several younger Kandhas, however, reiterated the similarities between Kandha and Hindu ontologies, and indigenous and Hindu cosmologies. They expressed nature-culture synergies in terms that were not bound and immutable but rather shifting and uneven, which demanded to be located within the pragmatics of a larger political and economic context. Kandhas' attempts to locate themselves within Hindu ethnonationalism were recapturing economic anxieties about uneven caste incorporations into a neoliberal economy, in which tribal recognition had failed to ensure economic commensuration despite acknowledging Adivasi land rights.[25]

As one Kandha elder explained to me, "We are not just begrudging the Panas their due. But explain to us, if they are advancing through Christian conversion, their young are getting educated, why are we not doing the same, why is it not happening to us? For years, we are watching them get ahead, their life has changed. They embraced another dharma, but that dharma made them rich. The few of ours that changed our dharma, we did not get rich like them, we remained where we were. That is why we know it is futile for us to change our religion, we will not sell the land of our nation by converting to Christianity because it is not taking us anywhere. At least we have some self-respect with Hindu dharma. Our land, it has feeling, it is not separate from us, it is all we have."

His son who had been intently listening to our conversation added, "We used to be okay with this, who is rich who is not, we did not think so much about it. Perhaps we had not thought too much about who is ahead of us, who is behind us, we were living our own lives. But these Hindu bhai mane, when they started explaining it to us, it is not just that Panas are getting rich by embracing the Christian dharma, they are now trying to get rich by claiming to be Adibasis to grab our land. It was not enough for them to change their dharma, why are they trying to claim our heritage? Our land?" Claims to land recaptured Kandhas' discontent that Christian capital had disproportionately benefited Dalit Christian converts to further Kandhas' marginalization within the local economy. Indeed, ethnonationalists had been insistent that Kandhas were unable to prosper materially, despite being engaged by missions and NGOs, because materially savvy Panas monopolized capital, and it was only local land that afforded Kandhas security, both economic and moral-cultural.

Jagannath Sahu, a Bajrang Dal leader, and I sat among a gathering of Kandha men who returned to describing Pana attempts to gain tribal status as encroachments upon their Adivasi entitlements. Sahu babu emphasized that Panas were different from Kandhas because they would not hesitate to fill their bellies regardless of the means through which they would do this, even if it meant "selling" the land of the nation to Christians through conversion. Reinvoking Dalit materialism in terms of Panas' seeming inability to place fidelity to nation and religion over the fulfillment of their material needs, Sahu babu said, "Our Kandha brothers know these Panas for what they are. Panas are scavengers, they will prey on the flesh of the dead. They will eat any filth anyone gives them. To fill their belly, they can be anything—Christian or Hindu, it doesn't matter to them. They are so devious and cunning that they will switch sides whenever it suits them."

Seated among Kandhas, two Vanvasi Kalyan Ashram workers, Pradhan babu and Mohapatra babu, puzzled over why Kandhas continued to be unable to advance economically despite receiving land rights by displacement. I attempted to steer the conversation toward how Panas too were economically suffering and had no legal recognition. Pradhan babu said, "It is clear that Panas have been talking to you and influencing you. These are their words, their feelings, not yours. They are so clever, look at what they have been telling you. They know you are not from here, that you are not aware of the long history of their mercenary and materialistic ways, and that you will believe them. They are trying to gain your sympathy to elicit something from you. Never believe them, they will swindle you. You don't have to believe us, ask the Kandhas. They will tell you how they have stolen from them for years, taken their dues from them. And even now, they are trying to take their Adivasi name, their land, which to them is everything. It is not a possession for them, it is something they cannot describe. They see it as a mother, like we do. You are an outsider, so you have fallen for their words. But everyone here in Kandhamal knows. Here we are trying to protect our nation as our mother. And they? They can even sell their own mother and sister in the bajaar (marketplace), they are that kind."

Pradhan babu and Sahu babu resignified a longer history of the different casteist construction of Kandhas and Panas to suture their Dalit identity to their Christian identity. Portraying Panas as scavenging crows recalled tropes of the animality of Dalits as well as their identification with ritually polluting labor, such as manual scavenging and the management of dead bodies, as distinct markers of Dalitness in order to layer them onto Christian identity. While this may be seen as an instance of what Joel Lee describes as "the socialization of the sensorium of the dominant—the over-cultivation of disgust among the privileged castes toward processes and forms of labor essential to life,"[26] Kandhas themselves observed purity and pollution taboos against Panas before their Hinduization and osmosis of caste Hindu strictures such as vegetarianism and staying away from alcohol. In that sense, Hindu ethnonationalist recalled historical referents of a strict caste hierarchy between Kandhas and Panas, while also layering other upper-caste valences onto Kandhas' endorsement of their embodied caste superiority over Panas. This meant recalling upper-caste disgust for professions associated with Dalit livelihoods while also reminding Kandhas of Panas as servile and lower than them, which associated them with ritual tasks for Kandhas that Kandhas themselves would not undertake.

Although Panas were warier of discussing their historical relationship and any claims of a shared heritage with Kandhas, they most frequently expressed their claim to indigeneity through their occupation of the lands of Kandhamal, where they bore similar conditions of rural poverty, infrastructural neglect, and lack of opportunity. Lorance Digal often invited me to his home to lament an enduring construction of Panas as outsiders and squatters on Adivasi land, musing that though his forefathers also lived here, he and his community were always framed as being from elsewhere and as such as unentitled to the land of Kandhamal.

Lorance mused, "They say we are from outside, from elsewhere. But where is this elsewhere? We do not know. As long as I have come to my senses, I know I am from here, my forefathers also. But they say I have no ties to this land, I have no reverence for it. If I do not have any special relationship to it, where else do we belong? Where else do we live, pray, raise our children?" A third-generation Christian, Lorance defiantly refused the ethnonationalist characterization of Christianity as a foreign religion (*bideshi dharma*), by simply pointing out that all his pastors and fellow Christians were from Bharata *desha*. He also astutely recapitulated a point that several Christians, mostly Pana, and even some Kandhas, reiterated during my fieldwork: there was no such thing as Hindu before the British came to India and consolidated several plural and fragmented practices under a new monolithic category of Hindu. If that was true, as Lorance continued, then both notions of Hindu and Christian could be seen as equally foreign to Adivasis and Dalits.

Although Lorance and other Panas had clear rejoinders for ethnonationalist indictments of them as outsiders who were selling the land of the nation by converting, they found it more difficult to address the question of ontological beliefs about land and Dharini Pennu in particular. Not only did these discussions remain shrouded in hesitation because of a deeply internalized sense of shame within both the Kandha and the Pana communities about meriah sacrifice and its connections to Dharini Pennu, Panas also struggled with outlining their heritage and their beliefs as distinct in relation to Kandhas.

Bala Digal, a young Pana friend, said, "They say you keep to your beliefs, do not claim you are Kandha, who are you? What shall we say who we are? When we say we have been so close to Kandhas, we have shared what they believe in, they say it is wrong. Such is our state. We are inseparable from them, but they say we can never be them." Bala's friend seated next to him clarified, "They say you have no heritage, no ties to land. What is our history? They say talk about only your own history. But we cannot say with pride, we have this history, we were someone once. That's why we want to become better in the present, study, go ahead we want to stop being identified with a past in which we are always bad. We want our children to have a different view of themselves. But they say angrily—don't take what is ours. This is only our heritage, our land."

Lorance's teenage son, John, often implored him to be more muted in his criticism of ethnonationalist rhetoric in our conversations; he and some other younger Panas instead reframed the debate in economic terms of land ownership through labor: "The Kandhas are working the land, they are cultivating crops on it, so yes, it is theirs. If we got a chance to own land and cultivate it, work on it, maybe it would also be seen as ours. But that is what becoming Kandhariya Pana is about. How else do we get land? If we never get it, never work on it, it will never be ours, we will never be seen as occupying what is rightfully ours. They are making it seem like we want to steal from others, but we will work on it and take care of it, if we get it."

In Kandhamal, Dalit entitlements to land seemed impossible to achieve not only because of the primacy accorded to Kandha land rights given their Adivasi status but also because of the disarticulation of Pana and Dalit identifications through loss of Scheduled Caste status following Pana conversion to Christianity.[27] Panas were then attempting to access land through being reclassified as tribal Kandhariya Panas. This would address Pana landlessness as not just an economic condition but also a condition of un-belonging, both local and (ethno)national. Together, Lorance and John addressed Dalit exclusion from land both as site of dharmic (religious) affinity and as economic entitlement, as outsiders in Kandhamal. Even as they did not explain their own ontological beliefs about land using nature-culture figuration, they described land as a place of belonging, a belonging that they were always burdened to prove. For Lorance's generation and that of his son, the only way to secure that belonging was to lay claim to indigeneity, which would officially designate them as indigenes with entitlements to land that they would toil on to claim as their own, emphasizing how critical labor was for Dalit assertions about land.

Adivasi ontological claims about land, and purported intimacies with Hindu cosmologies, provided a critical foil against which Dalits were (re)constructed as materialistic outsiders with no sacred regard for land and as converts to Christianity motivated only by a materialism that allowed them to embrace Christian capital. Ethnonationalists characterized Christian capital as sullying the moral fiber of Adivasi lands through a defilement of Adivasi land as a nature-culture figure. They captured anxieties about Christian capital and the threat of Dalit economic mobility in ways that were imagined to be usurpations of Adivasi economic claims. When we engage Adivasi land as a nature-culture figure around which indigenous ontologies were central to indigenous political-economic claims, we see how indigenous ontologies may become another modality through which indigenous economic claims are seemingly upheld to the detriment of landless minorities like Dalits, excluded from dominant regimes of caste capital. Indigenous ontologies are revealed to be unstable and porous as well as capable of becoming harmonious with tropes of authentic belonging, autochthony, and economic entitlements animating conservative politics.

Ontological Claims in Economic Precarity

Scholars have pointed out that the ontological turn within anthropology hinges on a South American Primitivity, positing that a "nonmodern" "Amerindian cosmology," or an "Amerindian multinaturalist ontology," offers a sharp counter to "modern, Western, European" "mononaturalist-multiculturalist" philosophy and the binaries of nature-culture on which this "modern ontology" is predicated.[28] Such a nonreductionist framework has placed indigenous ontologies at the heart of a hopeful politics in the age of the Anthropocene. As Eduardo Kohn specifies, animism is no longer a "mistaken belief in an animated nature"[29] but a more capacious and hopeful form of social relationality with nonhumans.[30] By taking indigenous cosmologies seriously as frameworks that force Western thought to rethink its own separation of nature from culture, the ontological turn suggests that we can undo the deleterious effects of cordoning off nature from culture, as well as gain a more expansive understanding of contemporary forms of politics.[31]

Critical analyses of the ontological turn have pointed to the colonial overtones in these attempts that purify the very categories they seek to dismantle. In their thorough critique, Lucas Bessire and David Bond sharply note that not only does the ontological turn purify the very categories of the indigenous and the modern, it also presumes the referential stability of Western categories of nature and culture. If indigenous ontologies not only become a framework through which Western thought can question its own ontological assumptions that separate the human and nonhuman but also replace such epistemological habits of categorization, can indigenous ontologies, in fact, further reify indigeneity as Other to modernity?

The ahistoricism of the ontological turn has resulted in a neglect of indigenous cosmologies as unstable and porous, rather than immutable and unchanging. When we take histories of the Hinduization of plains-dwelling Adivasis in India into account, Adivasi indigenous ontologies clearly come into view as sites where political and economic control have been exercised over indigenous communities, including patronage and assimilation under Hindu kingship and Othering and censure under British colonial governance. Moreover, Adivasi ontologies become visible as highly porous, permeable, and in flux, rather than static, stable, and unchanging. Acknowledging and theorizing this porosity and mutability, and indeed *muddiness*, of indigenous ontologies is critical to theorizing about indigenous communities that does not rehearse romantic tropes of pure and allochronistic indigenous cosmologies but instead attends to the multiplicity and heterogeneity within indigenous ontological understandings, as nature-culture figurations exist alongside and support dominant political and economic regimes and ideologies.

As Kandhas called attention to their singular vision of land as Dharini Pennu to assert their proprietary claims on land as property as well as a site of cultural-religious belonging, the multiplicity and plurality within ontologies of land resisted any singular account of Kandha attachments to land as a sentient, revered figure and land as heritage and, thus, rightful economic entitlement. As Michael Cepek so forcefully argues, anthropologists must take seriously that their indigenous subjects' ontological statements are propositions that disclose multiple real worlds.[32] To comprehend the intellectual agency of indigenous interlocutors, we need to acknowledge rather than ignore the social, pragmatic, and epistemological contours of their discourse, cosmological or otherwise. Cepek sharply rebukes ontological investigations that focus on the bare content of abstract propositions, while paying little attention to their pragmatic function, epistemological stance, affective tone, and position in a division of linguistic and conceptual labor.[33] Ignoring these factors, Cepek argues, results in a failure to engage indigenous subjects as critical intellectual agents whose analytic capacities are just as powerful, vexed, and complex as our own. At its worst, it traffics in the abstraction, antihumanism, and interpretive excess of theoretical traditions as structuralism while maintaining no necessary relationship to accurate ethnography, ethical methodology, or liberatory politics.[34]

Cepek's critiques and others, such as those advanced by Bond and Bessire, must be borne in mind while attending to the pragmatics of Kandha ontological claims in a larger political economic discursive field shaped by neoliberal economic uncertainty and a turn to majoritarian politics. Observing Kandha attempts at stating, restating, and negotiating the accommodation of

Dharini Pennu as a nature-culture figure in an ethnonationalist tradition of geopiety, we see how ontological claims can become implicated in upholding a Hindu majoritarian economic regime of land, one in which indigenes claim their economic rights to land but remained economically disenfranchised, to ultimately reactivate the economic abjection of Dalits as landless minorities.

Discussions of tribal participation in Hindu nationalism in India have been mired in a language of purity that denies the ontologically porous and politically unruly experiences of contemporary tribal communities. Dialoguing between Subaltern and Critical Indigenous Studies, Jodi Byrd and Michael Rothberg present productive incommensurations as a point of convergence[35] between the subaltern and indigenous positions. The subalternity of Adivasis might be seen, Gyan Prakash has argued, as signifying "that which the dominant discourse cannot appropriate completely, an otherness that resists containment," "dominance fails to appropriate the radical incommensurability of the subaltern, it registers only the recalcitrant presence of subalternity, records impressions of that which it cannot contain." Subaltern Studies insists that these impressions are disruptive because they are situated *inside* power and discourse, rather than exterior to them. Byrd and Rothberg recall this disruptive potential as a significant dovetailing between indigeneity and subalternity, quoting Prakash's formulation that subaltern traces force dominant discourse "into contradictions, by making it speak in tongues."[36]

In Kandhamal, Hindutva as a neocolonial discourse is forced to adopt conflicted and contradictory positions in its recognition of Adivasi indigeneity. In such a context, Kandha claims on land tie together religious cosmology and political economy, becoming a site where debates over recognition via ethnonationalism showcase indigenous ontologies of land as complex and heterodox. These claims show that indigenous lifeworlds are capable of being absorbed into dominant political and economic regimes in ways that render indigeneity a crucial political technology through which exclusions of majoritarian reterritorializations are reproduced and reactivated. Adivasis' claims to land that unevenly suture land as property to land as sentient nature-culture figure to make clear the insufficiency of understanding tribal politics as not just unequivocally resistant to dominant political-economic processes and legal discourses.[37] Instead, indigenous invocations of nonhuman actors that challenge nature-culture divides might be folded into a "politics as usual" while articulating struggles for indigenous rights and entitlements. These uneven translations of ontological claims uphold dominant economic inequities as land as nature-culture figure becomes another modality through which ethnonationalists craft and hail indigenous authenticity. Ethnonation-alists engage tribal as indigenous recognition and Adivasis' proprietary legal status by engaging their distinct veneration of land as a sentient being, and thereby caste Hindu economic dominance by continuing to reproduce Dalits as indigeneity's Others with no entitlements to land, both as property and as site of religious-cultural belonging.

Even as indigenous ontologies have been presented as a hopeful panacea to forms of modern politics in the age of the Anthropocene, Adivasi ontologies of land emerge as far from pure, stable, and, thus, unimplicated within modern politics.[38] Rather, their activations of exclusionary xenophobic imaginings of Panas as landless Dalit converts force a rethinking of the ontological turn's hopeful but highly speculative futurism in which romanticized indigenous ontologies are imagined as a panacea to forms of contemporary politics.[39]

CHAPTER 6

Carnality of Capital

From the very first time I sat down with Laxmananda Saraswati in Jalespata, his laments about the corrosive effects of Christian conversion did not convey conversion merely in terms of a religious-symbolic challenge to the ethos of the Hindu nation. Rather, Laxmananda emphasized the economic dimensions of conversion as he denigrated conversion as inciting a corrosive materialism by dangling economic lures in front of minorities to convince them to "sell" the nation. His charged statements attested to conversion within nationalist ideology as a challenge to both the material and the symbolic dimensions of caste. Laxmananda unevenly acknowledged that mission engagement of material uplift and service provision perhaps marginally improved caste minorities' economic circumstances. But he emphatically insisted that these engagements fundamentally changed their moral character, rendering them materialistic and dependent on missions and Christian aid organizations for handouts. While in his view Kandhas had now awakened to the materialism of missions as ultimately destructive for their religion (dharma) and Adivasi heritage (sanskruti), Dalits were particularly vulnerable to this immoral materialism and were natural prey for missions.

"These Christians and these NGOs," he said, "they have made Kandhamal's culture a culture of begging. People here have gotten used to begging for the means to live their life. These Kandhas, even if they had nothing else, they had pride in their culture. This pride was systematically destroyed by Christians. Christianity has made everyone greedy—they have made these poor people used to handouts and made them willing to sell their religion. They just want more money in their palms, they are ready to sell their own heritage for money."

To describe Christians' strategy for converting the residents of Kandhamal, Laxmananda used a mnemonic-like ethnonationalist catchphrase, which

I would hear recited almost commonsensically in the district: "lady, paddy, hen, pen." This mnemonic pithily summarized persistent refrains within ethnonationalist rhetoric: women, and sexual relations with them, were the gateway to a life steeped in a Western materialism that rendered Dalits dangerously economically mobile. To explain the fourfold strategy through which caste minorities were lured to convert, Laxmananda—and several other ethnonationalist workers from the Vishwa Hindu Parishad, the Vanvasi Kalyan Ashram, and the Bajrang Dal—insisted that the missions deployed Christian women with a free, even bestial, sexuality to lure potential converts; filled their stomachs with illicit but pleasurable substances such as alcohol and meat; and finally educated them. "And not educated in our great books, our values," Laxmananda said, "but educated in English-medium mission schools where they teach you about Jesus, and about Western values where they learn about life in other countries but not about our own heritage (*sanskruti*)."

Laxmananda elaborated further, "These nuns, they actually act as lures. They entice men physically and sleep with them to convert them. You know, these big gatherings they have, these mass prayers. They show images of people having sex to arouse them, titillate people with these lurid images. They use these Christian women, these women of loose morals, to entice them at that time. Then they say you have to marry her, you have to become Christian. The priests too. You know what they do, these so-called celibate priests, they have sex with poor women, they rape them. Yes, rape them! . . . All the illegitimate children born from all these illicit relationships are dumped into a well. Everyone knows. People will tell you about wells that are filled with the bodies of these illegitimate infants. The stink, the rotting smell of these babies stink up entire villages, you can smell the stench from these wells from far away."

To describe the illicit and illegal strategies of Christian conversion, Laxmananda insistently evoked both sexual relations and sensory experiences such as the stench of rotting flesh to link immorality with bodily disgust. He swiftly moved from the themes of unbound, illicit sexuality and its distasteful consequence to gore and physical violence: "They use every force they can to convert you. And you know how they do it, they call it baptism. They dunk you in water, in water filled with feces, cow flesh, and menstrual blood so that you are so dirty, so disgusting that no Hindu will accept you after that. That is how they make you a Christian. And if you say no, I will not become Christian, they put a blanket over you and stamp on you till your bones are broken and all life is squeezed out of you. They suffocate you till you lose consciousness and then they bury you alive."

Laxmananda was emotive as he described the immoral and illicit actions of Christians. To conclude his conversation, he expressed the pride that Hindu ethnonationalism was taking in the reclamation of Adivasis from such Christian depravity and how such a reclamation had elevated Adivasis like Kandhas to newfound respectability, shifting earlier perceptions of them as ritually polluting and impure in the social hierarchy of caste society. In Laxmananda's oratory, the role of language and speech ascertained a proper order of things in the world coded in Hindu aesthetics, as Barnard Bate has shown, wherein what is proper is determined through aesthetic or gut-level embodied appraisals.[1]

Ethnonationalists invoked sex in graphic and spectacular ways in Kandhamal to mobilize a history of caste hierarchy thrown into disarray in a time of uneven caste incorporations and advancements in a neoliberal economic order. Their charged vitriolic speech recaptured indictments of Dalit materialism, often by directly invoking the legal derecognition of Dalits and bans on religious conversion. Words carry their socially produced contexts within them; the context of the individual utterance of the word is crucial to the extent to which utterances are interpreted and, thus, able to cause injury. Ethnonationalist rhetoric then could be seen as recapturing and resignifying a historical and legal context in which Dalits are constructed and reconstructed as materialistic and suspect. As in Judith Butler's formulation of hate speech as excitable speech, ethnonationalist political oratory was not the *primary* scene of injury. Rather it could be seen as *repeating* injury to minorities through a resignification of a landless Dalit condition in terms of a rapacious Dalit materialism that usurped economic commensuration from other minorities such as Kandhas.

In the vitriolic speech of Hindu ethnonationalists, a distinct upper-caste aesthetics of disgust for Dalits was channeled and remobilized toward disgust for Christians. Joel Lee reasons that what has been assumed to be the invocation of Hindu disgust toward the mobilization of anti-Muslim sentiment within recent religious conflicts is, in fact, the culmination of a longer history in which upper-caste disgust is cultivated and channeled from the Dalit as untouchable toward the Muslim by reformist movements such as the Arya Samaj.[2] These attempts have formed a crucial substrate further built on by Hindu ethnonationalist outfits such as the Vishwa Hindu Parishad. And yet, while the aesthetic register employed by ethnonationalists was distinctly encoded in a grammar of upper-caste Hinduism, themes of economic victimization, usurpation of the due of a once-dominant group, and notions of economic "fairness" emerged that resonated with other emergent right-wing politics and populisms.

This chapter engages the graphic, sexually charged oratory of ethnonationalist workers in Kandhamal and its world-making capacities[3] through its incitement of a moral panic about a rapacious and threatening Christian Dalit sexuality. Ethnonationalist reliance on sex to recapture and resignify Dalit materialism showcases sexuality as a privileged system of signification, which allows economic discontents to be indexed through the material body, and bodily arousal to be engaged as an aesthetic resource to lend these discontents visceral charge. Ethnonationalist political speech relies on the material body as a presumptive "natural" resource to trigger and harness embodied, aesthetic appraisals. Ethnonationalists engage in a discursive denial of the material body to deny sex as un-Hindu, engaging sex to resignify Dalit materialism in terms of a threatening economic ascendency that thwarts and usurps Kandha Adivasi economic commensuration and dominance. Fears and discontents about the uneven incorporation of Adivasis and Dalits in the new economy are lent a visceral, embodied charge through political rhetoric, engaging caste in aesthetic and affective terms. This final chapter attempts to resolve an impasse between structural conditions and embodied violence by showing how religious aesthetics allow for the uneven and charged capture and resignification of caste capitalism. Such an ethnonationalist capture of longstanding economic discontents showcases how religion abets continuities between caste capitalism and emergent forms of conservative politics by providing the conditions of possibility for unlikely alliances within them, gesturing to how and why minorities build identifications with majoritarian politics that only further their economic marginalization. To engage with religion as a continued force in caste capitalism, then, we must examine how the domain of the religious mobilizes a set of aesthetic and affective political appraisals that marshal, redirect, and resignify political economic discontents to spur deeply embodied rejection, avoidance, and panic, which are manifested in caste and racial violence.

Hindu Ethnonationalist Preoccupations with Sex

South Asian feminists have long noted a Hindu nationalist obsession with the unbound sexuality of vilified Others. At once reprehensible and powerful, this sexuality is contrasted to the figure of weak and sexually moral

Hindus as a perpetual foil; against the "hypersexualized, demonized image" of the religious rival is the image of the "gentle, spiritual, and celibate Hindu."[4] Drawing on Slavoj Zizek, Amrita Basu has suggested that these preoccupations with the excessive sexuality of vilified Others gestures to a displaced envy on the part of Hindu ethnonationalists.[5] In the late nineteenth century, Hindu ideological contestations shaped the Indian nationalist project to sow the seeds for ambivalence around sex well before contemporary Hindu ethnonationalism's conflation of religious and national identity.[6] An ideal Hindu body modified by post-Enlightenment rationality provided a set of guidelines for self-cultivation or *anushilan*, taking into account both "rationality" and "spirituality."

Sexuality endangered the rational and spiritual purity of the body, leading nationalists such as Gandhi to ponder sexuality's role in crafting and disrupting spiritual asceticism at the service of the nation. On the one hand, control over sexuality was mastery over the self at the service of the nation; on the other, sexuality was, in fact, a potent wellspring of spiritual vitality.[7] Struggles with the materiality of the sexual body in relation to spiritual aspirations provided the "symbolic material for a relentless national self-purification."[8] A Hindu ethnonationalist subject emerged as a "ghostly double" of an ascetic nationalist subject, even though Gandhian bodily asceticism came to be seen by Hindu ethnonationalism's founding fathers, Vinayak Savarkar and Madhav Sadashiv Golwalkar, as rendering Hindu masculinity weak and effete through the repudiation of violence. Even prior to India's independence from British rule in 1947, the early twentieth century saw the emergence of newly aggressive Hindu ethnonationalism distinct from nationalist assertion against British colonial rule.

The movement was institutionalized with the establishment of the Rashtriya Swayamsevak Sangh in 1925, the apex authority that oversees a family of right-wing organizations known as Sangh Parivar. After a brief ban on Rashtriya Swayamsevak Sangh following its involvement in Gandhi's assassination, the movement gained momentum from the 1980s onward. With India's economic liberalization in the late 1990s, the state embraced free market capitalism while upholding cultural and economic conservatism.[9] The movement promotes regimented bodily masculinity[10] and sexual renunciation alongside capitalist materialism. As an aspirational upper-caste bodily asceticism has served as the guiding ideology of the national subject, Hindu ethnonationalism has refined a set of upper-caste bodily and community purification practices to secure a distinctly masculinist Hindu somatic nationalism.[11] For tribal communities such as those in Kandhamal, these practices cleanse their "uncivilized" habitus[12] to secure national belonging. In these ways, sex polices and reproduces caste hierarchy,[13] being linked to notions of bodily purity and pollution that serve as the foundation of Brahminical orthopraxy in religious ritual, and to maintain a national bodily purity which is feared to be compromised through illicit sex with aggressive, virile religious Others.

India is hardly distinct in placing the triumvirate of caste as race/class, gender, and sexuality at the heart of an idealized national subject. These debates illustrate foundational insights of feminist historiography that showcase struggles over "nationalism" as necessarily waged along axes of gender, sexuality, and race.[14] Sex as religious aggression against victimized Hindus has been ubiquitous in the revitalized Hindu ethnonationalism since the late 1980s. Its invocations threaten fault lines of caste, gender, and sexuality to renew the need for the policing of these embodied and relational boundaries. A national disavowal of sexuality consistently rears its head. Politicians, lawmakers, and filmmakers vacillate between this disavowal and an anticipation that suppression only furthers an obsession with sex as a forbidden site of mystification and titillation within an Indian public incapable of regulating itself without censorship.[15]

Hindu ethnonationalism's metamorphosis into right-wing populism builds on these recurrent sexualized refrains within Indian public culture. At the same time, it resonates with—or more properly, anticipates—neoliberal disaffections across other populist resurgences such as discontent with elite and establishment politics, interrogation of liberal ideals like secularism, vigilante supplantation of the rule of law, and economic uncertainties. Populist sex panics deny the sexuality of Hindus to summon fears about an ascetic, self-denying masculine subject as an idealized embodiment of the Hindu demos under siege in global capitalism. Here, the feminized indulgences of the material body threaten the renunciatory sexual discipline of the Hindu man. Such a feminization of material excess conveys a growing ambivalence toward the market, which economically marginalizes the Hindu man to render him emasculated, if not effete. These panics realign gender, caste/race, and sexuality relationally to stoke fears about the endangerment of the Hindu nation apprehended through the bodily security of "the people." Right-wing claims about Hindu people as the subject of sexual wrongs connect compromised civilizational bodily purity to the usurpation of economic entitlements and thus provoke calls for an increasingly muscular and masculinist Hindu "reclamation" of the Indian nation-state.[16]

The Feminization of Dalit Materialism

Laxmananda spoke of illicit sexual relations between priests and female Christian converts; in so doing, he recalled feminized depictions of a coerced, sexually victimized feminine nation while also engaging a gender switch to suture caste to religion, Dalitness to Christianity, inverting scripts of the pure, unmarked Hindu woman as the true patriotic subject of the Hindu nation,[17] and indeed the very embodiment of the nation, against whom male religious Others commit violence. Right-wing workers marked Christian women as lustful femmes fatales who lured and trapped Hindu men. These inversions gestured to the salience of caste rather than merely religious identity. Feminist historian Charu Gupta has noted that under British colonial rule Indian nationalists attempted to delineate and outline the role of sexuality at the service of the nation. As monogamous and heterosexual marriage was being envisaged as imperative for a modern, civilized Hindu nation, female reproduction became critical to the nation in that it could lead to the birth of healthy, male progeny. Against a backdrop of such Hindu civility, gendered and sexed fears reflect the collective unconscious of upper-caste Hindus in which perceived Dalit sexualities become constructed as deviant, as a threat both to civilized norms of sexual behavior and, thus, to civilizational integrity.[18]

Caste then rests upon endogamy, with women featuring as "gateways to caste through whom caste purity could be threatened and caste status could be claimed."[19] Yet purity concerns do not safeguard Dalit women against sexual predations of dominant upper-caste men.[20] Recalling the victim blaming of Dalit women in casteist sexual violence, ethnonationalists inverted long-observed scripts of the female Hindu woman as the victimized embodiment of the nation to indict Dalit, and Christian, women, as sexual aggressors against local men in Kandhamal. Their rhetoric incited panic about alluring, lustful Dalit Christian women who weaponized their feminine wiles and free sexuality to lure Kandhas and Hindu men into Christian capitalist indulgence. Sexuality became a fecund device through which a Dalit economic mobility that threatened upper-caste monopoly over capital was resignified as usurpation of naturalized blood-and-soil entitlements of Kandhas.

Gyan Pandey emphasizes that for Dalits religious conversion was a conversion to the "modern," signified by a sensibility, comportment, and rules of social and political engagement that countered Hindu orthodoxy.[21] Concomitantly, debates about Dalit conversion have been implicated in securing full citizenship for Dalits through the abolition of untouchability, the instituting of universal adult franchise, and the extension of legal and political rights to all citizens, providing the conditions of possibility for Dalit emancipation.[22] As we have seen, conversion is a distinctive democratic challenge to an all-pervasive Hindu orthodoxy; it is also a site of reinscription of Dalits as "bad" converts whose inalienable materialism rather than interiorized belief drives them to convert, both in nationalist thought[23] and within Christian missions.

Ethnonationalists sought to convey Christian Dalit women as the embodiment of moral decay and as posing the threat of liberating women from caste and religious conventions. Yet conversion to Christianity has also had particularly contradictory implications for women[24] and has hardly liberated women from the moral strictures of an idealized chaste domesticity. In fact, as Charu Gupta reminds us, missionary women self-consciously undertook their work among their non-Christian "sisters" in the colonial empires as a "mission of domesticity," in order to school them in marriage, education, household work, childcare, cleanliness, and a particular outlook.[25] They rued, however, that their efforts hardly rendered Dalit women straightforward and good, "clean" Christian wives and mothers.

Missions attempted to reform Dalit women after conversion by restructuring every aspect of converted Dalit women's daily lives, including physical appearance, sartorial styles, marital relations, customs, language, and social milieu; as a result, these women's religious and social practices reflected highly eclectic borrowing and adaptation.[26] Even when seemingly engaging in processes of imitation and mimicry, Dalit women selectively appropriated, reconstituted, and subverted ideals of upper-caste and missionary life, imbuing them with their own sensibilities and practices. Difficult and contradictory implications of Dalit conversion and, as David Mosse has suggested, their echoes and reinvocation within ethnonationalist rhetoric are then particularly visible in the case of Dalit women. Missions, intent on schooling them in domesticity, acknowledge the difficulty of making them good, "clean" Christian wives and mothers, and ethnonationalists decry their loose sexuality, echoing a distrust of Dalit women as the very embodiment of an excessive Dalit materialism. In ethnonationalist rhetoric, much as in Christianity, Dalit women were particularly paradigmatic of Dalitness—embodying resistant bodily materialities[27] that exceeded and subverted "purely" spiritual and ideological/ideational fidelity, causing discomfort to missions and Hindu-reformist nationalists alike.

When violence broke out in Kandhamal in 2008 after months of ethnonationalist rhetoric had circulated panics about Dalit sexuality, a Christian nun

was gang-raped by Hindu men. In the months before the incident, ethnonationalist rhetoric insistently framed Christian women as sexually depraved
and thus morally reprehensible. Such a framing cast sexually free Christian women as signifying the moral bankruptcy of a life of pleasures aided
by Christian capital. More subtly, however, such an indictment of Christian
women secured a critical inversion that sutured caste to religion, Dalitness
to Christianity—as Dalit female converts came to be cast as sexually free,
aggressive, and, thus, only rightly subject to violence. The workings of caste,
particularly its perpetuation through Brahminical patriarchy[28] and the distinct vulnerability of Dalit women to caste violence as sexual violence, mandate an analysis of interlinking caste-class-gender dynamics.[29] Mainstream
savarna, or fourfold caste Hindu feminism, continues to neglect caste, while
even some Dalit critiques of caste overlook patriarchy. Ambedkarite thought,
however, has long asserted the foundation of caste to rest upon sexual regulation,[30] with Ambedkar's call for intercaste marriages and the reform of
family laws aiming to precisely unravel the reproduction and sexual policing
of caste hierarchy in order to fundamentally destabilize caste order. Writing
against the tendency to describe violent events as either caste atrocities or
sexual atrocities, Sharmila Rege calls on us "to map the ways in which woman
as a category is . . . differently reconstituted within patriarchal relations of
gendered caste inequalities," and Gabriele Dietrich emphasizes the particular
consequences for Dalit women as subjects of violence both by upper-caste
men and by Dalit men.[31] As Anupama Rao forcefully argues, sexual violence
becomes particularly indecipherable as caste violence, even as it may be properly understood, in fact, as the *epitome* of caste violence.[32] Through a Dalit
feminist perspective, we see how an upper-caste, ethnonationalist feminization of Dalit materialism rendered Christian Dalit women particularly vulnerable through the provocation of sexual violence and how such violence
pedagogically functioned to reinforce the socialization of caste norms.[33]

Fantasies of Christian Capital

Jagannath Prasad Sahu, a young Bajrang Dal leader whom I met several
months after my initial arrival at Kandhamal, echoed Laxmananda's insistence on the purposive use of material lures by Christians as carnal pleasures.
At first, Sahu babu did not broach the topic of Christian sex and hedonism
with me; indeed, it would be unseemly to discuss these issues freely with me

as an upper-caste woman. But as my continued presence in the district made him more carefree in our conversations, Sahu babu began to speak with me about conversion and Christian deployment of sex as a means of securing spurious conversion, a motif that would recur across conversations with local residents. To inaugurate these conversations, Sahu babu and other ethnonationalists drew on the readily available discourse of Christian conversion as engaging illegal strategies in its use of material lures to attract minorities, invoking Odisha's anti-conversion law. While ethnonationalists castigated such conversions as illegal because of their purposive use of material inducement to Christian conversion, they became newly animated and emotive to render such inducement to be an excess of immoral and illicit material pleasures that lured caste minorities to convert. Sahu babu described a key modality through which Christian proselytization as material excess was conducted: jungle feasts (*bana bhojis*), held in remote forested areas, which were marked by an illicit—indeed, even unspeakable—depravity, where locals would be lured to join Christianity.

"You know they take these people into the forest where no one can see them," he said. "They build these fires, roast tens of chickens, and ply people with meat and alcohol. They have these women there, these loose women they get from different parts of the country who speak English. When the people gathered become drunk, they encourage them to have sex with these women. Imagine, these so-called religious people encourage people to have orgies like common animals. They encourage them to become hedonists with no morality, just do whatever they want. That is how they get to you, they use every material lure, break all our moral rules."

Seeing my discomfort with this depiction of Christians, a Kandha panchayat leader seated next to me shouted out in distaste, "He is right. They are ruining our sanskruti, they are like animals, fornicating, eating, doing whatever with whoever. When you think about it, it is horrible. You think, can it be true? But it is, sister. It makes us ashamed to even discuss these things with you. But believe him, it is true."

Bana bhojis were represented as gatherings where participants would sing and dance, drink alcohol, eat animal flesh, and be encouraged to have unfettered orgiastic sex. Sahu babu described them as spaces of moral lawlessness, of rampant indulgence unfettered by social norms, spaces at once fantasy and nightmare, replete with sensory gratification, bodily pleasures, and sin. Like Laxmananda, Sahu babu engaged a graphic imagery that relied on impure and polluting substances within an upper-caste Hindu aesthetic framework, such as menstrual blood, animal flesh, and alcohol as well as illicit acts, such as covert and unbound sex, bodily violence, and monetary greed and excess.

These graphic images created a lurid fantasy world that elicited strong moral reactions in audiences. The images that were conjured were cinematic and fantastical, titillating and arousing for both ethnonationalist speakers and their Kandha audiences. Such titillation and arousal were quickly channeled toward disgust as right-wing workers presumed sex to be a "natural" somatic resource for activating affective-embodied modes of political appraisal. As they titillated, they quickly moved to close titillation with disgust to threaten their audiences and emphasize the need for boundaries between Hindus and their Christian Others.[34] Sexual acts, cow flesh, and alcohol are not "naturally" offensive. Rather, juxtaposed alongside sensory experiences such as the smell of rotting flesh and the sight of blood, they were cultivated as such. Ethnonationalist workers marked the sacred and the profane within an ideological upper-caste Hindu framework to delineate an aesthetic "proper" of the nation as a "hierarchical cum aesthetic distinction, based on the practices and evaluations of people located in a place of privileged evaluation, some hegemonic center."[35] These appraisals were not counter to ideology; rather, they informed ideological evaluations, spurring shifts in language, thought, and emotion that are not deterministic. As Charles Hirschkind reiterates,[36] these moral and political judgments were seated in evaluations outside the purview of consciousness to orientations grounded in the visceral registers of human existence. At the same time, ethnonationalist political speech called upon historical referents to mobilize caste in order to make it current to construct and reconstruct reality for political actors.

In Kandhamal, the sexualized rhetoric about Christians secured a thorough carnalization of capital, in which sex became synonymous with hedonistic pleasures of consumerist and capitalist excess that were un-Hindu to invite a xenophobic rejection of Christian converts as outsiders to a Hindu nation. Critical to this sexualized rhetoric was Hindu ethnonationalism's ability to cast bodily indulgence in sex as a gateway into a world of material excesses and hedonism abetted by Christian capital. Ethnonationalists insisted that the material lure dangled by missionaries was not restricted to modest sums for sacks of rice and building houses. Rather, they engaged in a fantastical exaggeration of Christian capital as material excess proffered by Christian aid workers and Christian tourists to enable a clamorous consumerism among Pana converts, including the purchase of radios, cycles, expensive food and clothing, and the ability to build better houses. Oftentimes Panas were routed into Christian networks of English rather than vernacular education through mission schools, which aided them in securing jobs as teachers' assistants and enabled their children to seek education in Phulbani. These subtle advantages gave Panas an economic mobility in the new economy that came to be imagined in terms of a material excess disproportionate to their standing in the local caste hierarchy as lower than Kandhas and once engaged by Kandhas as their employees.

Mediational aspects of religion—the volatile production and reproduction of a social order[37]—were evident in the distinctly modern attempts of ethnonationalist political speech to engage fantasy as a social practice to fabricate social life.[38] As Birgit Meyer reminds us, such fantastical imaginings are crucial in understanding malaises of globalization and modernity and the power of images in the "(re) creation of persons and societies," in which fantasy comes to the fore as a constitutive social practice, rather than asserting fantasy and reality to be mutually exclusive categories.[39] Hindu ethnonationalists wove together depictions of unbound, illicit sexuality of religious rivals and highly graphic images of gore and violence, creating a lurid fantasy world capable of bringing forth strong moral reactions that linked carnality to capital, and various iterations of materialism variously evoked by Pana, Dalit, and Christian identities. Engaging distinct upper-caste Hindu aesthetics of purity and pollution in varied permutations and combinations to create fantastical mise-en-scènes to remobilize disgust for Dalits as disgust for Christians, they engaged "ways of seeing" that have been crucial within Hindu religious practice,[40] suffused with aesthetic and visual signifiers, icons, and idolatry.

As religious imagery and iconography were deployed in a distinctly modern production and consumption of images, ethnonationalist fantasies enabled "mimetic travels" for Kandhas in which passions and anxieties difficult to express in everyday life were confronted.[41] These fantastical spaces and their upper-caste Hindu aesthetics revealed what Marx called "the religion of everyday life," serving as revelations of the fantasy dimension of global capitalism,[42] with religion itself serving as a practice of mediation. As Meyer notes, images of blood, sex, and money woven together allow complex negotiations to be made between "the desires for transgression of the moral order, the longing to feel morally superior, and the striving for knowledge to understand one's world."[43] The graphic imagery invoked in Hindu nationalist speech served to mediate an imagined world of religious Others in visceral terms for Kandhas as distinct upper-caste Hindu aesthetics served to experience and produce the transcendental through the senses.[44]

The sex panic that sutured Christian and Dalit materialism in Kandhamal worked, as Ravinder Kaur suggests, as a great spectacle in which images translated economic facts into animated dreamworlds of the future.[45] These spectacular imaginings and renderings facilitated an affective translation of the field of economy—translating economic facts, rendering them accessible, and making them common sense. Through these spectacular images, Kandhas reencountered a familiar world inhabited by recognizable figures of Hindus and Panas bound together in unfamiliar roles and power hierarchies. Yet, as Kaur reminds us, what rearranged these images remained "hidden in plain sight": an uneven global capitalism that fueled ethnonationalist economic anxieties and an uneven and differential economic growth for Kandhas and Panas in the local order. Right-wing workers summoned sex as spectacle to craft dreamworlds that bound Dalit and Christian together in unfamiliar roles and power hierarchies in relation to Hindu and Kandha, transposing state economic neglect and dispossession of Kandhas with xenophobic suspicions about Christian capital.

Eliding the neoliberal entrenchment of Kandhas' inability to achieve economic mobility, right-wing workers displaced Kandhas' economic despair onto the canny materialism of Dalit converts. Mobilizing a Westernized and, thus, liberated Christian sexuality to stand in for Dalit hankering for capital, ethnonationalists urged Kandhas to turn away from Christian conversion, precisely as a form of democratization that unraveled a patriarchal caste Hindu hegemony to render Dalits dangerously mobile. Even as missions struggled with Dalits as "rice Christians," right-wing workers insisted that missions used such material lures purposefully, debasing proselytizing as a form of "bribing" that reduced caste minorities to supplicating for handouts.

Engaging sex as spectacle, ethnonationalists activated caste as aesthetic infrastructure in order to link a national populism, in which economically abjected Dalits were reconfigured as materialistic converts threatening the civilizational integrity of the nation to challenge their straightforward exclusion from capital to a local populism, in which a locally salient construction of Panas as wily, mercenary, and exploitative obscured their vulnerability as landless. These links were secured not through an erasure of caste, and Adivasi identity, but through their resignification. Ethnonationalists lauded Adivasi indigenous authenticity by insisting that Kandhas had too much pride in their dharma and their heritage to be corrupted by capital, resignifying a pejorative simplicity and unworldliness of Adivasis as a noble, self-denying abjuration of Christian capital. They insisted that Kandhas as Adivasis were

willing to eat only "from what they worked on with their own hands," fus-
ing Adivasi "pure labor" and incorruptibility by capital with an upper-caste
ascetic Hindu masculinity in order to position Kandhas against a hostile,
threatening, and immoral Dalit materialism. This fusion allowed a horizontal
boundary marking between a national Us and Them, between caste Hindus
and Dalits, to be conflated with the vertical boundary marking between the
Kandhas and Panas.

Masculinity, Disgust, and Upper-Caste Aesthetics

As these depictions of Pana reliance on Christian mission services as materialistic were more intensely circulated in the political speech of ethnonationalists, Kandhas continued to angrily point out the failures of recognition in
ensuring their economic commensuration. They spoke of the extreme and
exceptional economic hardships faced by their community, which rarely
enjoyed the fruits of their toil and labor. With performative anger and exaggerated pride, Kandhas, however, impressed upon me that it was better for
them to starve than to accept grain or material benefits through Christian
networks of capital as Panas were. One young man, Hari, who had spent
many days speaking to me about the value of toil among Kandhas, described
how they took great pride in their capacity for honest labor. His family sometimes did not have enough to eat, but he would only eat what he was able
to secure himself through his toil and would rather perish than accept any
material aid from Christians.

"I may be poor," he said, "but I am not disgusting. I have some dignity. I am
not a beggar. Maybe I will starve but I as a Kandha, I have self-respect. I cannot
sell my Kandha heritage, my religion. Otherwise no one will come to even
cremate me on my dying day. I will be shunned by everyone. If I stay hungry,
I am used to it. At least I will not lose my self-respect. If I accept these tainted
things from others, these Christians, everyone in the community will forsake
me for being disgusting. Perhaps I will not even get a place in *narka* (hell)."

One day, after many such heated discussions between ethnonationalists
and Kandhas to discuss Pana attempts at reclassification as merely another
sign of their clamorous greed for capital, I lingered after ethnonationalist
workers had left. I sat as young Kandhas put away their implements and
tended to their children before dusk fell, when they would retreat indoors to
eat their evening meal and prepare for sleep. The men were tired, and their

time was precious, but I wanted to know how they felt after hearing about the goings-on of the district as described by ethnonationalists.

A young man, Purba, mopped his brow and said, "What should I say, ask everyone—what they think, what they say? One can hardly believe it, but then you are reminded—these are Panas. They are not straightforward, they are capable of a kind of deceit, a kind of doubleness that you and I cannot imagine. Listening to all this makes our blood boil. Who will not get angry when people are doing such foul things? They are hurting the land by filling it with filth, they are exploiting our land. Soon the air starts smelling from their presence, they are becoming that disgusting. Should we just stand by and listen?"

Kandhas reported that hearing ethnonationalists tell "the truth about what was really going on" provoked them to anger and made them want to stand up for their community and their motherland. Kandhas expressed the impact the words had on them in sensual, visceral terms themselves, describing how these words willed them to act in some way, rather than be mute witnesses to the events unfolding in the district. The speech-act quality of ethnonationalist speech was underscored by the immediacy of its effects in moving Kandhas into states of feeling and acting; Kandhas described their rejection and disgust, engaging caste as aesthetic infrastructure of caste as spatial-sensory order.

Contrasting Kandhas' alternately melancholic and prideful assertions about their denial of capital, Panas could only weakly protest the damning portrayal of their Christian personhood as unchecked materialism. They wearily denied their continued investment in Christianity to be not motivated by greed. They returned to discussing the ethos of care that was modeled by their pastors and the support extended to them through Christian networks, including through capital, education, and healthcare, which secured their attachment to Christianity. Capital and care, aspiration and affection were so deeply intertwined as to be inseparable in Pana orientations towards Christianity. Away from caste Hindu and Kandha settings, my friend Pastor Digal indignantly and tearfully demanded to know why Dalits were being vilified for what he saw to be a very natural desire—to seek uplift for oneself and one's community. As a man of the cloth, he refused to explicitly discuss the sexualized rhetoric that was being deployed by ethnonationalists, even in the defense of his community. His face burned with shame, he said, to hear Panas being accused of engaging in sins that no observant Christian would ever contemplate.

Kandhas have long been described by engaging tropes of an aggressive masculinity. As Ajay Skaria writes of British colonial gendering of "wild tribes," not only did European traditions around contract theory place the patriarchal family at the very origins of social life, the tribal as noble savage hearkened back to a presumed moment of unfettered masculinity after the sexual contract but *before* the social contract. The very notion of "wild tribes," derived from ideas of the state of nature, was fundamentally gendered from its inception, and within this gendered context, honesty, loyalty, truthfulness, independence, and warlike qualities were ascribed to tribes, by colonists but also by caste Hindus, both before and after colonialism.[46] When Kandhas expressed disgust at Christian sex and its world of depravity, they asserted a cleansed, civilized Adivasi masculinity. Indeed, caste Hindus have historically indicted Adivasis of engaging in the very same immoral bodily excesses described in bana bhojis: singing, dancing, imbibing alcohol and impure animal flesh, and displaying sexual freedom. While expressing disgust for Christian Panas, Kandhas distanced themselves from pejorative characterizations of their own primitive savagery, fashioning a Kandha masculine civility that rejected bodily freedoms of sex and other material indulgences. Instead, they belabored that they would rely solely on their own labor and land even if it meant "starving," to mark their distinction from Panas.

Fears about Christian Dalit sexuality captured the idealization of a masculinist protectionism that purportedly linked upper-caste ethnonationalists and Kandha Adivasis as sons of the female Hindu rashtra, who would protect it at all costs. Ethnonationalist workers directly engaged an idealized Brahminical protectionism of women fused with an assumed aggressive masculinity for Adivasis to claim that Dalit men were failing to espouse such protectionist rectitude. Instead, Dalit men were cast as capable of "selling" women in a marketplace of sexual relations and exploitation. Such a fused Hindu-Kandha masculinity contrasted directly with a Dalit masculinity that not only failed to protect women but also blatantly exploited them for material gain, making them capable of "selling" the nation. In this depiction of the Dalit moral universe, the sexual exploitation of women for material gain was normalized, in contrast to an upper-caste gendered order in which women were, above all, repositories of caste and religious community honor.

Using sexuality as an aesthetic resource to arouse and channel disgust, ethnonationalists cast the clamorous materialism of Panas as leading to the disintegration of a casteist moral order expressed in embodied, gendered terms to suggest a threatening breakdown of caste economic dominance and hierarchy. At the same time, Kandhas were simultaneously invited to perform a masculinist Hindu protectionism of the nation as a gendered maternal figure by resignifying their own economic deprivation, both in terms of an upper-caste ascetic renunciation and an indigenous nobility that willingly abjured capital. Ethnonationalist workers depicted the capital and material resources flowing through faith-based nonprofits, Christian aid organizations, and mission outreach services as materialistic and immoral allures that cheapened the noble, self-denying virtuous Kandhas, debasing them by appealing to them as they would to materialistic Dalits.

Sex and Economic Victimization

In "Thinking Sex," Gayle Rubin provides a by now commonsensical understanding of how and why social anxieties and attendant emotional intensities are displaced onto sex, leading to the reemergence of conflicts over sexuality in times of social stress.[47] Rubin asserts the undeniably symbolic nature of sexuality. With no intrinsic meaning and no singular material reality, sex accrues social anxieties that resurface in panics that reactivate and reconstitute social relations in the face of a real or perceived threat of moral decline and disrepair, allowing power to be exercised in moral, social, and political arenas.[48]

Rubin's formulation shows sex to be a cipher onto which disparate meanings are projected to reflect political and economic anxieties. Her emphasis on the semiotic capacities of sex as a floating signifier, however, elides the material body as a means through which the purity and stability of fictional but embodied boundary markers such as gender, race, and sexuality[49] are threatened in order to provoke embodied affective appraisals. Sexuality has no inherent and absolute physical attributes even as it is socially produced. Understanding how it is framed, contextualized, understood, and interpreted requires a materialist, historicized approach.[50] Conversely, sexuality's ability to invoke bodily naturalness even as it is inextricable from society[51] makes it a distinct signifier of social and political economic conditions. Sex panics rely as much on the material embodiment of sex as "natural" signifier as they do on the social-economic as signified. Reading sex in this way intervenes in a long-standing tendency to discuss sexual violence as a mere ruse that distracts from "real" political economic agendas, viewing sexual violence as, at its core, an economic phenomenon.[52] Sex evokes anxieties because the material body and its semiosis of social-economic conditions are inseparable in citizens' meaning making, a fusion anticipated and harnessed in Hindu ethnonationalist speech.

Engaging sex's capacity to shore up social and economic anxieties, eth-nonationalists index conversion as a suite of material-ideological and mate-rial valences concerning the unraveling of caste as a political-economic order. They deploy an essentialist understanding of sex as a "natural" embodied means of bodily arousal, rendering structural and political economic uncer-tainties into intimate, embodied terms. An ethnonationalist aporia evident in a discursive denial and material indulgence of the body as a resource for political communication becomes a critical means through which national economic uncertainties become tied to a local economic populism.

As Ravinder Kaur and Thomas Blom Hansen discuss, a critical paradox of caste has emerged in a neoliberal India in which the vision of a new India is created by "leaving behind" or even erasing what does not fit in with the imagi-nary of a prosperous, techno-friendly, mobile consumer nation. Such a caste paradox becomes central to creating a vision of a economically victimized, dominant upper caste; caste elites masquerade as the "common man" whose claims to political legitimacy are entirely dependent upon speaking on behalf of the dispossessed and the powerless citizenry.[53] This erasure of one's upper- and middle-class identity in some ways parallels what Satish Deshpande has called the paradox of "castelessness"[54] in contemporary India: profiting from one's upper-caste privilege without having to acknowledge that privilege.

In this "casteless" upper-caste discourse of merit and intellect, economic gains through caste-based reservations and affirmative action made by low-caste groups that have historically suffered discrimination are considered threatening. In this reconception of the common man, claims of castelessness also abet claims to classlessness; class distinctions are blurred even as the poor are increasingly excluded from the benefits of the growth of a new economy. An aesthetics of spectacle plays a critical role in smoothing over and recon-ciling contradictions in these processes, playing a critical role in how market society negates its own essence to suggest an increasing submission of the previously unoccupied areas of social life to market forces. In such a context, Hindu ethnonationalists conjured up spectacles of sexual and bodily excess as unfettered material indulgence to suggest older anxieties of alienation and negation—the separation of the humanity from its essence and its projection on to God, nation, or other ideological fantasies.

In Kandhamal, ethnonationalists' engagement of sex as spectacle and religious aesthetics did not seek erasure of caste and class to foment claims of castelessness in transforming economic facts and attendant uncertainties into accessible, alluring, and even threatening dreamworlds. Rather, religious aesthetics became a critical means through caste, and class—or rather caste as class—was resignified as new obfuscations and relationships were forged between caste, capital, and economic identity. These obfuscations and resignifications became clear as Kandhas claimed economic unfairness and exploitation while expressing affinities with an upper-caste Hindutva. Kandha and Pana caste and class identities are resignified in terms of Adivasi authenticity and Dalit materialism in a context in which, as David Mosse argues,[55] caste has emerged as a dynamic aspect of the modern Indian economy, with market-led neoliberal development both weakening and reproducing caste inequalities privileged as the basis of social and economic capital. Kandhamal showcases how a fused category of a Hindu Kandha Adivasi as economic victim was created by engaging Dalits as clamorous and threatening usurpers of tribal recognition and Adivasi economic commensuration.

The economic particulars of Kandhas and Panas' uneven incorporation are a regionally specific instantiation of how Adivasi-Dalit economic hierarchy is both continued, disrupted and restored, underscoring that caste in the neoliberal economy must be engaged in the long durée of caste capitalism. The salience of the bestial, rapacious sexuality of the Other has been a particularly idiosyncratic Hindu ethnonationalist idiom. Yet, ethnonationalist engagements of sexual tropes to express the economic victimization of Kandhas and Hindus have broader resonances with many right-wing resurgences across contexts where notions of economic victimization and fairness rear their head.[56] Not only do these right-wing resurgences reengage motifs of gender, sexuality, and race that undergird an idealized national subject, religious symbolism, as in Kandhamal, recaptures new economic anxieties. Since the late 1980s, a revitalized Hindu ethnonationalism has increasingly sought to make the vision of sex as religious aggression against victimized Hindus ubiquitous, with its invocations precisely threatening fault lines of caste, gender, and sexuality. While these sexual refrains renew the need for the policing of these embodied and relational boundaries, their use of religious aesthetics in reframing economic discontents to suture religious intensities to economic discontents must be understood as part of a larger shift in modern politics.

Previously, we saw Kandhas repeatedly describing the advent of Hindu ethnonationalism as a resumption of historical intimacies between Kandha and Hindu kingship. Invoking such historical intimacy with Hindu kingship in which Kandhas were subjects of Hindu religious-political incorporations, Kandhas understood the political speech of ethnonationalists as forceful and legitimate, relying on the explicitly dharmic identity adopted by ethnonationalists. Kandhas did not mark a strict ontological separation between the religious and political[57]—to which we can add the economic. Even as state discourse understood Desia Kandhas to be Hinduized after having undergone a process of passive assimilation into Hinduism, Kandhas continued to mark their distinct indigenous cosmologies. These cosmologies resolutely refused distinctions between the material, the political, and the religious, while accommodating and absorbing Hindu religious and political notions. Hindu ethnonationalism further purposively blurred the aesthetic and affective connections between religious and political authority in its signification of sex as Dalit materialism in its political rhetoric.

The political speech of ethnonationalists, then, became a site of dissolution for secular analytic divisions between religious and political authority. As Bernard Bate has observed, the logic of political practice partakes of the same logic that forms religious practices associated with the worship of God.[58] For example, followers observe no clear division between religion and politics, relating to powerful leaders as being akin to deities.[59] In his ethnosociological model of Indian society, McKim Marriott advances a model of Hindu society in which all beings are understood to be gradable by shakti, a kind of political power that is synonymous with both religious virtue and effective world dominance, revealing the fluidity of exchange between religion and political power in South Asia.[60] Kandhas who identified as participants in the ethnonationalist movement did not explicitly gloss all ethnonationalist workers' political speech as *pravachans*, or religious discourses, as Kalyani Devaki Menon notes of the speech of ethnonationalist sadhvis, or female renouncers. Yet they characterized ethnonationalist perspectives as "truths"—not a commentary about how they should see things differently but rather a description of things as they really were—by describing ethnonationalist political speech as the "talk of dharmic people," showing just how the legitimacy of ethnonationalists, and the truth effects of their vitriolic speech, derived in large part from their religious authority. In ethnonationalist oratory in Kandhamal, the dissolution of religious, political, and economic aspects became critical in engaging caste as aesthetic infrastructure to render capital carnal.

Hindu ethnonationalist political oratory is, then, distinctly modern in its quest to suture religious and caste aesthetics to political economic uncertainties, addressing political subjects in a register simultaneously spectacular and intimate. Birgit Meyer reminds us of the proliferating deployment of sensuous and sensational forms in the domain of the religious in the wake of what Max Weber famously postulated to be a progressive disenchantment—a purported rationalization and secularization of the world with the rise of capitalism. We may debate the extent to which such a thesis of disenchantment was, in fact, realized in the West, to say nothing of its limits in India, which has crucially challenged canonical notions of an idealized secular public sphere. Yet the political speech of ethnonationalists evidences the self-conscious engagement of a distinct upper caste Hindu aesthetic framework in the resignification of Kandhas as immaterial indigenes and Dalits as their clamorous materialistic Others. Ethnonationalists engaged caste as a deeply visceral, charged script to render economic discontents to be moral transgressions in ways that resist narration through arid secular categories.

Sex's ability to index material excesses while operating as an aesthetic strategy functioned in a dual sense. On the one hand, it triggered embodied political appraisals while upholding the nation in highly ideological aesthetic terms that mandated a performance of upper-casteness as national belonging. Through their call for protection of the moral fiber of their land, Kandhas performed an aspirational upper-caste masculinist protectionism while they defended their economic entitlements from being usurped by Christian Dalits clamoring for capital. Ethnonationalist political oratory suggested a spectacular reimagining of a local political economy of caste in which Dalit materialism threatened Kandha economic dominance or even commensuration, even as such a commensuration had never been realized. At the same time, this aesthetic framework not only remobilized the rejection of Panas as Dalits in sensuous terms but also resignified, and laminated, Adivasi authenticity with upper-caste Hindu masculinity. Reviving religious ethnonationalist tropes of sex as warfare against Hindus, ethnonationalists elicited a strenuous disavowal of the material body, by casting a noble, self-denying Kandha indigenous identity and its affinity with an idealized masculine ascetic Hinduism as endangered by neoliberal femininized material excess. Using disgust to challenge embodied boundaries and arouse panic, ethnonationalist linked Kandhas' religious identity with their gender and caste identifications to redirect animus about economic marginalization in an uneven neoliberalism.

The uneven, differential incorporation of Kandha Adivasis and Pana Dalits into a neoliberal local economic order showcases how uneven caste incorporations are culminating in a resurgent casteism in which Dalits have nationally become even more vulnerable to discrimination and violence,[61] including a resurgence in sexual violence. On an uneven socioeconomic terrain without guarantees, Hindu ethnonationalist rhetoric about the sexual excesses of Panas, and by extension Christians, performatively generated rather than merely suppressed politics[62] as a national anti-Dalitness was sutured to a local casteist resurgence against Christian Panas. Feminized Christian Dalit materialism served as a proxy for Pana economic mobility as Pana conversion threatened upper-caste monopoly over capital. In right-wing rhetoric, however, Pana Christianity was resignified as the usurpation of the naturalized blood-and-soil entitlements of Kandhas.

Ethnonationalist political rhetoric suggested that Kandhas perform an aspirational upper-caste masculinist protectionism that was at once an aspirational performance of an upper-caste ethnonationalist masculinity and an assertion of their indigenous authenticity. In riots that occurred weeks and months later, Kandhas torched Christian Pana houses and churches, and engaged in sexual violence against Christian nuns, showing how such violence resisted being read as either caste or sexual atrocity. Though it was described as religious in character, this violence was symptomatic of an ongoing ambivalence toward the market.[63] Sexual violence became indecipherable as caste violence, even as it performed a pedagogical socialization of caste norms[64] by hemming Dalits back into economic disenfranchisement as normative to caste hierarchy and provoking a resurgent casteism against them.

Conclusion

We return now to the outbreak of violence with which we began.

In December 2007, the various strands and registers in which Kandha-Pana hostilities were expressed in months prior—economic, aesthetic, and ontological—began to uneasily coalesce under the sign of religion. At this time, on the day before Christmas, a conflict between Hindus and Christians broke out in Bamunigam, Daringbadi. Hindu villagers tore down Christmas decorations in the village square. The celebration, they insisted, was a deliberate, malicious ploy by Pana Christians to defile the site where Durga Puja had been celebrated only a few months before. The Ambedkar Banika Sangha, the local Dalit Ambedkarite traders' guild that organized the event, asserted Christians' right to freely celebrate their religious festivals. Upon protesting, Christians were beaten by Hindus until they were bloodied and unconscious. Soon after, differing claims were made about who instigated the violence. Hindus reported that they resorted to violence in self-defense, as Panas had begun the fight. Christian Panas, in turn, insisted that they were decorating the site peacefully until an angry Hindu crowd accosted them.

"Truth"—indeed, "truths"—was slippery at this time in Kandhamal. Repeated accusations by Hindu Kandhas and Christian Panas were leveled at one another with increasing frequency in the later months of my fieldwork spanning December 2007 to April 2008. The violence in Bamunigam confirmed the escalating climate of mistrust, secrecy, and fear in which Hindu Kandhas and Christian Panas accused one another of a salvo of aggressions. Sibu, the owner of the tea stall I frequented, voiced the views of the Hindu and Kandha residents of the district: Pana Christians were cunning and materialistic, they had always been that way, and their most recent claims to victimization were merely another manipulative attempt at eliciting sympathy to gain benefits from the state. A Dalit Christian aid worker, Peter

Digal, roundly critiqued these accusations by presenting the Dalit Christian perspective.

Hindus insisted that Christians were engaging in assertive and tactical pollution of a Hindu sacred space. Peter, however, asserted that it was more the case that Christians' public celebration of Christmas was challenging the increasing Hindu ethnonationalist imperative that Christians practice their religion privately and not convert others. Peter insisted that the only way Christians could live in the district without being threatened by violence at every turn was if they became "invisible," practicing their religion within the confines of their homes, as if ashamed of their Christian Pana identity. The violence in Bamunigam portended an attempt to drive Panas out of the district—quite literally, an ethnic cleansing—as Hindu Kandhas aggressively engaged tropes of purity and pollution to insist that Pana Christians were outsiders and usurpers on Kandha lands, defiling them with their presence. Peter drew attention to the repeated caste Hindu hierarchy characterization of Panas as Dalits who were ritually polluting, who did "dirty" menial jobs, to emphasize that the vitriolic rejection of Pana Christians was necessarily tied to their caste identity as Dalits.

Kandhas dismissed narratives of equality and shared political-economic struggle with Panas. Once the economic patrons and employers of Panas, they now saw them as audaciously attempting to usurp their Adivasi heritage to usurp their proprietary Adivasi status. As Peter verbally sparred with the tea shop owner, he drew together the recurring motifs that have reared their heads repeatedly in these pages: Kandhas as Adivasis were simple, unworldly indigenes exploited by Panas as wily, materialistic Dalits, which justified violence against them. Even as these racialized casteist scripts were invoked once again in terms of immutable essences, they had clearly accrued new political and economic anxieties in an uncertain, uneven terrain of Indian multiculturalism.

Within hours of the incident at Bamunigam, the atmosphere in Baliguda, the district subdivision, was tense. Matchbox cars with saffron flags ferrying members of the Bajrang Dal patrolled as if conducting vigils to rouse fear among Christians and signal protection for Hindus. In my neighborhood behind the Baliguda market, people stayed up later than usual, huddled together at the entrances of their houses around kerosene lamps. The night passed uneasily. By the morning of Christmas Day, riots spread throughout the district, starting in Bamunigam and spreading to the peripheries of Baliguda as churches, mission schoolhouses, and Christian houses were set on fire by Hindus—several, if not all, of them Kandha Adivasis.

A few days later, Pastor Digal came to my house. The pastor, a slight, spry, and ever-smiling man, often sought me out for conversations about the need to uplift his Dalit Christian parishioners. On this day, however, he looked gaunt and fatigued, his usually pristine white clothes stained and muddied. Refusing the chair I offered him, he squatted on his haunches on the floor. When he opened his mouth to speak, whimpers gave way to sobs that wracked his entire body. His house had been torched, along with those of his neighbors in the Christian *sai* (neighborhood). The pastor had lost the materials he stored for his parishioners: textbooks for schoolchildren, warm blankets to be distributed at Christmas, toys, secondhand clothes collected in church collection drives in the United States. Also lost were hundreds of signatures he had collected from Christian Panas petitioning to be reclassified as Kandhariya Panas (Panas like Kandhas) in order to gain recognition by the Indian state as a Scheduled Tribe. "They wanted a better life, they trusted me with their future, now what will I tell them," Pastor Digal said through his tears.

The next day, I went to meet Pastor Digal and his neighbors, having promised him that I would visit. Approaching the Christian sai, I saw torched houses, now mostly reduced to rubble. One wall of the pastor's house remained standing, now used as a base for a stretched tarp that protected him and his wife from the elements. Pastor Digal looked haggard. "It is hard to sleep," he said. "I always fear someone is coming, something else will happen."

As we conversed, some people came to the doorstep, asking who I was. When the pastor's wife said that I was one of their people, I hastened to clarify that I was not a missionary, since the local administration had forbidden missionaries and Hindu nationalists, fearing they were escalating religious disharmony. Afterward, some of the pastor's neighbors speculated that they were local police conducting checks on Hindu or Christian workers entering riot sites and stirring conflict. I asked the pastor why the police were not in uniform and if they had come around before. He replied that he too had been puzzled about their plain clothes but that they had come around a few times, stating their good intentions and desire to keep a protective eye on the community. My journalist friend, Santosh Digal, later clarified that these men were not policemen but rather Maoist insurgents patrolling the area to find out more about Hindu ethnonationalist instigation of hostilities between the two communities.

The pastor's neighbors came into what remained of his house. With a trembling voice, one man described how their families' harvested grain for the year and other belongings—clothing, blankets, food items—had been consumed by the blaze. Frightened, they ran to hide in the surrounding forests. After a week, fearing they might perish, they returned but remained terrified that they would be burned alive in their own homes. Several Panas planned to leave for relief camps set up by the state government in Phulbani, the district capital, and Bhubaneswar, the state capital. Leaving their homes, however, would mean that they would become entirely dispossessed.

As Dalits, Panas had no ancestral or legal claims to land. Their houses were built on land found by chance, which was never formally registered in their names, on which they were seen squatters. "It is our fate to wander. To be without home and land. It is all written in your *bhaagya* (fate) when you are born a Pana. Panas are fated to be homeless. Where is our land? It is nowhere," one man said, his face expressionless. Kandhas had angrily insisted on their economic victimization as authentic indigenes, but in the days that followed what became apparent was the profound vulnerability of their purported aggressors as landless Dalit converts. Dalits were economically marginalized by their inability to claim land as property. Landlessness also reinscribed Dalits as without a home in the Indian nation-state, a condition in which they were constantly compelled to account for their fidelity to both religion and nation while being subjected to centuries of caste violence that suffused their workings.

The violence around Christmas 2007 would foreshadow the outbreak of violence months later that would go on to become the largest incident of anti-Christian violence in the Indian nation-state's history. In August 2008, Maoist insurgents would assassinate Laxmananda Saraswati, my chief ethnonationalist interlocutor, in the compound of the Jalespata girls' school where I interviewed him, as a dire warning to Hindu ethnonationalists to stop instigating religious and communal strife in the district. Ethnonationalist organizers would parade his body through crowds of Kandhas gathered to pay their respects to him as a father figure, an iconic benefactor who had revitalized the community by restoring pride in Kandha identity. Indeed, it was under Laxmananda's charismatic leadership that economic dissatisfaction, caste aspiration, and indigenous dominance had come together to consolidate aggressive local populism against Christian Panas. Following ethnonationalist resignifications of Dalit materialism, its links to Christian capital, and now Maoist violence against Hindu religious leaders, Kandhas began a rampage that would displace forty-five thousand Dalit Christians. Over a decade later, more than half of these displaced Dalits continue to be scattered in rehabilitation camps, most losing claims to their dwellings in the absence of any formal claims to land and property in their villages.

Since Kandhamal, violence against Dalits has dramatically risen, emphasizing Dalits as the constitutive outside of caste Hindu society who become particularly scapegoated in conditions of economic uncertainty in which right-wing populism flourishes. Such violence harnesses foundational exclusions of Dalits, which Aishwary Kumar describes as "a symptomatic blockage, constitutive of liberalism's civilisational prejudice that guards, like a 'barbed wire,' the rules and logics of India's questionably urbane civility."[1] The vulnerability of Dalits to ethnonationalist violence, when held up alongside the escalation of anti-Black, anti-Asian, and anti-Muslim violence in right-wing conditions globally, emphasizes that resurgent caste and racial violence within contemporary right-wing populisms must be understood as neoliberal revelations of legal and democratic exclusions, which are foundational to nation-states.

Cruel Optimisms

Minority citizens make highly imaginative, charged assertions linking state patronage, religious identity, and capital, and their promises of "unachievable fantasies of a good life through assurances of upward mobility, job security, and political and social equality,"[2] attesting to their attachments as what Lauren Berlant would see as forms of cruel optimism. Despite recognition's failures and exclusions, minorities only return to it as a motor of caste capitalism. In neoliberal conditions of economic pessimism and stymied political assertions, minorities increasingly seek, rather than refuse, recognition. These growing minority claims on indigeneity in the Global South show how the violence of recognition is wrought precisely *through* its doubleness, securing attachments through its failures that make a hopeful and emancipatory refusal impossible for the most vulnerable.

Recognition motors a differential economic casteism against Adivasis and Dalits to differentially implicate them within ethnonationalist violence in India. These differential minority trajectories assert the inadequacy of idealized visions of shared subalternity and racial coalition building, to instead recenter caste and race as critical to engaging ossifying divergences between minorities' economic and political trajectories within nation-states. Taken together, these developments showcase the dystopic deadlock of caste and race in late capitalism: minorities recursively return to majoritarian recognition, both in the law and in conservative politics, forms of mis-recognition that they attempt to bear in economic precarity, as in Berlant's formulation. Recognition within (neo)colonial majoritarian regimes continually renews the violence *of* caste and race as shape-shifting yet durable fictions.

Analyzing ethnonationalist violence as caste violence, we see how caste and race secure an intimate, processual suturing of a local populism to an (ethno) national populism. Casteist and racialized formations of Adivasi authenticity and Dalit materialism emerge at the interface of legal and ethnonational logics of minority recognition. We see religion churning the structural through the affective-aesthetic as structures of majoritarian hierarchies of recognition are upheld through the processual recapture and resignification of caste and race in economic precarity. Religion thus, enables majoritarian regimes of caste capitalism to be upheld by making possible unlikely political allegiances and attachments among minority communities that ultimately only continue their economic disenfranchisement.

In Kandhamal, despite its doctrinal denial of Adivasiness as a condition of prior claims undermining Hindu primacy in the Indian nation-state, we see a deeply raced neocolonial Hindu ethnonationalism speak in tongues while confronting Adivasi lifeworlds, to return to Jodi Byrd and Michael Rothberg's words. Charting these varying, and sometimes contradictory, attempts to absorb and accommodate Adivasi indigeneity in its evolving right-wing populist avatar, we see a ever-capacious evolution of ethnonationalist and right-wing movements in their absorption of seemingly progressive discourses and formations, even when they seem to variously dilute their stated ideological emphases. For instance, Hindu ethnonationalism has engaged nature-culture symbolism not just to reabsorb indigenous ontologies of land but also to straddle religious symbolism and ecological protectionism, such as the protection of rivers, revered as personified sacred goddesses in Hinduism. These developments show how nature-culture symbolism is engaged in an emergent counterintuitive eco-ethnonationalism, in which a history of politicization of Hindu icons and deities is in conversation with transnational legal and political environmentalism elsewhere. Hindu ethnonationalism has long been bracketed as an unusual and singular political movement; it, in fact, foreshadows critical contradictions and evolutions in global right-wing populisms as they absorb progressive discourses, and minority politics, into their logics to render pessimisms into cruel optimisms.

Unruly Indigeneities

Nowhere is the perverse nature of attachments to recognition more profoundly visible than it is in the case of indigeneity. Indigeneity has become a key trope in minority politics across South Asia in the past two decades. As Townsend Middleton reminds us, proliferating demands for tribal status in India should be understood in the context of the global proliferation of indigenous movements that have placed indigeneity and its distinctive claims to culture, identity, and difference at the forefront of claims in multicultural orders across geographies. Adivasi and Dalit claims on tribal recognition show how indigeneity as a condition of entitlements to land and territory provides an increasingly charged register of autochthony through which minorities seek to claim their economic entitlements from the Indian state.[3]

A vexed economic conundrum has emerged amid these developments, however. Adivasis have been unable to achieve economic commensuration despite tribal recognition, remaining the most economically disadvantaged group in the Indian nation-state.[4] And yet bids for tribal recognition proliferate among other ethnic groups, precisely engaging tribal recognition as a privileged means of economic uplift in neoliberal precarity. A critical paradox underlies the violence of tribal recognition in South Asia. Tribal recognition, seen as de facto indigenous recognition, is fetishized and clamored for as a guarantor of economic commensuration and mobility. Yet, simultaneously, tribal recognition serves as the very means through which Adivasi groups such as Kandhas continue to be reinscribed as unable to economically benefit from recognition and its mandates through a reconstruction of Adivasi authenticity.

Moreover, indigenous recognition's exclusions and consequences for indigeneity's landless Others perpetuate their differential entrenchment within caste capitalism. As Adivasis and Dalits struggle over who economically benefits from recognition in what ways and who deserves economic uplift, recognition emerges as a crucible of religion, caste, and class—or, more properly, *caste as class*. The sociolegal scripts that emerge in these claims accrue new valences in political and economic uncertainty to revitalize xenophobic characterizations of Dalits as indigeneity's Others and, ultimately, outsiders to the nation. Adivasis, the most economically disenfranchised group in the Indian nation-state, lag behind Dalits despite recognition. Dalits, on the other hand, are excluded from recognition upon religious conversion, showing a continued insistence that caste is enclosed within Hinduism despite ample evidence to the contrary.

Recognition for both is contested and exclusionary, entrenching rather than ameliorating their differing exclusions from capital.[5] Adivasi and Dalit contestations over recognition show how Adivasi indigeneity operates as a fulcrum of caste capitalism to reactivate the violent anti-Dalitness of Indian multiculturalism. Recognition emerges as a critical site of ethnonationalist and populist violence's continuities with caste capitalism. Dalits, whose conversion to Christianity exacerbates their vulnerability as landless minorities, become subject to new fictions of economic canniness and materialism. These fictions show how caste shape-shifts; Adivasi indigeneity reactivates Dalit exclusions from legal and nationalist regimes of recognition, rendering them newly vulnerable to xenophobic violence. Adivasi indigeneity, then, clearly brings into view the darker possibilities of indigeneity as a political formation in conditions of economic precarity and political pessimism, which sharply rebukes recursive attempts within anthropology to repurify and reengage indigeneity as a formation that promises political panacea and romantic resistance in a time of economic and ecological crisis.

Scholars of recognition note the way that indigeneity cunningly entraps communities into logics of authenticity[6] and entrenches indigenous exclusion from capital,[7] in order to call for a refusal of recognition as a project of colonial determinism.[8] Anthropologists emphasize the political and ethical power in the refusal of indigenous recognition, as in Audra Simpson's study of the Kahnawà:ke Mohawks and their choice to refuse the "gifts" of American and Canadian citizenship. Such refusal challenges what is assumed to be a finished, settled project of colonialism.[9] And yet, Nicholas Copeland notes that such a "principled refusal, which bleeds into notions of choice," is a luxury scarcely afforded by minorities. Accordingly, it might serve as standard of "judging the existence or authenticity of radical desire, which rarely appears in such uncontaminated forms,"[10] and thus might give us a more nuanced understanding of how indigenous radical imaginaries may be embedded within seemingly perverse alignments of indigenous politics with conservative regimes.

The increasing minority turns toward tribal-as-indigenous recognition in India argue against the concept of an always radical indigenous politics. The uncannily resonant patterns in the construction and governance of Indian indigeneity noted in this analysis, as well as their implications for landless

minorities such as Dalits, require us to interrogate India's exclusion from settler colonial geographies.[11] In his analysis of ethnological logics underlying
tribal recognition in India, Middleton describes the racialization of Adivasis
as tribes, which has led them to occupy the margins of a "peculiarly Euro-
Brahminical imaginary." The concept of the indigenous Adivasi was consolidated in the British colonial imaginary through processes of racialization
with uncanny settler colonial resonance. Colonial knowledge, followed by
governance by the postcolonial Indian state, crafted Adivasis as a sensuous,
bodily primitive Other of Indian liberalism.[12] As such, Adivasis have been
critical figures in the maintenance of a temporal experience of modernity for
colonists as well as caste Hindus,[13] and Adivasiness's continued circulation
as racialized indigeneity has been described a condition of ongoing internal
colonization within caste society.[14]

A romantic racialization of Adivasis as indigenes has also led to them
representing an "idealized radical political horizon,"[15] despite their steady
mobilization into an aggressive, masculinist Hindu ethnonationalism in
India. Hindu ethnonationalists have reframed the Adivasi (original settler)
as the vanvasi (forest dweller) in a struggle over notions of authentic Indian
identity and lineage as rooted in the Indian soil.[16] This struggle is based in
a denial of the Aryan-invasion theory that posits Adivasi tribals as original
settlers and Aryan Hindus as outsiders, undermining caste Hindu primacy
in the nation-state. Hindu ethnonationalist reframing of Adivasi as vanvasi
is an act of semantic aggression against indigenous identity and politics.[17]
Mobilizers, however, engage Adivasis as indigenes rooted in land to naturalize their connection to a Hindu nation. They marshal religious intimacies
between Adivasis and Hindus to invoke a long history of incorporation and
assimilation, intimacies that have been obscured by a secular dismissal of the
force of religion in Adivasi lives.[18]

Hindu ethnonationalists symbolically valorize Adivasiness as a vital
moral "essence" of the nation, deploying Adivasi authenticity in ways that
confirm fears about the indigenous movement's naturalization of ideas of
blood and soil.[19] Hindu ethnonationalism is believed to undermine indigeneity as a condition of prior claims to the Indian nation-state and its lands.[20] Yet
ethnonationalists figure the Adivasi as indigene to abet future forms of value
extraction and exploitation of Adivasis by caste Hindus as well as to configure
Dalits as materialistic infidels unrooted to land, religion, and thus nation. In
the ethnonationalist affirmation of Adivasi claims in order to deny economic
commensuration for Dalits, we see confirmation of Alpa Shah's caveat that we

inquire about just how rhetorics of indigenous rights are mobilized, by whom and to what ends.[21] As Copeland argues of conservative turns in indigenous politics in Latin America,[22] conditions of economic and political pessimism thwart progressive indigenous politics.

From the vantage point of its Dalit Others, Adivasi indigeneity emerges as an unruly political-economic technology in which "becoming Adivasi" emphasizes the multiplicity of uneven and contradictory events, sites, and representations through which Adivasi indigeneity is, and has been, constructed and negotiated.[23] Emphasizing such a becoming of Adivasi over tribe, which has "strong evolutionist connotations," as David Hardiman points out, also highlights the historical processes with distinct economic consequences that consolidated Adivasi indigeneity: the nineteenth-century subjugation, economic oppression, and dispossession of a wide variety of communities that, before the colonial period, had remained free.[24] Following historian Sangeeta Dasgupta, focusing on "becoming Adivasi" rather than "being Adivasi" better accommodates "the range of multiple histories around the singular subject of the [A]divasi."[25] Acknowledging Adivasi indigeneity as an unruly becoming that is also yet a distinct political technology joins a new historiographical turn that emphasizes how the Adivasi condition is embedded in a politics of representation. In this frame, the Adivasi is foregrounded as modern subject negotiating with modern state power, displaying plural identities that are "radically contingent, impermanent, changeable habitations."[26]

Adivasi politics has gained new currency with the emergence of global indigenous-rights movements, neoliberal developmental initiatives of the Indian state, and Maoist insurgency.[27] Amid these developments, Adivasi indigeneity needs to be reconceptualized as a distinct political technology that resists easy categorization in contemporary India. This highlights the necessity for a historically, socially, and politically situated approach to the ways in which particular forms of resistance are depicted as Adivasi at particular times.[28] Against any purifying narratives, indigeneity must be engaged as an ontologically porous and unruly category[29] for a more critical engagement with indigenous politics. From a Dalit perspective, the unruliness of the contemporary Adivasi identification and its ability to hold together contradictory and laminated political claims to the detriment of Dalits allow for the continual remaking of Adivasi indigeneity as a fulcrum of caste capitalism. Contemporary ethnonationalist politics reengage Adivasi indigeneity to mobilize xenophobic violence against landless Dalits, emphasizing the Adivasi condition,

as Lucas Bessire has said, not as a stable radical alterity but rather as a condition of semantic implosions, which nonetheless serves as a neoliberal political
technology crucial for policing who should live and in the name of what.[30] A
complex and unruly Adivasi indigeneity rooted in land reactivates and remo-
bilizes the anti-Dalitness of Indian multiculturalism.

NOTES

Introduction

1. I use the term "Adibasi," an Odia variant of Adivasi, as it was used in my informants' speech.

2. Nathaniel Roberts, *To Be Cared For: The Power of Conversion and Foreignness of Belonging in an Indian Slum* (Oakland: University of California Press, 2016).

3. Roberts, *To Be Cared For.*

4. Anand Teltumbde, *Republic of Caste: Thinking Equality in the Time of Neoliberal Hindutva* (New Delhi: Navayana, 2018).

5. Marc Galanter, *Competing Equalities: Law and the Backward Classes in India* (New Delhi: Oxford University Press, 1991).

6. Stuart Corbridge, "Competing Inequalities: The Scheduled Tribes and the Reservations System in India's Jharkhand," *Journal of Asian Studies* 59, no. 1 (2000): 62–85 at 64.

7. Jawaharal Nehru, *The Adivasis* (Delhi: Ministry of Information and Broadcasting, 1955).

8. See Ramachandra Guha, *Savaging the Civilized: Verrier Elwin, His Tribals, and India* (Chicago: University of Chicago Press, 1999); and Galanter, *Competing Equalities,* 153.

9. Corbridge, "Competing Inequalities."

10. For a thorough analysis of how Dalits have come to be claimed as always Hindu via the attempts of twentieth-century Indian nationalists to encompass Dalit religion within a newly imagined Hindu body politic, and a majoritarian Hinduization of Dalits, see Joel G. Lee, *Deceptive Majority: Dalits, Hinduism and Underground Religion* (New York: Cambridge University Press, 2021).

11. Townsend Middleton, *The Demands of Recognition: State Anthropology and Ethnopolitics in Darjeeling* (Stanford, CA: Stanford University Press, 2015).

12. Anupama Rao, *The Caste Question: Dalits and the Politics of Modern India* (Berkeley: University of California Press, 2009).

13. Chinnaiah Jangam, *Dalits and the Making of Modern India* (Oxford: Oxford University Press, 2019).

14. See Nicolas Jaoul, "Beyond Citizenship: Adivasi and Dalit Political Pathways in India," *Focaal* 76 (2016): 3–14.

15. David Mosse, "The Modernity of Caste and the Market Economy," *Modern Asian Studies* 54, no. 4 (2020): 1225–71.

16. See Jodi Melamed, "Racial Capitalism," *Journal of Critical Ethnic Studies* 1, no.1 (2015): 76–86; Nikhil Pal Singh, "On Race, Violence and So-Called Primitive Accumulation," *Social Text* 34, no. 3 (2016): 27–50; and Cedric Robinson, *Black Marxism: The Making of the Black Radical Tradition* (Chapel Hill: University of North Carolina Press, 1983); in the South Asian context, see David Mosse's work, Jan Breman's work, and Rao, *Caste Question.*

17. See also K. Satyanarayana, "Dalit Reconfiguration of Caste: Representation, Identity and Politics," *Critical Quarterly* 56, no. 3 (2014): 46–61.

18. Rawat and Satyanarayana, *Dalit Studies* (Durham, NC: Duke University Press, 2016), 4.

19. Rawat and Satyanarayana, *Dalit Studies,* 17.

20. Nikhil Pal Singh, "Race, Violence and So-Called Primitive Accumulation," *Social Text,* 34 no. 3 (2016): 27–50.

21. Rao, *Caste Question.*

22. Mosse, "Modernity of Caste."

23. I adapt this formulation from Rupa Viswanath's caste-state nexus that she uses to describe how an alliance between British and Indian officials and native high-caste employers of Pariahs elide and avoid the economic disenfranchisement of Dalits. See Rupa Viswanath, *The Pariah Problem: Caste, Religion, and the Social in Modern India* (New York: Columbia University Press, 2014), 3.

24. Navyug Gill, "Limits of Conversion: Caste, Labor, and the Question of Emancipation in Colonial Panjab," *Journal of Asian Studies* 78, no. 1 (2019): 3–22.

25. Rawat and Satyanarayana, *Dalit Studies,* 4.

26. Glen Sean Coulthard, *Red Skin White Masks: Rejecting The Colonial Politics of Recognition* (Minneapolis: University of Minnesota Press, 2009), 34.

27. See Harihar Panda, "History of Orissa," *Cuttack, 1997* (2008): 272.

28. Debasree De, "Development-Induced Displacement: Impact on Adivasi Women of Odisha," *Community Development Journal* 50, no. 3 (2015): 448–62.

29. Miriam Driessen, "Rural Voids," *Public Culture* 30, no. 1 (2018): 61–84.

30. James Ferguson, *The Anti-Politics Machine: "Development," Depoliticization, and Bureaucratic Power in Lesotho* (Minneapolis: University of Minnesota Press, 1994).

31. João Biehl, *Vita: Life in a Zone of Social Abandonment* (Berkeley: University of California Press, 2005).

32. Jan Breman, *Footloose Labour: Working in India's Informal Economy* (Cambridge: Cambridge University Press, 1996).

33. Pralay Kanungo, "Hindutva's Entry into a 'Hindu Province': Early Years of RSS in Orissa," *Economic and Political Weekly* 38, no. 31 (2003): 3293–3303.

34. For a detailed account of mission presence and activity in Odisha, see Manjushri Dhall, *The British Rule: Missionary Activities in Orissa, 1822–1947* (New Delhi: Har-Anand, 1997).

35. Harish Wankhede, "The Political Context of Religious Conversion in Orissa," *Economic and Political Weekly* 44, no. 15 (2009): 33–38.

36. Alpa Shah and Sarah Shneiderman, "The Practices, Policies, and Politics of Transforming Inequality in South Asia," *Focaal* 65 (2013): 3–12.

Chapter 1

1. Laura Dudley Jenkins, "Competing Inequalities: The Struggle over Reserved Legislative Seats for Women in India," *International Review of Social History* 44 (1999): 53–75 at 54.

2. Stuart Corbridge, "Competing Inequalities: The Scheduled Tribes and the Reservations System in India's Jharkhand," *Journal of Asian Studies* 59, no. 1 (2000): 62–85.

3. A notable exception is Townsend Middleton's *Demands for Recognition*, which explicitly states the way that tribal recognition secures a position of pejorative privilege for minorities within the Indian state. See Middleton, *The Demands of Recognition: State Anthropology and Ethnopolitics in Darjeeling* (Stanford, CA: Stanford University Press, 2015).

4. Aishwary Kumar, "What Is Dalit Studies: A Review," *Indian Economic and Social History Review* 56, no. 2 (2019): 227–45 at 240.

5. See Bhrigupati Singh, "Agonistic Intimacy and Moral Aspiration in Popular Hinduism: A Study in the Political Theology of the Neighbor," *American Ethnologist* 38, no. 3 (2011): 430–50; and Michael Herzfeld, "It Takes One to Know One: Collective Resentment and Mutual Recognition among Greeks in Local and Global Contexts," in *Counterworks: Managing the Diversity of Knowledge*, ed. Richard Fardon (London: Routledge, 1995), 118–36.

6. Edward Simpson et al., "A Brief History of Incivility in Rural Postcolonial India: Caste, Religion, and Anthropology," *Comparative Studies in Society and History* 60, no. 1 (2018): 58–89 at 62.

7. Simpson et al., "Brief History of Incivility."

8. I am indebted to Moishe Postone's reading of anti-semitism as a form of vulgar anti-capitalism in his essay "Anti-Semitism and National Socialism: Notes on the German Reaction to 'Holocaust,'" *New German Critique* 19 (1980): 97–115, as well as his later *Time, Labor, and Social Domination: A Reinterpretation of Marx's Critical Theory* (Cambridge: Cambridge University Press, 1993), for the understanding of expansion of capital as an abstract, impersonal form of domination, which posits a fundamental critique of Marxist approaches that understand domination in terms of overt social relations, such as the concrete domination of the working class by the capitalist class. Iyko Day reworks Postone in her book *Alien Capital: Asian Racialization and the Logic of Settler Colonial Capitalism* (Durham, NC: Duke University Press, 2016) to show the racialization of Asian immigrants to Canada and the United States through the historical alignment of Asian bodies and labor with capital's abstract and negative dimensions became one of settler colonialism's foundational and defining features. Though the history and trajectory of capital cannot be equated in Europe, settler colonial North

America, and South Asia, the aim here is to observe fruitful comparisons across projects of racialization that are critical to the abstract domination, rather than merely concrete class domination, through which capital operates.

9. James George Frazer, *The Golden Bough: A Study in Magic and Religion* (London: Wordsworth, 1993), originally published in 1890; Henri Hubert and Marcel Mauss, *Sacrifice: Its Nature and Functions* (Chicago: University of Chicago Press, 1981), originally published in 1964.

10. Barbara M. Boal, *The Konds: Human Sacrifice and Religious Change* (Warminster, U.K.: Aris and Phillips, 1982); Felix Padel, *The Sacrifice of Human Being: British Rule and the Konds of Orissa* (Delhi: Oxford University Press, 1995).

11. Rebecca Basso, "Music, Possession and Shamanism among Khond Tribes," *Culture and Religion* 7, no. 2 (2006): 177–97.

12. See Padel, *Sacrifice of Human Being*, 116–17.

13. Padel, *Sacrifice of Human Being*, 121.

14. Verrier Elwin, *The Tribal World of Verrier Elwin: An Autobiography* (London: Oxford University Press, 1964), 178.

15. Tina Otten and Edward Simpson, "F. G. Bailey's Bisipara Revisited," *Economic and Political Weekly* 2, nos. 26–27 (2016): 25.

16. F. Fawcett, "The Dombs of Jeypore, Vizagapatnam District, Madras," *Man* 1 (1901): 34–38.

17. Padel, *Sacrifice of Human Being*, 55–56.

18. Padel, *Sacrifice of Human Being*, 119.

19. Padel, *Sacrifice of Human Being*, 111.

20. Padel, *Sacrifice of Human Being*, 112.

21. Padel, *Sacrifice of Human Being*, 137.

22. Padel, *Sacrifice of Human Being*, 138.

23. F. G. Bailey, *Tribe, Caste, and Nation: A Study of Political Activity and Political Change in Highland Orissa* (Manchester: Manchester University Press, 1960), 130.

24. Bailey, *Tribe, Caste, and Nation*, 100.

25. Bailey, *Tribe, Caste, and Nation*, 133.

26. Bailey, *Tribe, Caste, and Nation*, 102.

27. My account of Kandha-Pana economic relations should be read alongside Piers Vitebsky's account of Sora-Pano relations in Odisha, where the same caste group serves as economic liaisons and traders within the Sora Adivasi community and is tasked with procuring buffalo from plains for them. Vitebsky details how these buffalo become tools of economic oppression of Soras, as Panas or Panos, as he prefers to call them, sell them at inflated prices, leading to intergenerational debt and loss of Sora land and harvest to Panos. For Vitebsky's explanation of how such "incomprehensively quantified cumulative debt" locks Soras and Panos in "ugly economic embrace" in perpetuity, see Piers Vitebsky, *Living without the Dead: Loss and Redemption in a Jungle Cosmos* (Chicago: University of Chicago Press, 2017), 30–31.

28. Bailey, *Tribe, Caste, and Nation*, 135.

29. F. G. Bailey, *The Civility of Indifference: On Domesticating Ethnicity* (Ithaca, NY: Cornell University Press, 1996), xvi.

30. Mohan Behera, *The Jayantira Pano: A Scheduled Caste Community of Orissa* (Bhubaneswar: Tribal and Harijan Research-cum-Training Institute, 1991).

31. Anand Pandian, *Crooked Stalks: Cultivating Virtue in South India* (Durham, NC: Duke University Press, 2009).

32. Elizabeth Povinelli, *The Cunning of Recognition: Indigenous Alterities and the Making of Australian Multiculturism* (Durham, NC: Duke University Press, 2002).

33. Prathama Banerjee, *Politics of Time: "Primitives" and History-writing in a Colonial Society* (New Delhi: Oxford University Press, 2006).

34. Kaushik Ghosh, "A Market for Aboriginality: Primitivism and Race Classification in the Indentured Labor Market of Colonial India," in *Subaltern Studies 10*, ed. Gautam Bhadra, Gyan Prakash, and Susie Tharu (New Delhi: Oxford University Press, 1999), 8–48.

35. Prathama Banerjee, "Debt, Time and Extravagance: Money and the Making of 'Primitives' in Colonial Bengal," *Indian Economic and Social History Review* 37, no. 4 (2000): 423–45.

36. Tania Murray Li thoroughly critiques the tendency to treat indigeneity and capitalism as wholly oppositional by showing how indigenous dispossession has not necessarily led landless indigenous peasants to dispute the legitimacy of the market processes through which they had become dispossessed, nor to call for a return to previous, more inclusive principles of land access that assume solidarity as integral to indigenous sociality. See Tania Murray Li, "Indigeneity, Capitalism, and the Management of Dispossession," *Current Anthropology* 51, no. 3 (2010): 385–414.

37. See Moishe Postone, *Time, Labor, and Social Domination: A Reinterpretation of Marx's Critical Theory* (Cambridge: Cambridge University Press, 1993); and Iyko Day, *Alien Capital.*

38. Caste capitalism as a fundamental reengineering of relations between persons, as well as people and the environment, is also echoed by scholars of racial capitalism such as Jodi Melamed in "Racial Capitalism," *Journal of Critical Ethnic Studies* 1, no. 1 (2015): 76–86.

39. Anastasia Piliavsky, "The 'Criminal Tribe' in India before the British," *Comparative Studies in Society and History* 57, no. 2 (2015): 323–54 at 324–25.

40. Ronald Inden, *Imagining India* (Bloomington: Indiana University Press, 1990), 1–2.

41. Sanjay Nigam, "Disciplining and Policing the 'Criminals by Birth,' Part 1: The Making of a Colonial Stereotype—The Criminal Tribes and Castes of North India," *Indian Economic and Social History Review* 27, no. 2 (1990): 131–64 at 133.

Chapter 2

1. I use the term "Kandha" instead of the British "Kond" to reflect the pronunciation that the Kandha tribals use themselves.

2. I use the term *Adibasi,* an Odia variant of Adivasi, in my discussions of local Kandha indigenous identity and politics, and retain it when mentioned in discussions with caste Hindu Odias and Kandhas. I use *Adivasi* to refer to the national formation and its discussions in policy and scholarship.

3. Keith Hart, *The Ethnography of Finance and the History of Money.* "New Perspectives in Economic Ethnography: Modalities of Exchange and Economic Calculation," (Rio de Janeiro: Museu National, 2011); Bill Maurer, "The Anthropology of Money," *Annual Review of Anthropology* 35 (2006): 15–36; Taylor C. Nelms and Bill Maurer, "Materiality, Symbol, and Complexity in the Anthropology of Money," in *The Psychological Science of Money,* ed. Erik Bijleveld and Henk Aarts (New York: Springer, 2014), 23.

4. Patrick Wolfe, "Land, Labor, and Difference: Elementary Structures of Race," *American Historical Review* 106, no. 3 (2001): 866–905.

5. Nikhil Pal Singh, "On Race, Violence and So-Called Primitive Accumulation," *Social Text* 34, no. 3 (2016): 27–50 at 31.

6. Jessica R. Cattelino, "From Locke to Slots: Money and the Politics of Indigeneity," *Comparative Studies in Society and History* 60, no. 2 (2018): 274–307; Prathama Banerjee, "Debt, Time and Extravagance: Money and the Making of 'Primitives' in Colonial Bengal," *Indian Economic and Social History Review* 37, no. 4 (2000): 423–45; and Kaushik Ghosh, "Between Global Flows and Local Dams: Indigenousness, Locality, and the Transnational Sphere in Jharkhand, India," *Cultural Anthropology* 21, no. 4 (2006): 501–34.

7. Banerjee, "Debt, Time and Extravagance," 429.

8. Ghosh, "Between Global Flows," 512.

9. Banerjee, "Debt, Time and Extravagance"; Ghosh, "Between Global Flows," 512.

10. Ghosh, "Between Global Flows," 512.

11. I am indebted to Kaushik Ghosh's interventions that provide the foundation of my analysis of Indian indigeneity as engaging similar motifs of racialization as in settler colonial contexts.

12. Bernard S. Cohn, *Colonialism and Its Forms of Knowledge: The British in India* (Princeton, NJ: Princeton University Press, 1996).

13. Cohn, *Colonialism and Its Forms.*

14. Michel-Rolph Trouillot, "Anthropology and the Savage Slot: The Poetics and Politics of Otherness," in *Recapturing Anthropology: Working in the Present,* ed. R. Fox (Santa Fe, NM: School of American Research Press, 1991), 17–44.

15. Uday Chandra, "Liberalism and Its Other: The Politics of Primitivism in Colonial and Postcolonial Indian Law," *Law and Society Review* 47, no. 1 (2013): 135–68.

16. See Govinda Chandra Rath, ed., *Tribal Development in India: The Contemporary Debate* (New Delhi: Sage, 2006), 77, 78.

17. Ramachandra Guha, *Savaging the Civilized: Verrier Elwin, His Tribals, and India* (Chicago: University of Chicago, 1999).

18. Ghosh, "Between Global Flows"; Amita Baviskar, "Indian Indigeneities: Adivasi Engagements with Hindu Nationalism in India," in *Indigenous Experience Today*, ed. Marisol de la Cadena and Orin Starn (Oxford and New York: Berg, 2007), 275–304.

19. Ghosh, "Between Global Flows," 512.

20. Jessica R. Cattelino, *High Stakes: Florida Seminole Gaming and Sovereignty* (Durham, NC: Duke University Press, 2008).

21. Nihar Ranjan Patnaik, *Economic History of Orissa* (New Delhi: Indus, 1997); Rath, *Tribal Development in India*, 77.

22. Jessica R. Cattelino, "Fungibility: Florida Seminole Casino Dividends and the Fiscal Politics of Indigeneity," *American Anthropologist* 111, no. 2 (2009): 190–200.

23. F. G. Bailey, *Tribe, Caste, and Nation: A Study of Political Activity and Political Change in Highland Orissa* (Manchester, UK: Manchester University Press, 1960).

24. Barbara M. Boal, *The Konds: Human Sacrifice and Religious Change* (Warminster, U.K.: Aris and Phillips, 1982); Felix Padel, *The Sacrifice of Human Being: British Rule and the Konds of Orissa* (Delhi: Oxford University Press, 1995).

25. Patnaik, *Economic History of Orissa*, 380.

26. Bailey, *Tribe, Caste, and Nation*.

27. Patnaik, *Economic History of Orissa*, 372.

28. Patnaik, *Economic History of Orissa*, 372.

29. Patnaik, *Economic History of Orissa*, 381.

30. Rath, *Tribal Development in India*, 80.

31. The Scheduled Tribes and Other Traditional Forest Dwellers (Recognition of Forest Rights) Act was passed in 2006 to restore the rights of forest-dwelling communities to land for agriculture and other uses. At the time of my fieldwork in early 2007, however, most of my Kandha interlocutors were not aware that this new law had restored their rights, not least because of the colonial signage issuing warnings about the illegality of slash-and-burn practices that remained scattered throughout the surrounding forest cover.

32. Ghosh, "Between Global Flows," 510.

33. Guha, *Savaging the Civilized*.

34. Adivasi governance is a particularly excellent site through which to observe how Foucauldian governmentality plays out in the Indian context, as indigenous citizens are governed through a promise of development as a nebulous yet all-pervasive ideal, reinforced by a plethora of state and nonstate actors drawing on both national and transnational discourses of indigenous uplift. For a larger discussion of how governmentality functions in India, particularly for rural citizens, through local state encounters informed by ideas circulated by the government and a larger development community and its role on the development of political society, see Stuart Corbridge, et al., *Seeing the State: Governance and Governmentality in India* (Cambridge: Cambridge University Press, 2005).

35. Sangeeta Kamat, *Development Hegemony: NGOs and the State in India* (New Delhi: Oxford University Press, 2002); Rath, *Tribal Development in India*, 13.

36. See Nayanika Mathur, "Effecting Development: Bureaucratic Knowledges, Cynicism, and the Desire for Development in the Indian Himalaya," in *Differentiating Development: Beyond an Anthropology of Critique*, ed. Soumhya Venkatesan and Thomas Yarrow (New York and Oxford: Berghahn Books, 2012), 193–209.

37. Nelms and Maurer, "Materiality, Symbol, and Complexity," 44.

38. Georg Simmel, *The Metropolis and Mental Life* (New York: Free Press, 1950).

39. Banerjee, "Debt, Time and Extravagance."

40. Ghosh, "Between Global Flows," 511.

41. Cattelino, "'No Such Thing as Money.'"

42. Padel, *Sacrifice of Human Being*.

43. For example, Alpa Shah points to the correlation between caste hierarchies and development in Jharkhand, a tribal-majority state neighboring Odisha, showing how rural elites harness development projects to maintain their economic dominance, sidelining Munda tribals from the benefits of state development. See Alpa Shah, *In the Shadows of the State: Indigenous Politics, Environmentalism, and Insurgency in Jharkhand, India* (Durham, NC: Duke University Press, 2010), 70.

44. Bailey, *Tribe, Caste, and Nation*; Boal, *The Konds*; Padel, *Sacrifice of Human Being*, 22.

45. Stuart Corbridge, *Jharkhand: Environment, Development, Ethnicity* (New Delhi: University Press, 2004).

46. See Townsend Middleton, "Across the Interface of State Ethnography: Rethinking Ethnology and Its Subjects in Multicultural India," *American Ethnologist* 38, no. 2 (2011): 249–66; and Middleton's *The Demands of Recognition: State Anthropology and Ethnopolitics in Darjeeling* (Stanford: Stanford University Press, 2015).

47. Stuart Corbridge, "Competing Inequalities: The Scheduled Tribes and the Reservations System in India's Jharkhand," *Journal of Asian Studies* 59, no. 1 (2000): 62–85.

48. Ghosh, "Between Global Flows," 511.

49. Patnaik, *Economic History of Orissa*, 25.

50. Literally "mother-father," used as an utterance of deference akin to filial deference to parental authority.

51. Hart, *Ethnography of Finance*; Maurer, "Anthropology of Money"; Nelms and Maurer, "Materiality, Symbol, and Complexity," 23.

52. Nancy Fraser, "Rethinking Recognition," *New Left Review* 3 (2000): 107–20.

53. See Patchen Markell, "Recognition and Redistribution," in *The Oxford Handbook of Political Theory*, ed. John S. Dryzek, Bonnie Honig, and Anne Phillips (Oxford: Oxford University Press, 2008), 450–69.

54. Glen Sean Coulthard, *Red Skin, White Masks: Rejecting the Colonial Politics of Recognition* (Minneapolis: University of Minnesota Press, 2014).

55. Jean and John Comaroff, eds. *Law and Disorder in the Postcolony* (Chicago: University of Chicago Press, 2006).

56. James Ferguson, *Global Shadows: Africa in the Neoliberal World Order* (Durham, NC: Duke University Press, 2006).

57. Kim Fortun, Mike Fortun, and Steven Rubenstein, "Editors' Introduction to Emergent Indigeneities," *Cultural Anthropology* 25, no. 2 (2010): 222–34.

Chapter 3

1. Webb Keane, *Christian Moderns: Freedom and Fetish in the Mission Encounter* (Berkeley: University of California Press, 2007), 40–41.

2. Bruno Latour, *We Have Never Been Modern* (Cambridge, MA: Harvard University Press, 1993).

3. See Joel Lee for a thorough critical examination of the assumption that the vast majority of India's Dalit population is, and always has been, in some meaningful sense, Hindu, and the conditions under which this assumption take shape.

4. Bengt G. Karlsson, "The Social Life of Categories: Affirmative Action and Trajectories of the Indigenous," *Focaal* 65 (2013): 33–41.

5. Karlsson distinguishes between an indigenous-rights approach and Scheduled Tribe recognition in the Indian state, marking their hybridization as a novel consequence of dialogue with transnational indigenous political movements. The way that Scheduled Tribe recognition was being claimed and understood by Kandhas and their Pana Dalit neighbors, however, made it clear that a politics of indigeneity fundamentally undergirded how Adivasi groups claimed tribal recognition and its mandates with detrimental consequences for themselves and others. Not only had indigeneity been a part of Adivasi identity formation and politics from the very outset but such a discourse of indigeneity had also been bolstered and consolidated through tribal recognition with unanticipated effects for other minorities, including Dalits.

6. Rupa Viswanath, "The Emergence of Authenticity Talk and the Giving of Accounts: Conversion as Movement of the Soul in South India, ca. 1900," *Comparative Studies in Society and History* 55, no. 1 (2013): 120–41.

7. Viswanath, "Emergence of Authenticity Talk," 130.

8. Barbara M. Boal, *The Konds: Human Sacrifice and Religious Change* (Warminster, U.K.: Aris and Phillips, 1982), 188.

9. Janet McIntosh, *The Edge of Islam: Power, Personhood and Ethnoreligious Boundaries on the Kenya Coast* (Durham, NC: Duke University Press, 2009), 188.

10. Laura Dudley Jenkins contextualizes the proliferation of anti-conversion legislation in India alongside sites such as Sri Lanka (largely in response to demands by Buddhist organizations) and Muslim-majority Algeria, motivated in part by the global growth of evangelical Christianity, which has had a significant impact on religious demographics as well as politics in the Americas, Africa, Asia, and former Soviet countries. In recent years, more and more states in India have enacted laws to restrict religious conversion, particularly targeting conversions via "force" or "allurement." Current laws stem back to colonial laws such as anti-conversion, apostasy, and public-safety acts in British India and several princely states. Implementing these laws seems to require judging the converts' states of mind by assessing their motives and volition or, in other words, determining whether converts were "lured" or legitimate.

11. Keane, *Christian Moderns,* 40–41.

12. David Mosse, "Outside Caste? The Enclosure of Caste and Claims to Castelessness in India and the United Kingdom," *Comparative Studies in Society and History* 62, no. 1 (2020): 4–34 at 8.

13. Nathaniel Roberts, *To Be Cared For: The Power of Conversion and Foreignnness of Belonging in an Indian Slum* (Oakland: University of California Press, 2016).

14. Kumkum Sangari, "Politics of Diversity: Religious Communities and Multiple Patriarchies," *Economic and Political Weekly* 30, no. 51 (1995): 3287–3310.

15. In contemporary India, government assessments of conversions' legitimacy tend to rely on two assumptions: first, that people who convert in groups might not have freely chosen conversion and, second, that certain groups are particularly vulnerable to being lured into changing their religion. These assumptions, which pervade anti-conversion laws as well as related court decisions and government committee reports, reinforce social constructions of women and lower castes as inherently naive and susceptible to manipulation. The language of these laws skirts the question of judging individual volition on a case-by-case basis by condoning the assumption that certain groups are more easily tricked into conversion. For example, those found to be converting lower castes (Scheduled Castes), tribals (Scheduled Tribes), women, or minors may face longer prison terms or higher fines in some states, attesting to a paternalistic protectionism of women and minorities that constructs them as vulnerable subjects who might not be able to ascertain their own volition or motivations in rational and transparent ways. Several states have required that people register their change of faith with a local official—in some states, prior to conversion—to enable state tracking of conversion patterns, particularly mass conversions.

16. Appointed by the national government, the Wadhwa Commission initially focused in its report on the killers' potential motives but frequently shifted to question the area converts' motives, concerned in particular with economically marginalized Adivasi populations. As Dudley Jenkins notes, a government inquiry into missionary killings devolved into an inquiry into converts' motives, showing the state and its legal mechanism's obsession with the duped minority convert whose volition cannot be fully ascertained, rather than majoritarian ethnonationalist violence. Presenting disenfranchised populations—especially poor and tribal converts—as passive and unagentive, the commission's report ended by strongly advocating for government surveillance of conversion activity and for more government scrutiny of numerical data on conversions and on shifting religious demographics to further curtail illegal, "coercive" conversions. Another government shortcut for assessing the conversion validity is to monitor and suspect "mass" conversions, underscoring the state's continued reliance on the singular, individual conversion as the legal ideal for authentic conversion.

17. Such paternalistic protectionism is particularly visible when religious leaders, including Hindu nationalists, are particularly preoccupied with saving women from traditional practices via conversion or, conversely, from conversion itself, mirroring the language of anti-conversion law. This may be due to the constitutive role of women

in religious and national communities, including reproducing the community, both biologically and ideologically, by giving birth to and training children and serving as tangible boundary markers of religious community. Missionary and colonial policies regarding women frequently took the form of "domesticating" converts into submissive roles that emulated ideals of femininity in the metropole. Yet female converts have exercised more agency than male religious leaders attributed to them, despite such leaders' own continuing fixations on domestic and social order and assumptions that women are victims.

18. Clarinda Still, "'They Have It in Their Stomachs but They Can't Vomit It Up': Dalits, Reservations, and 'Caste Feeling' in Rural Andhra Pradesh," *Focaal* 65 (2013): 68–79.

19. André Béteille, *Society and Politics in India: Essays in a Comparative Perspective* (London: Routledge, 1991); Christopher J. Fuller, "Introduction," in *Caste Today*, ed. Christopher J. Fuller (Oxford: Oxford University Press, 1996), 1–31.

20. Clarinda Still, "The State in the Palli: Dalit Perspectives on the State in Andhra Pradesh," *Contemporary South Asia* 19, no. 3 (2011): 315–29.

Chapter 4

1. For an excellent discussion of the role of female renouncers, or *sadhvis*, in Hindu nationalism that details how doctrinal understanding of renunciation is invoked in counterintuitive ways as a form of violent political practice within Hindu nationalism and how it has secured great visibility for women within the movement, see the chapter "Violent Dharma" in Kalyani Devaki Menon's *Everyday Nationalism: Women of the Hindu Right* (Philadelphia: University of Pennsylvania Press, 2012), 80–104.

2. André Béteille, *The Backward Classes in Contemporary India* (Delhi: Oxford University Press, 1992).

3. Uday Chandra, "Liberalism and Its Other: The Politics of Primitivism in Colonial and Postcolonial Indian Law," *Law and Society Review* 47, no. 1 (2013): 149; Alpa Shah, *In the Shadows of the State: Indigenous Politics, Environmentalism, and Insurgency in Jharkhand, India* (Durham, NC: Duke University Press, 2010); and Townsend Middleton, *The Demands of Recognition: State Anthropology and Ethnopolitics in Darjeeling* (Stanford, CA: Stanford University Press, 2015).

4. For another discussion that questions the insistent seclusion of India from settler colonies, see Uditi Sen, "Developing *Terra Nullius*: Colonialism, Nationalism, and Indigeneity in the Andaman Islands," *Comparative Studies in Society and History* 59, no. 4 (2017): 944–73.

5. For a discussion of Adivasi communities' incorporation into Hindutva within indigenous and native studies, see Jodi A. Byrd and Michael Rothberg, "Between Subalternity and Indigeneity: Critical Categories for Postcolonial Studies," *Interventions* 13, no. 1 (2011): 1–12.

6. Peggy Froerer, *Religious Division and Social Conflict: The Emergence of Hindu Nationalism in Rural India* (New Delhi: Social Science Press, 2007).

7. Christophe Jaffrelot, *The Hindu Nationalist Movement and Indian Politics: 1925 to the 1990s* (New Delhi: Penguin, 1999), 449.

8. See Froerer, *Religious Division and Social Conflict*.

9. For an excellent analysis of long-standing Hindu nationalist views of conversion as a form of violence toward Hinduism, see Nathaniel Roberts, *To Be Cared For: The Power of Conversion and Foreignness of Belonging in an Indian Slum* (Oakland: University of California Press, 2016).

10. Barbara M. Boal, *The Konds: Human Sacrifice and Religious Change* (Warminster, U.K.: Aris and Phillips, 1982); Felix Padel, *The Sacrifice of Human Being* (Delhi: Oxford University Press, 1995).

11. See Shah, *In the Shadows of the State*; Talal Asad, *Genealogies of Religion: Discipline and Reasons of Power in Christianity and Islam* (Baltimore: Johns Hopkins University Press, 1993); and David Hardiman, *The Coming of the Devi: Adivasi Assertion in Western India* (Delhi: Oxford University Press, 1987).

12. See Gauri Vishwanathan, *Outside the Fold: Conversion, Modernity, and Belief* (Princeton, NJ: Princeton University Press, 1998); and Roberts, *To Be Cared For*.

13. Donna J. Haraway, *Staying with the Trouble: Making Kin in the Chthulucene* (Durham, NC: Duke University Press, 2016). See also Radhika Govindrajan, *Animal Intimacies: Interspecies Relatedness in India's Central Himalayas* (Chicago: University of Chicago Press, 2018).

14. For a summary of debates on the colonial "invention" of Hinduism, see David N. Lorenzen, "Who Invented Hinduism?" *Comparative Studies in Society and History* 41, no. 4 (1999): 630–59.

15. See Burkhard Schnepel, "Durga and the King: Ethnohistorical Aspects of Politico-Ritual Life in a South Orissan Jungle Kingdom," *Journal of the Royal Anthropological Institute* 1, no. 1 (1995): 145–66; Akio Tanabe, "Ethnohistory of Land and Identity in Khurda, Orissa: From Pre-Colonial Past to Post-Colonial Present," *Journal of Asian and African Studies* 56 (1998): 75–112; Nandini Sundar, "Debating Dussehra and Reinterpreting Rebellion in Bastar District, Central India," *Journal of the Royal Anthropological Institute* 7, no. 1 (2001): 19–35.

16. Dipesh Chakrabarty, *Provincializing Europe: Postcolonial Thought and Historical Difference* (Princeton, NJ: Princeton University Press, 2007), 12–13.

17. Chakrabarty, *Provincializing Europe*, 12–13.

18. For more on this debate and a suggested reconceptualization, see Uday Chandra, "Rethinking Subaltern Resistance," *Journal of Contemporary Asia* 45, no. 4 (2015): 563–73.

19. For how the vexing problem of Adivasi participation in Hindutva is narrated as a chilling crisis, see Amita Baviskar, "Adivasi Encounters with Hindu Nationalism in MP," *Economic and Political Weekly* 40, no. 48 (2005): 5105–13.

20. Audra Simpson, "Settlement's Secret," *Cultural Anthropology* 26, no. 2 (2011): 205–17 at 208.

21. Amita Baviskar, "The Politics of Being 'Indigenous,'" in *Indigeneity in India*, ed. Bengt G. Karlsson and Tanka B. Subba (London: Kegan Paul, 2006), 33–50.

22. See Sumit Sarkar, *Beyond Nationalist Frames: Postmodernism, Hindu Fundamentalism, History* (Bloomington: Indiana University Press, 2002); and Menon, "Violent Dharma."

23. Nandini Sundar, "Teaching to Hate: RSS's Pedagogical Program," *Economic and Political Weekly* 39, no. 16 (2004): 1605–12.

24. See Padel, *Sacrifice of Human Being*.

25. Both Kandhas and Hindus regard menstruating women to be ritually impure, a belief that Kandha women affirmed to be another instance of a practice for all time rather than a Hinduization of Kandha beliefs.

26. Mary Douglas, *Purity and Danger: An Analysis of Concepts of Pollution and Taboo* (London: Routledge, 2002), 13.

27. Lauren Berlant, "Critical Inquiry, Affirmative Culture," *Critical Inquiry* 30, no. 2 (2004): 445–51 at 449.

28. Berlant, "Critical Inquiry, Affirmative Culture," 449.

29. Charles Hirschkind, "The Ethics of Listening: Cassette-Sermon Audition in Contemporary Egypt," *American Ethnologist* 28, no. 3 (2001): 623–49.

30. Michael T. Taussig, *Mimesis and Alterity: A Particular History of the Senses* (New York: Routledge, 1993). Taussig notes that colonial first encounters between colonial officers, explorers, and even naturalists such as Darwin tend to emphasize the "mimetic ability of primitives" or the ways in which "primitive savages" were thought to possess extraordinary ability to mimic the acts of colonizers, as Darwin said, "due to their more practiced habits of perception and keener senses, common to all men in a savage state" (81).

31. Mysore Narasimhachar Srinivas, *Social Change in Modern India* (Berkeley: University of California Press, 1969).

32. Bhrigupati Singh, "Agonistic Intimacy and Moral Aspiration in Popular Hinduism: A Study in the Political Theology of the Neighbor," *American Ethnologist* 38, no. 3 (2011): 430–50.

33. See Boal, *The Konds*; Padel, *Sacrifice of Human Being*; and Rebecca Basso, "Music, Possession and Shamanism among Khond Tribes," *Culture and Religion* 7, no. 2 (2006): 177–97.

34. Stephano Beggiora, "Tiger, Tiger Spirits and Were-Tigers in Tribal Orissa," *Religions of South Asia* 7, no. 1–3 (2013): 93–107.

35. Schnepel, "Durga and the King," 145–66.

36. Lucas Bessire, *Behold the Black Caiman: A Chronicle of Life among the Ayoreo* (Chicago: University of Chicago Press, 2014).

37. Biswamoy Pati, *Identity, Hegemony, Resistance: Towards a Social History of Conversions in Orissa, 1800–2000* (New Delhi: Three Essays Collective, 2003), xiii. Also cited in Rowena Robinson and Joseph Marianus Kujur, eds., *Margins of Faith: Dalit and Tribal Christianity in India* (New Delhi: Sage, 2010).

38. The missionaries were also seen to provide a threat to the social status of those they sought to convert. The missionaries had gone to the Adivasi villages with the belief that "tribals" did not rank their various communities in terms of status or purity, as was the case with castes in the plains regions. This was a miscalculation, for there were in fact strong hierarchies, with certain communities being judged higher and purer than others. Particular groups, such as the Katkaris and Kolghas, were even considered to be "untouchable" by other Adivasis. What this meant was that most Adivasis had before them a model of what they did not want to become, and individuals feared that conversion to Christianity would lead to their being put out of their community and condemned to such a status. One consequence of this was that it was often the Adivasis of lowest status who proved most amenable to the missionaries. In the Vyara area of South Gujarat, for example, it was reported in 1920 that non-Christian Adivasis considered themselves to be of "better caste" than the Christians. The large majority of converts in this tract were from the Gamit community, which was considered inferior in the hierarchy to the larger Chodhri and Dhodiya communities. See David Hardiman, "Christianity and the Adivasis of Gujarat," in *Labour, Marginalisation and Migration: Studies on Gujarat, India*, ed. Ghanshyam Shah, Mario Rutten, and Hein Streefkerk (New Delhi: Sage, 2002), 8.

39. F. G. Bailey, *Tribe, Caste, and Nation: A Study of Political Activity and Political Change in Highland Orissa* (Manchester, U.K.: Manchester University Press, 1960). See also Hardiman, *Coming of the Devi*.

40. Bailey, *Tribe, Caste, and Nation*; Roland Hardenberg, *Fierce People of the Mountains: Society, Ritual and Cosmology of the Orissa Hills* (Muenster: University of Muenster, 2005).

41. See Hardiman, *Coming of the Devi*; Shah, *In the Shadows of the State*.

42. See also Roberts, *To Be Cared For*; Vishwanathan, *Outside the Fold*.

43. Vishwanathan, *Outside the Fold*.

44. See Hermann Kulke, "Kshatriyaization and Social Change: A Study in Orissa Setting," in *Aspects of Changing India: Studies in Honour of Prof. G. S. Ghurye*, ed. S. Devadas Pillai (Bombay: Popular Prakashan, 1976), 398–409.

45. Vishwanathan, *Outside the Fold*.

46. See also Menon, "Violent Dharma."

47. Padel, *Sacrifice of Human Being*.

48. See the discussion in Pati, *Identity, Hegemony, Resistance*.

49. Veena Das in Padel, *Sacrifice of Human Being*, xi.

50. Boal, *The Konds*, 38. See also Padel, *Sacrifice of Human Being*, 35–62.

51. See Padel, *Sacrifice of Human Being*, 132. Kandhas said to McPherson, "We use the Rajah as a spoon to taste the food from the fire. That way the spoon gets burnt but not the mouth." The British misunderstood this relationship between the rajas and Kandhas when they assumed that they could proclaim new laws through the mediation of rajahs. Rajas, however, were firm that it be clear to the Kandhas that they were acting not as free agents but as agents of colonial rule when they asked to hand over meriah children to British officials.

52. For a discussion of the role within Hindu ethnonationalism of kar sevaks, literally "hand servants," who provide free labor for a religious cause, see Jaffrelot, *Hindu Nationalist* Movement, 420–31, 455–57.

53. Bailey, *Tribe, Caste, and Nation*, 159.

54. Frantz Fanon, *Black Skins, White Masks*.

55. Lois McNay, *Against Recognition* (Cambridge: Polity, 2008).

56. Pralay Kanungo, "Hindutva's Entry into a 'Hindu Province': Early Years of RSS in Orissa," *Economic and Political Weekly* 38, no. 31 (2003): 3293–3303; Harish Wankhede, "The Political Context of Religious Conversion in Orissa," *Economic and Political Weekly* 44, no. 15 (2009): 33–38.

57. For an excellent discussion of animality as colonial trope, see Radhika Govindrajan's introduction to *Animal Intimacies*, 1–31.

58. Menon, "Violent Dharma."

59. Simpson, "Settlement's Secret," 205–17.

60. Orin Starn, "Here Come the Anthros (Again): The Strange Marriage of Anthropology and Native America," *Cultural Anthropology* 26, no. 2 (2011): 179–204.

61. For another discussion of a hearts-and-minds formulation in South Asia, see Jennifer Huberman's "The Mind and Hearts of Children," a chapter on the hearts and minds of children in Varanasi, in her *Ambivalent Encounters: Childhood, Tourism, and Social Change in Banaras, India* (New Brunswick, NJ: Rutgers, 2012), 93–117.

62. Menon, "Violent Dharma."

63. See Anand Pandian's discussion of fragmentary traditions of moral virtue in India, which persist through scattered forms of moral argumentation, rival narratives, and images of a moral selfhood and are articulated through diverse domains of ethical practice. Pandian, "Tradition in Fragments: Inherited Forms and Fractures in the Ethics of South India," *American Ethnologist* 35, no. 3 (2008): 466–80.

64. See Richard Handler's review "Debating Authenticity: Concepts of Modernity in Anthropological Perspective," *American Anthropologist* 116, no. 1 (2014): 205–6.

65. Christophe Jaffrelot, "The Sangh Parivar between Sanskritization and Social Engineering," in *The BJP and the Compulsions of Politics in India*, ed. Christophe Jaffrelot and Thomas Blom Hansen (Delhi: Oxford University Press, 1998), 22–71; Thomas Blom Hansen, *The Saffron Wave: Democracy and Hindu Nationalism in Modern India* (Princeton, NJ: Princeton University Press, 1999), 107.

66. For an excellent discussion of such incorporations of Dalits into religious majoritarianism, see Joel G. Lee, "Lāl Beg Underground: The Passing of an 'Untouchable God,'" in *Objects of Worship in South Asian Religions: Forms, Practices and Meanings*, ed. Knut A. Jacobsen, Mikael Aktor, and Kristina Myrvold (London: Routledge, 2014), 143–62.

67. Middleton, *Demands of Recognition*, 9.

68. Kaushik Ghosh, "Between Global Flows and Local Dams: Indigenousness, Locality, and the Transnational Sphere in Jharkhand, India," *Cultural Anthropology* 21, no. 4 (2006): 501–34.

69. See also Baviskar, "Adivasi Encounters."

70. See Bessire, *Behold the Black Caiman*.

71. For an excellent discussion of how heritages of ambivalences and ambiguities provide the foundation of neoliberal indigenous identities and articulations, see Fernando Armstrong-Fumero's discussion of "a heritage of ambiguity," in "A Heritage of Ambiguity: The Historical Substrate of Vernacular Multiculturalism in Yucatán, Mexico," *American Ethnologist* 36, no. 2 (2009): 300–316; and his *Elusive Unity: Factionalism and the Limits of Identity Politics in Yucatán, Mexico* (Boulder: University Press of Colorado, 2013), in which he details how forms of official multiculturalism and emergent forms of neoliberal governmentality are experienced by indigenous groups in ways that reflect a greater degree of continuity with older institutions and styles of politics. While Armstrong-Fumero invokes this ambiguous heritage as one that secures continuities between modern and neoliberal governmentality and, thus, multiculturalism, my aim is to reach beyond the modern in the postcolonial state to precisely emphasize the temporal unruliness of indigeneity within neoliberal multiculturalism in India. Biswamoy Pati also discusses the possibility of such ambiguities and how ethnographers such as Padel might have played up Adivasi-Odia binaries by ignoring how Odias might have emerged from Adivasis themselves. See Pati, *Identity, Hegemony, Resistance*.

72. See Sanjib Baruah, "Territoriality, Indigeneity and Rights in the North-East India," *Economic and Political Weekly* 43, no. 12 (2008): 15–19.

73. Edward Anderson and Arkotong Longkumer, "'Neo-Hindutva': Evolving Forms, Spaces, and Expressions of Hindu Nationalism," *Contemporary South Asia* 26, no. 4 (2018): 371–77.

74. Menon, "Violent Dharma."

75. Gyan Prakash, "The Impossibility of Subaltern History," *Nepantla: Views from South* 1, no. 2 (2000): 287–94 at 293. I am grateful to Jodi Byrd and Michael Rothberg's engagement of Gyan Prakash that alerted me to this formulation, which I have reworked here.

76. Glen Sean Coulthard, *Red Skin, White Masks: Rejecting the Colonial Politics of Recognition* (Minneapolis: University of Minnesota Press, 2014).

Chapter 5

1. Joel G. Lee, "Odor and Order: How Caste Is Inscribed in Space and Sensoria," *Comparative Studies of South Asia, Africa and the Middle East* 37, no. 3 (2017): 470–90.

2. Marisol de la Cadena, "Indigenous Cosmopolitics in the Andes: Conceptual Reflections beyond 'Politics,'" *Cultural Anthropology* 25, no. 2 (2010): 334–70.}

3. Lucas Bessire and David Bond, "Ontological Anthropology and the Deferral of Critique," *American Ethnologist* 41, no. 3 (2014): 440–56.

4. For regimes of capital, see Glen Sean Coulthard, *Red Skin, White Masks: Rejecting the Colonial Politics of Recognition* (Minneapolis: University of Minnesota Press, 2014). For more on land, see Uday Chandra, "Beyond Subalternity: Land, Community, and the State in Contemporary Jharkhand," *Contemporary South Asia* 21, no. 1 (2013): 52–61.

5. See also Amita Baviskar, *In the Belly of the River: Tribal Conflicts over Development* (New Delhi: Oxford University Press, 1997); Alpa Shah, *In the Shadows of the State: Indigenous Politics, Environmentalism, and Insurgency in Jharkhand, India* (Durham, NC: Duke University Press, 2010); Kaushik Ghosh, "Between Global Flows and Local Dams: Indigenousness, Locality, and the Transnational Sphere in Jharkhand, India," *Cultural Anthropology* 21, no. 4 (2006): 501–34; and the introduction to Townsend Middleton, *The Demands of Recognition: State Anthropology and Ethnopolitics in Darjeeling* (Stanford, CA: Stanford University Press, 2015).

6. Kim Fortun, Mike Fortun, and Steven Rubenstein, "Editors' Introduction to Emergent Indigeneities," *Cultural Anthropology* 25, no. 2 (2010): 222–34; Jessica R. Cattelino, "The Double Bind of American Indian Need-Based Sovereignty," *Cultural Anthropology* 25, no. 2 (2010): 235–62.

7. Rebecca Basso, "Music, Possession and Shamanism among Khond Tribes," *Culture and Religion* 7, no. 2 (2006): 177–97.

8. Tina Otten and Edward Simpson, "F. G. Bailey's Bisipara Revisited," *Economic and Political Weekly* 51, no. 26–27 (2016): 25–32 at 25.

9. Mihir K. Jena et al., *Forest Tribes of Orissa: Lifestyle and Social Conditions of Selected Orissan Tribes*, vol. 2, *The Kuttia Kondh* (New Delhi: D. K. Printworld, 2006); Klaus Seeland, "Indigenous Knowledge of Trees and Forests in Non-European Societies," in *Nature Is Culture: Indigenous Knowledge and Socio-Cultural Aspects of Trees and Forests in Non-European Cultures*, ed. Klaus Seeland (London: IT, 1997), 101–12. Other pronouncements by Kandhas confirmed their endorsement of fluid and permeable boundaries between human and nonhuman others, as well as between the human and the divine, including theriomorphic Kandha tales of the *palta bagha*, in which man became tiger, tiger became goddess, and back into man. See Stephano Beggiora, "Tiger, Tiger Spirits and Were-Tigers in Tribal Orissa," *Religions of South Asia* 7, no. 1–3 (2013): 93–107.

10. Felix Padel, *The Sacrifice of Human Being: British Rule and the Konds of Orissa* (Delhi: Oxford University Press, 1995).

11. Burkhard Schnepel, "Durga and the King: Ethnohistorical Aspects of Politico-Ritual Life in a South Orissan Jungle Kingdom," *Journal of the Royal Anthropological Institute* 1, no. 1 (1995): 145–66.

12. Bruce Mannheim, "Iconicity," *Journal of Linguistic Anthropology* 9, nos. 1–2 (1999): 107–10.

13. Christophe Jaffrelot, "The Hindu Nationalist Reinterpretation of Pilgrimage in India: The Limits of Yatra Politics," *Nations and Nationalism* 15, no. 1 (2009): 1–19.

14. Chetan Bhatt, *Hindu Nationalism: Origins, Ideologies and Modern Myths* (London: Bloomsbury Academic, 2001), 181.

15. Bhatt, *Hindu Nationalism*, 181.

16. Anne McClintock, Aamir Mufti, and Ella Shohat, eds., *Dangerous Liaisons: Gender, Nation, and Postcolonial Perspectives* (Minneapolis: University of Minnesota Press, 1997).

17. Sumathi Ramaswamy, *The Goddess and the Nation: Mapping Mother India* (Durham, NC: Duke University Press, 2010), 11.

18. Mrinalini Sinha, "Reading Mother India: Empire, Nation, and the Female Voice," *Journal of Women's History* 6, no. 2 (1994): 6–44.

19. See also Charu Gupta, "Hindu Women, Muslim Men: Love Jihad and Conversions," *Economic and Political Weekly,* 44, no. 51 (2009): 13–15; and Pinky Hota, "Populist Panics: Sex as Excess in Right Wing India," *Anthropology Quarterly* 93, no. 3 (2020): 377–400.

20. Otten and Simpson, "F. G. Bailey's Bisipara Revisited," 26.

21. Parvis Ghassem-Fachandi, *Pogrom in Gujarat: Hindu Nationalism and Anti-Muslim Violence in India* (Princeton, NJ: Princeton University Press, 2012).

22. For a discussion of this, see Radhika Govindrajan, *Animal Intimacies: Interspecies Relatedness in India's Central Himalayas* (Chicago: University of Chicago Press, 2018).

23. See Sumit Sarkar, *Beyond Nationalist Frames: Postmodernism, Hindu Fundamentalism, History* (Bloomington: Indiana University Press, 2002); and Kalyani Devaki Menon, "Violent Dharma," in *Everyday Nationalism: Women of the Hindu Right* (Philadelphia: University of Pennsylvania Press, 2012), 80–104.

24. Piergiorgio Di Giminiani, "The Becoming of Ancestral Land: Place and Property in Mapuche Land Claims," *American Ethnologist* 42, no. 3 (2015): 490–503. For Gilles Deleuze and Félix Guattari's concept of reterritorialization, see their *A Thousand Plateaus: Capitalism and Schizophrenia* (Minneapolis: University of Minnesota Press, 1987).

25. Hota, "Populist Panics"; see also Virginius Xaxa, "Protective Discrimination: Why Scheduled Tribes Lag Behind Scheduled Castes," *Economic and Political Weekly of India* 36, no. 29 (2001): 2765–72.

26. Joel G. Lee, "Disgust and Untouchability: Towards an Affective Theory of Caste," *South Asian History and Culture* 12, nos. 2–3 (2021): 310–27 at 315.

27. Anand Teltumbde, *Republic of Caste: Thinking Equality in the Time of Neoliberal Hindutva* (New Delhi: Navayana, 2018), 372, 377. For a sustained examination of Dalit struggles for land in Gujarat, see pages 203–28. Anand Teltumbde reminds us of the particular vulnerability of rural landless Dalits who lead crisis-ridden lives as landless laborers, small-scale farmers, and slum-dwelling casual workers. He writes of Ambedkar's realization in his later years that he had neglected to adequately highlight the particular vulnerability of the landlessness of the rural Dalit condition while he had attempted to secure the rights and entitlements of Dalits by advancing Dalit representation, emphasizing the participation of educated Dalits in state structures, where they would be able to influence state policy. Even as Ambedkar recognized the urgent need for land redistribution among rural Dalits, he was also aware that securing land rights for Dalits would not be easy.

28. For the first, see Bessire and Bond, "Ontological Anthropology."

29. See Eduardo Kohn, for the quote, in Edward Burnett Tylor, *Primitive Culture: Researches into the Development of Mythology, Philosophy, Religion, Art, and Custom,* vol. 2 (Cambridge: Cambridge University Press, 2010), first published in 1871.

30. Phillippe Descola, *In the Society of Nature: A Native Ecology in Amazonia* (Cambridge: Cambridge University Press, 1996). See also Bruno Latour, *We Have Never Been Modern* (Cambridge, MA: Harvard University Press, 1993); Nurit Bird-David, "'Animism' Revisited: Personhood, Environment, and Relational Epistemology," *Current Anthropology* 40, no. 1 (1999): s67–91; David Harvey, *A Brief History of Neoliberalism* (Oxford: Oxford University, 2005); and Rane Willerslev, *Soul Hunters: Hunting, Animism, and Personhood among the Siberian Yukaghirs* (Berkeley: University of California Press, 2007).

31. De la Cadena, "Indigenous Cosmopolitics."

32. Michael Cepek, "There Might Be Blood: Oil, Humility, and the Cosmopolitics of a Cofán Petro-Being," *American Ethnologist* 43, no. 4 (2016): 623–35.

33. Hilary Putnam, *Mind, Language and Reality* (Cambridge: Cambridge University Press, 1975).

34. Cepek, "There Might Be Blood," 624.

35. Jodi A. Byrd and Michael Rothberg, "Between Subalternity and Indigeneity: Critical Categories for Postcolonial Studies," *Interventions* 13, no. 1 (2011): 1–12 at 9.

36. Gyan Prakash, "The Impossibility of Subaltern History," *Nepantla: Views from South* 1, no. 2 (2000): 287–94 at 293.

37. For a reconceptualization of subaltern politics, see Uday Chandra, "Rethinking Subaltern Resistance," *Journal of Contemporary Asia* 45, no. 4 (2015): 563–73; and Rajshree Chandra, "Understanding Change With(in) Law: The Niyamgiri Case," *Contributions to Indian Sociology* 50, no. 2 (2016): 137–62. For the way that neoliberal orders proliferate struggles over indigenous politics and recognition, see Stuart Corbridge, "Competing Inequalities: The Scheduled Tribes and the Reservations System in India's Jharkhand," *Journal of Asian Studies* 59, no. 1 (2000): 62–85; and Middleton, *Demands of Recognition*.

38. See, for instance, Eduardo Kohn, *How Forests Think: Toward an Anthropology beyond the Human* (Berkeley: University of California Press, 2013).

39. Bessire and Bond, "Ontological Anthropology."

Chapter 6

1. Bernard Bate, *Tamil Oratory and the Dravidian Aesthetic: Democratic Practice in South India* (New York: Columbia University Press, 2009).

2. Joel G. Lee, "Disgust and Untouchability: Towards an Affective Theory of Caste," *South Asian History and Culture* 12, nos. 2–3 (2021): 310–27 at 9.

3. William Mazzarella, "The Anthropology of Populism: Beyond the Liberal Settlement," *Annual Review of Anthropology* 48, no. 1 (2019): 45–60 at 52.

4. Partha Chatterjee, "Colonialism, Nationalism, and Colonialized Women: The Contest in India," *American Ethnologist* 16, no. 4 (1989): 622–33; Mrinalini Sinha, *Colonial Masculinity: The "Manly Englishman" and the "Effeminate Bengali" in the Late Nineteenth Century* (Manchester: Manchester University Press, 1995).

5. Amrita Basu, *The Challenge of Local Feminisms* (Boulder, CO: Westview Press, 1995).

6. Milind Wakankar, "Body, Crowd, Identity: Genealogy of a Hindu Nationalist Ascetics," *Social Text* 45 (1995): 45–73.

7. Sudhir Kakar, *Intimate Relations: Exploring Indian Sexuality* (Chicago: University of Chicago Press, 1990).

8. Wakankar, "Body, Crowd, Identity," 56.

9. Arvind Rajagopal, *Politics after Television: Hindu Nationalism and the Reshaping of the Public in India* (Cambridge: Cambridge University Press, 2001).

10. Joseph S. Alter, "Indian Clubs and Colonialism: Hindu Masculinity and Muscular Christianity," *Comparative Studies in Society and History* 46, no. 3 (2004): 497–534; Arafaat A. Valiani, "Physical Training, Ethical Discipline, and Creative Violence: Zones of Self-Mastery in the Hindu Nationalist Movement," *Cultural Anthropology* 25, no. 1 (2010): 73–99.

11. Joseph S. Alter, "Somatic Nationalism: Indian Wrestling and Militant Hinduism," *Modern Asian Studies* 28, no. 3 (1994): 557–88.

12. Peggy Froerer, *Religious Division and Social Conflict: The Emergence of Hindu Nationalism in Rural India* (New Delhi: Social Science Press, 2007).

13. Uma Chakravarti, "Conceptualising Brahmanical Patriarchy in Early India: Gender, Caste, Class and State," *Economic and Political Weekly* 28, no. 14 (1993): 579–85.

14. Svati P. Shah, "Sedition, Gender, and Gender Identity in South Asia," *South Asia Multidisciplinary Academic Journal* 20 (2019), https://doi.org/10.4000/samaj.4925.

15. William Mazzarella, *Censorium: Cinema and the Open Edge of Mass Publicity* (Durham, NC: Duke University Press, 2013), 169.

16. Paola Bacchetta, *Gender in the Hindu Nation: RSS Women as Ideologues* (New Delhi: Women Unlimited, 2004).

17. Tanika Sarkar, *Hindu Wife, Hindu Nation: Community, Religion and Cultural Nationalism* (New Delhi: Permanent Black, 2003), 228.

18. Charu Gupta, "Writing Sex and Sexuality: Archives of Colonial North India," *Journal of Women's History* 23, no. 4 (2011): 12–35 at 16.

19. Padma Velaskar, "Theorising the Interaction of Caste, Class, and Gender: A Feminist Sociological Approach," *Contributions to Indian Sociology* 50, no. 3 (2016): 389–414 at 391.

20. Hugo Gorringe, "Afterword: Gendering Caste: Honor, Patriarchy and Violence." *South Asia Multidisciplinary Academic Journal* 19 (2018), https://doi.org/10.4000/samaj.46.

21. Gyanendra Pandey, "The Time of the Dalit Conversion," *Economic and Political Weekly* 41, no. 18 (2006): 1779–88.

22. Pandey, "Time of the Dalit Conversion."

23. Nathaniel Roberts, *To Be Cared For: The Power of Conversion and Foreignness of Belonging in an Indian Slum* (Oakland: University of California Press, 2016).

24. Chad M. Bauman, *Christian Identity and Dalit Religion in Hindu India, 1868–1947* (Grand Rapids, MI: Wm. B. Eerdmans, 2008); Jane Haggis, "Ironies of Emancipation: Changing Configurations of 'Women's Work' in the 'Mission of Sisterhood' to

Indian Women," *Feminist Review* 65, no. 1 (2000): 108–26; and Eliza Kent, *Converting Women: Gender and Protestant Christianity in Colonial South India* (New York: Oxford University Press, 2004).

25. Charu Gupta, "Intimate Desires: Dalit Women and Religious Conversions in Colonial India," *Journal of Asian Studies* 73, no. 3 (2014): 661–87 at 688.

26. Kent, *Converting Women*.

27. David Mosse, *Cultivating Development: An Ethnography of Aid Policy and Practice* (London: Pluto, 2014), 674.

28. See B. R. Ambedkar and Sharmila Rege, *Against the Madness of Manu: B. R. Ambedkar's Writings on Brahmanical Patriarchy* (New Delhi: Navayana, 2013), 20; Bhimrao Ambedkar, *Annihilation of Caste* (Nagpur: Prabuddha Bhart Pustkalya, 2011); and Chakravarti, "Conceptualising Brahmanical Patriarchy."

29. As Hugo Gorringe exhorts in "Afterword," 275.

30. See also Anupama Rao, *The Caste Question: Dalits and the Politics of Modern India* (Berkeley: University of California Press, 2009); and V. Geetha, "Bereft of Being: The Humiliations of Untouchability," in *Humiliation: Claims and Context*, ed. G. Guru (New Delhi: Oxford University Press, 2009), 95–107.

31. See Ambedkar and Rege, *Against the Madness*, 20; and Gabriele Dietrich, *A New Thing on Earth: Hopes and Fears Facing Feminist Theory: Theological Ruminations of a Feminist Activist* (Delhi: ISPCK, 2001).

32. Rao, *Caste Question*, 222.

33. Rao, *Caste Question*, 234.

34. Sara Ahmed, *The Cultural Politics of Emotion* (Edinburgh: Edinburgh University Press, 2004).

35. Bate, *Tamil Oratory*.

36. Charles Hirschkind, *The Ethical Soundscape: Cassette Sermons and Islamic Counterpublics* (New York: Columbia University Press, 2006).

37. Dominic Boyer, "From Media Anthropology to the Anthropology of Mediation," in *The Sage Handbook of Social Anthropology*, ed. Richard Fardon et al. (London: Sage, 2012).

38. Arjun Appadurai, *Modernity at Large: Cultural Dimensions of Globalization* (Minneapolis: University of Minnesota Press, 1996), 54.

39. Birgit Meyer and Peter Pels, eds., *Magic and Modernity: Interfaces of Revelation and Concealment* (Stanford, CA: Stanford University Press, 2003); Birgit Meyer, "Introduction: From Imagined Communities to Aesthetic Formations: Religious Mediations, Sensational Forms, and Styles of Binding," in *Aesthetic Formations: Religion/Culture/Critique*, ed. Birgit Meyer (New York: Palgrave Macmillan, 2009), 1–28.

40. Andy Rotman, *Thus Have I Seen: Visualizing Faith in Early Indian Buddhism* (New York: Oxford University Press, 2009).

41. Meyer, "Introduction: From Imagined Communities."

42. Meyer and Pels, *Magic and Modernity*, 15.

43. Meyer and Pels, *Magic and Modernity*, 15.

44. Meyer, "Introduction: From Imagined Communities," 13.

45. Ravinder Kaur, *Brand New Nation: Capitalist Dreams and Nationalist Designs in Twenty-First-Century India* (Stanford, CA: Stanford University Press, 2020).

46. Ajay Skaria, "Shades of Wildness: Tribe, Caste, and Gender in Western India," *Journal of Asian Studies* 56, no. 3 (1997): 726–45 at 734.

47. Gayle Rubin, "Thinking Sex: Notes for a Radical Theory of the Politics of Sexuality," in *Pleasure and Danger: Exploring Female Sexuality*, ed. Carole S. Vance (London: Pandora, 1992), 267–93.

48. For more on the real or perceived threat, see Roger N. Lancaster, *Sex Panic and the Punitive State* (Berkeley: University of California Press, 2011). For power, see Gilbert Herdt, ed., *Moral Panics, Sex Panics: Fear and the Fight over Sexual Rights* (New York: New York University Press, 2009).

49. Linda Peake, "Gender, Race, Sexuality," in *The Sage Handbook of Social Geographies*, ed. Susan J. Smith, Rachel Pain, Sallie A. Marston, and John Paul Jones III (Los Angeles: Sage, 2009).

50. Rubin, "Thinking Sex."

51. Margaret Lock, "Cultivating the Body: Anthropology and Epistemologies of Bodily Practice and Knowledge," *Annual Review of Anthropology* 22, no. 1 (1993):133–55; Ajantha Subramanian, *The Caste of Merit: Engineering Education in India* (Cambridge, MA: Harvard University Press, 2019), 97.

52. Rosalind C. Morris, "The Mute and the Unspeakable: Political Subjectivity, Violence Crime, and 'the Sexual Thing' in a South African Mining Community," in *Law and Disorder in the Postcolony*, ed. John L. and Jean Comaroff (Chicago: University of Chicago Press, 2006), 57–101.

53. Ravinder Kaur and Thomas Blom Hansen, "Aesthetics of Arrival: Spectacle, Capital, Novelty in Post-Reform India," *Identities* 23, no. 3 (2016): 265–75.

54. Satish Deshpande, "Caste and Castelessness: Towards a Biography of the 'General Category,'" *Economic and Political Weekly of India* 48, no. 15 (2013): 32–39.

55. David Mosse, "Caste and Development: Contemporary Perspectives on a Structure of Discrimination and Advantage," *World Development* 110 (2018): 422–36.

56. Katherine Smith, "Rhetoric and the Everyday—Fairness as Rhetorical Force and the Micro-Politics of Intentionality in a North Manchester Town," in *Rhetoric in British Politics and Society*, ed. Judi Atkins, Alan Finlayson, James Martin, and Nick Turnbull (London: Palgrave Macmillan, 2014), 160–72.

57. Nicholas Dirks, "The Original Caste: Power, History and Hierarchy in South Asia," *Contributions to Indian Sociology* 23, no. 1 (1989): 59–77; Dirks, *Castes of Mind: Colonialism and the Making of Modern India* (Princeton, NJ: Princeton University Press, 2001).

58. Bate, *Tamil Oratory*, 136.

59. Bate, *Tamil Oratory*, 144.

60. McKim Marriott, *Hindi Transactions: Diversity without Dualism* (Chicago: University of Chicago, 1976).

61. Smriti Sharma, "Caste Based Crimes and Economic Status: Evidence from India," *Journal of Comparative Economics* 43, no. 1 (2014): 204–26; Mosse, "Caste and Development."

62. Raminder Kaur and William Mazzarella, eds., *Censorship in South Asia: Cultural Regulation from Sedition to Seduction* (Bloomington: Indiana University Press, 2009), 13; Shah, "Sedition, Sexuality, Gender, and Gender Identity."

63. For more on either caste or sexual atrocity, see Ambedkar and Rege, *Against the Madness*, 20. For ambivalence toward the market, see Sareeta Amrute, "Moving Rape: Trafficking in the Violence of Postliberalization," *Public Culture* 27, no. 2 (2015): 331–59 at 333.

64. Rao, *Caste Question*, 222, 234.

Conclusion

1. Aishwary Kumar, "What Is Dalit Studies: A Review," *Indian Economic and Social History Review* 56, no. 2 (2019): 227–45 at 240.

2. Lauren Berlant, *Cruel Optimism* (Durham, NC: Duke University Press, 2011).

3. See Townsend Middleton, *The Demands of Recognition: State Anthropology and Ethnopolitics in Darjeeling* (Stanford, CA: Stanford University Press, 2015).

4. Virginius Xaxa, "Protective Discrimination: Why Scheduled Tribes Lag Behind Scheduled Castes," *Economic and Political Weekly of India* 36, no. 29 (2001): 2765–72.

5. Xaxa, "Protective Discrimination."

6. Elizabeth Povinelli, *The Cunning of Recognition: Indigenous Alterities and the Making of Australian Multiculturism* (Durham, NC: Duke University Press, 2002).

7. Glen Sean Coulthard, *Red Skin, White Masks: Rejecting the Colonial Politics of Recognition* (Minneapolis: University of Minnesota Press, 2014).

8. Audra Simpson, *Mohawk Interruptus: Political Life across the Borders of Settler States* (Durham, NC: Duke University Press, 2014).

9. Simpson, *Mohawk Interruptus*.

10. Nicholas Copeland, Book Review of Simpson, Audra. 2014. *Mohawk Interruptus: Political Life across the Borders of Settler States*. Durham, NC: Duke University Press, *North American Dialogue* 20, no. 2 (Fall 2017): 47–49.

11. Uditi Sen, "Developing *Terra Nullius*: Colonialism, Nationalism, and Indigeneity in the Andaman Islands," *Comparative Studies in Society and History* 59, no. 4 (2017): 944–73.

12. As Uday Chandra, Kaushik Ghosh, and Romila Thapar have shown, tribal bodies served as a particular resource in the development of upper-caste Hindu modernity and the national imaginary. See Uday Chandra, "Liberalism and Its Other: The Politics of Primitivism in Colonial and Postcolonial Indian Law," *Law and Society Review* 47, no. 1 (2013): 135–68; Kaushik Ghosh, "Between Global Flows and Local Dams: Indigenousness, Locality, and the Transnational Sphere in Jharkhand, India," *Cultural Anthropology* 21, no. 4 (2006): 501–34; and Romila Thapar, "The Image of the Barbarian in Early India," *Comparative Studies in Society and History* 13, no, 4 (October 1971): 408–36.

Tribal bodies have been variously imagined as particularly suited for colonial economic agendas through hard labor, a site of savagery where development could intervene via projects of public health and hygiene, reservoirs of unconstrained sexuality that evoked sexual envy and fantasy by "savage wars" and punishment that could not be governed adequately by the modern Indian state. See, respectively, Kaushik Ghosh, "A Market for Aboriginality: Primitivism and Race Classification in the Indentured Labor Market of Colonial India," in *Subaltern Studies X,* ed. Gautam Bhadra, Gyan Prakash, and Susie Tharu (New Delhi: Oxford University Press, 1999), 8–48; David Hardiman, "A Subaltern Christianity: Faith Healing in Southern Gujarat," in *Medical Marginality in South Asia: Situating Subaltern Therapeutics,* ed. David Hardiman and Projit Bihari Mukharji (Abingdon, U.K.: Routledge, 2012), 126–51; Verrier Elwin, *The Muria and Their Ghotul* (Oxford: Oxford University Press, 1947); Felix Padel, *The Sacrifice of Human Being: British Rule and the Konds of Orissa* (Delhi: Oxford University Press, 1995); and Devika Bordia, "The Ethics and Politics of Governance in the Tribal Regions of Western India" (Ph.D. diss., Yale University, 2009).

13. Prathama Banerjee, "Debt, Time and Extravagance: Money and the Making of 'Primitives' in Colonial Bengal," *Indian Economic and Social History Review* 37, no. 4 (2000): 423–45.

14. Banerjee, "Debt, Time and Extravagance"; Debasree De, "Development-Induced Displacement: Impact on Adivasi Women of Odisha," *Community Development Journal* 50, no. 3 (2015): 448–62.

15. Prathama Banerjee, "Writing the Adivasi: Some Historiographical Notes," *Indian Economic and Social History Review* 53, no. 1 (2016): 131–53.

16. Amita Baviskar, "Indian Indigeneities: Adivasi Engagements with Hindu Nationalism in India," in *Indigenous Experience Today,* edited by Marisol de la Cadena and Orin Starn (Oxford: Berg, 2007), 275–304.

17. Sumit Sarkar, "Conversions and Politics of Hindu Right," *Economic and Political Weekly* 34, no. 26 (1999): 1691–1700; Kalyani Devaki Menon, *Everyday Nationalism: Women of the Hindu Right in India* (Philadelphia: University of Pennsylvania Press, 2010).

18. Alpa Shah, *In the Shadows of the State: Indigenous Politics, Environmentalism, and Insurgency in Jharkhand, India* (Durham, NC: Duke University Press, 2010).

19. Adam Kuper, "The Return of the Native," *Current Anthropology* 44, no. 3 (2003): 389–402.

20. Contradictory pulls to alternately dismantle and fortify indigeneity outline the contours of what Anderson and Longkumer call Neo-hindutva, a contemporary ethnonationalism that engages a "diffuse logic" that serves as "a mediating discourse in its own right." Hindu ethnonationalism's attempts at dissolving and playing up Adivasiness as indigenous distinction might be seen as particularly illustrative of its hybrid nature, replete with "vernacular forms that negotiate local legal, social, moral, and political environments in ways that variously concentrate or dilute its ideological emphases." See Edward Anderson and Arkotong Longkumer, "'Neo-Hindutva': Evolving Forms, Spaces, and Expressions of Hindu Nationalism," *Contemporary South Asia* 26, no. 4 (2018): 371–77.

21. Shah, *In the Shadows of the State.*

22. Nicholas Copeland, *The Democracy Development Machine: Neoliberalism, Radical Pessimism, and Authoritarian Populism in Mayan Guatemala* (Ithaca, NY: Cornell University Press, 2019). Copeland shows how the failure of Left mobilizations has triggered factionalism among indigenous communities, normalizing political disengagement and resulting in counterintuitive political alliances including with corrupt authoritarian populists.

23. For the quote, see D. J. Rycroft and S. Dasgupta, eds., *The Politics of Belonging in India: Becoming Adivasi* (Abingdon, U.K.: Routledge, 2011), 3. For the rest, see their preface, xiv.

24. Ranajit Guha, *Elementary Aspects of Peasant Insurgency in Colonial India* (New Delhi: Oxford University Press, 1983), 8.

25. Tanika Sarkar, "View from outside the Field: An Afterword," *Indian Economic and Social History Review* 53, no. 1 (2016): 155–57 at 155.

26. For more on the modern subject, see Sangeeta Dasgupta, "Adivasi Studies: From a Historian's Perspective," *History Compass* 16, no. 10 (2018); and Rajshree Chandra, *The Cunning of Rights: Law, Life, Biocultures* (Delhi: Oxford University Press, 2016). For plural identities, see Tanika Sarkar, "Rebellion as Modern Self-Fashioning: A Santal Movement in Colonial Bengal," in *The Politics of Belonging in India: Becoming Adivasi*, ed. D. J. Rycroft and S. Dasgupta (Abingdon, U.K.: Routledge, 2011), 66–67.

27. For more on the emergence of indigenous rights movement across the globe, see Ramachandra Guha, *Savaging the Civilized: Verrier Elwin, His Tribals, and India* (Chicago: University of Chicago, 1999); and Shah, *In the Shadows of the State.* For information on the neoliberal developmental initiatives of the Indian state, see Felix Padel and Samarendra Das, *Out of This Earth: East India Adivasis and the Aluminum Cartel* (New Delhi: Orient BlackSwan, 2010); and Alf Gunvald Nilsen and Srila Roy, *New Subaltern Politics: Reconceptualizing Hegemony and Resistance in Contemporary India* (Oxford: Oxford University Press, 2013). For the Maoist insurgency in the country, see Alpa Shah and Judith Pettigrew, *Windows into a Revolution: Ethnographies of Maoism in India and Nepal* (Abingdon, U.K.: Social Science Press, 2012); and Nandini Sundar, *The Burning Forest: India's War in Bastar* (Delhi: Juggernaut, 2016).

28. Crispin Bates and Alpa Shah, *Savage Attack: Tribal Insurgency in India* (New Delhi: Social Science Press, 2014), 2.

29. Lucas Bessire, *Behold the Black Caiman: A Chronicle of Life among the Ayoreo* (Chicago: University of Chicago Press, 2014).

30. Bessire, *Behold the Black Caiman*, 21.

BIBLIOGRAPHY

Ahmed, Sara. *The Cultural Politics of Emotion*. Edinburgh: Edinburgh University Press, 2004.

Alter, Joseph S. "Indian Clubs and Colonialism: Hindu Masculinity and Muscular Christianity." *Comparative Studies in Society and History* 46, no. 3 (2004): 497–534.

———. "Somatic Nationalism: Indian Wrestling and Militant Hinduism." *Modern Asian Studies* 28, no. 3 (1994): 557–88.

Ambedkar, Bhimrao. *Annihilation of Caste*. Nagpur: Prabuddha Bhart Pustkalya, 2011.

Ambedkar, B. R., and Sharmila Rege. *Against the Madness of Manu: B. R. Ambedkar's Writings on Brahmanical Patriarchy*. New Delhi: Navayana, 2013.

Amrute, Sareeta. "Moving Rape: Trafficking in the Violence of Postliberalization." *Public Culture* 27, no. 2 (2015): 331–59.

Anderson, Edward, and Arkotong Longkumer. "'Neo-Hindutva': Evolving Forms, Spaces, and Expressions of Hindu Nationalism." *Contemporary South Asia* 26, no. 4 (2018): 371–77.

Appadurai, Arjun. *Modernity at Large: Cultural Dimensions of Globalization*. Minneapolis: University of Minnesota Press, 1996.

Armstrong-Fumero, Fernando. *Elusive Unity: Factionalism and the Limits of Identity Politics in Yucatán, Mexico*. Boulder: University Press of Colorado, 2013.

———. "A Heritage of Ambiguity: The Historical Substrate of Vernacular Multiculturalism in Yucatán, Mexico." *American Ethnologist* 36, no. 2 (2009): 300–316.

Asad, Talal. *Genealogies of Religion: Discipline and Reasons of Power in Christianity and Islam*. Baltimore: Johns Hopkins University Press, 1993.

Bacchetta, Paola. *Gender in the Hindu Nation: RSS Women as Ideologues*. New Delhi: Women Unlimited, 2004.

Bailey, F. G. *The Civility of Indifference: On Domesticating Ethnicity*. Ithaca, NY: Cornell University Press, 1996.

———. *Tribe, Caste, and Nation: A Study of Political Activity and Political Change in Highland Orissa*. Manchester: Manchester University Press, 1960.

Banerjee, Prathama. *The Politics of Time: 'Primitives' and History-writing in a Colonial Society*. Delhi: Oxford University Press, 2006.

———. "Debt, Time and Extravagance: Money and the Making of 'Primitives' in Colonial Bengal." *Indian Economic and Social History Review* 37, no. 4 (2000): 423–45.

———. "Writing the Adivasi: Some Historiographical Notes." *Indian Economic and Social History Review* 53, no. 1 (2016): 131–53.

Baruah, Sanjib. "Territoriality, Indigeneity and Rights in the North-East India." *Economic and Political Weekly* 43, no. 12 (2008): 15–19.

Basso, Rebecca. "Music, Possession and Shamanism among Khond Tribes." *Culture and Religion* 7, no. 2 (2006): 177–97.

Basu, Amrita. *The Challenge of Local Feminisms*. Boulder, CO: Westview Press, 1995.

Bate, Bernard. *Tamil Oratory and the Dravidian Aesthetic: Democratic Practice in South India*. New York: Columbia University Press, 2009.

Bates, Crispin, and Alpa Shah. *Savage Attack: Tribal Insurgency in India*. New Delhi: Social Science Press, 2014.

Bauman, Chad M. *Christian Identity and Dalit Religion in Hindu India, 1868–1947*. Grand Rapids, MI: Wm. B. Eerdmans, 2008.

Baviskar, Amita. "Adivasi Encounters with Hindu Nationalism in MP." *Economic and Political Weekly* 40, no. 48 (2005): 5105–13.

———. "Indian Indigeneities: Adivasi Engagements with Hindu Nationalism in India." In *Indigenous Experience Today*, edited by Marisol de la Cadena and Orin Starn, 275–304. Oxford: Berg, 2007.

———. *In the Belly of the River: Tribal Conflicts over Development in the Narmada Valley*. Oxford: Oxford University Press, 1995.

———. "The Politics of Being 'Indigenous.'" In *Indigeneity in India*, ed. Bengt G. Karlsson and Tanka B. Subba, 33–50. London: Kegan Paul, 2006.

Beggiora, Stephano. "Tiger, Tiger Spirits and Were-Tigers in Tribal Orissa." *Religions of South Asia* 7, nos. 1–3 (2013): 93–107.

Behera, Mohan. *The Jayantira Pano: A Scheduled Caste Community of Orissa*. Bhubaneswar: Tribal and Harijan Research-cum-Training Institute, 1991.

Berlant, Lauren. "Critical Inquiry, Affirmative Culture." *Critical Inquiry* 30, no. 2 (2004): 445–51.

———. *Cruel Optimism*. Durham, NC: Duke University Press, 2011.

Bessire, Lucas. *Behold the Black Caiman: A Chronicle of Life among the Ayoreo*. Chicago: University of Chicago Press, 2014.

Bessire, Lucas, and David Bond. "Ontological Anthropology and the Deferral of Critique." *American Ethnologist* 41, no. 3 (2014): 440–56.

Béteille, André. *The Backward Classes in Contemporary India*. Delhi: Oxford University Press, 1992.

———. *Society and Politics in India: Essays in a Comparative Perspective*. London: Routledge, 1991.

Bhatt, Chetan. *Hindu Nationalism: Origins, Ideologies and Modern Myths*. London: Bloomsbury Academic, 2001.

Biehl, João. *Vita: Life in a Zone of Social Abandonment*. Berkeley: University of California Press, 2005.

Bird-David, Nurit. "'Animism' Revisited: Personhood, Environment, and Relational Epistemology." *Current Anthropology* 40, no. 1 (1999): s67–91.

Boal, Barbara M. *The Konds: Human Sacrifice and Religious Change.* Warminster, U.K.: Aris and Phillips, 1982.

Bordia, Devika. "The Ethics and Politics of Governance in the Tribal Regions of Western India." Ph.D. diss., Yale University, 2009.

Boyer, Dominic. "From Media Anthropology to the Anthropology of Mediation." In *The Sage Handbook of Social Anthropology*, ed. Richard Fardon et al. London: Sage, 2012.

Breman, Jan. *Footloose Labour: Working in India's Informal Economy.* Cambridge: Cambridge University Press, 1996.

Butler, Judith. *Excitable Speech: A Politics of the Performative.* New York: Routledge, 1997.

Byrd, Jodi A., and Michael Rothberg. "Between Subalternity and Indigeneity: Critical Categories for Postcolonial Studies." *Interventions* 13, no. 1 (2011): 1–12.

Cattelino, Jessica R. "The Double Bind of American Indian Need-Based Sovereignty." *Cultural Anthropology* 25, no. 2 (2010): 235–62.

———. "Fungibility: Florida Seminole Casino Dividends and the Fiscal Politics of Indigeneity." *American Anthropologist* 111, no. 2 (2009): 190–200.

———. *High Stakes: Florida Seminole Gaming and Sovereignty.* Durham, NC: Duke University Press, 2008.

———. "From Locke to Slots: Money and the Politics of Indigeneity." *Comparative Studies in Society and History* 60, no. 2 (2018): 274–307.

Cepek, Michael. "There Might Be Blood: Oil, Humility, and the Cosmopolitics of a Cofán Petro-Being." *American Ethnologist* 43, no. 4 (2016): 623–35.

Chakrabarty, Dipesh. *Provincializing Europe: Postcolonial Thought and Historical Difference.* Princeton, NJ: Princeton University Press, 2007.

Chakravarti, Uma. "Conceptualising Brahmanical Patriarchy in Early India: Gender, Caste, Class and State." *Economic and Political Weekly* 28, no. 14 (1993): 579–85.

Chandra, Rajshree. *The Cunning of Rights: Law, Life, Biocultures.* Delhi: Oxford University Press, 2016.

———. "Understanding Change With(in) Law: The Niyamgiri Case." *Contributions to Indian Sociology* 50, no. 2 (2016): 137–62.

Chandra, Uday. "Beyond Subalternity: Land, Community, and the State in Contemporary Jharkhand." *Contemporary South Asia* 21, no. 1 (2013): 52–61.

———. "Liberalism and Its Other: The Politics of Primitivism in Colonial and Postcolonial Indian Law." *Law and Society Review* 47, no. 1 (2013): 135–68.

———. "Rethinking Subaltern Resistance." *Journal of Contemporary Asia* 45, no. 4 (2015): 563–73.

Chatterjee, Partha. "Colonialism, Nationalism, and Colonialized Women: The Contest in India." *American Ethnologist* 16, no. 4 (1989): 622–33.

Cohn, Bernard S. *Colonialism and Its Forms of Knowledge: The British in India.* Princeton, NJ: Princeton University Press, 1996.

Comaroff, Jean and John, eds. *Law and Disorder in the Postcolony*. Chicago: University of Chicago Press, 2006.

Copeland, Nicholas. Book Review of Simpson, Audra. 2014. *Mohawk Interruptus: Political Life across the Borders of Settler States*. Durham, NC: Duke University Press. *North American Dialogue* 20, no. 2 (2017): 47–49.

———. *The Democracy Development Machine: Neoliberalism, Radical Pessimism, and Authoritarian Populism in Mayan Guatemala*. Ithaca, NY: Cornell University Press, 2019.

Corbridge, Stuart. "Competing Inequalities: The Scheduled Tribes and the Reservations System in India's Jharkhand." *Journal of Asian Studies* 59, no. 1 (2000): 62–85.

———. *Jharkhand: Environment, Development, Ethnicity*. New Delhi: University Press, 2004.

Corbridge, Stuart, Glyn Williams, Manoj Srivastava, and Réne Véron. *Seeing the State: Governance and Governmentality in India*. Cambridge: Cambridge University Press, 2005.

Coulthard, Glen Sean. *Red Skin, White Masks: Rejecting the Colonial Politics of Recognition*. Minneapolis: University of Minnesota Press, 2014.

Dasgupta, Sangeeta. "Adivasi Studies: From a Historian's Perspective." *History Compass* 16, no. 10 (2018).

Day, Iyko. *Alien Capital: Asian Racialization and the Logic of Settler Colonial Capitalism*. Durham, NC: Duke University Press, 2016.

De, Debasree. "Development-Induced Displacement: Impact on Adivasi Women of Odisha." *Community Development Journal* 50, no. 3 (2015): 448–62.

de la Cadena, Marisol. "Indigenous Cosmopolitics in the Andes: Conceptual Reflections beyond 'Politics.'" *Cultural Anthropology* 25, no. 2 (2010): 334–70.

Deleuze, Gilles, and Félix Guattari. *A Thousand Plateaus: Capitalism and Schizophrenia*. Minneapolis: University of Minnesota Press, 1987.

Descola, Phillippe. *In the Society of Nature: A Native Ecology in Amazonia*. Cambridge: Cambridge University Press, 1996.

Deshpande, Satish. "Caste and Castelessness: Towards a Biography of the 'General Category.'" *Economic and Political Weekly of India* 48, no. 15 (2013): 32–39.

Dhall, Manjushri. *The British Rule: Missionary Activities in Orissa, 1822–1947*. New Delhi: Har-Anand, 1997.

Dietrich, Gabriele. *A New Thing on Earth: Hopes and Fears Facing Feminist Theory: Theological Ruminations of a Feminist Activist*. Delhi: ISPCK, 2001.

Di Giminiani, Piergiorgio. "The Becoming of Ancestral Land: Place and Property in Mapuche Land Claims." *American Ethnologist* 42, no. 3 (2015): 490–503.

Dirks, Nicholas. *Castes of Mind: Colonialism and the Making of Modern India*. Princeton, NJ: Princeton University Press, 2001.

———. "The Original Caste: Power, History and Hierarchy in South Asia." *Contributions to Indian Sociology* 23, no. 1 (1989): 59–77.

Douglas, Mary. *Purity and Danger: An Analysis of Concept of Pollution and Taboo*. London: Routledge, 2002.

Dudley Jenkins, Laura. "Competing Inequalities: The Struggle over Reserved Legislative Seats for Women in India." *International Review of Social History* 44 (1999): 53–75.

———. "Legal Limits on Religious Conversion in India." *Law and Contemporary Problems* 71, no. 2 (2008): 109–28.

Driessen, Miriam. "Rural Voids." *Public Culture* 30, no. 1 (2018): 61–84.

Elwin, Verrier. *The Muria and Their Ghotul.* Oxford: Oxford University Press, 1947.

———. *The Tribal World of Verrier Elwin: An Autobiography.* London: Oxford University Press, 1964.

Fawcett, F. "The Dombs of Jeypore, Vizagapatnam District, Madras." *Man* 1 (1901): 34–38.

Ferguson, James. *The Anti-Politics Machine: "Development," Depoliticization, and Bureaucratic Power in Lesotho.* Minneapolis: University of Minnesota Press, 1994.

———. *Global Shadows: Africa in the Neoliberal World Order.* Durham, NC: Duke University Press, 2006.

Fortun, Kim, Mike Fortun, and Steven Rubenstein. "Editors' Introduction to Emergent Indigeneities." *Cultural Anthropology* 25, no. 2 (2010): 222–34.

Fraser, Nancy. "Rethinking Recognition." *New Left Review* 3 (2000): 107–20.

Frazer, James George. *The Golden Bough: A Study in Magic and Religion.* London: Wordsworth, 1993.

Froerer, Peggy. *Religious Division and Social Conflict: The Emergence of Hindu Nationalism in Rural India.* New Delhi: Social Science Press, 2007.

Fuller, Christopher J. "Introduction." In *Caste Today,* ed. Christopher J. Fuller, 1–31. Oxford: Oxford University Press, 1996.

Galanter, Marc. *Competing Equalities: Law and the Backward Classes in India.* New Delhi: Oxford University Press, 1991.

Geetha, V. "Bereft of Being: The Humiliations of Untouchability." In *Humiliation: Claims and Context,* ed. G. Guru, 95–107. New Delhi: Oxford University Press, 2009.

Ghassem-Fachandi, Parvis. *Pogrom in Gujarat: Hindu Nationalism and Anti-Muslim Violence in India.* Princeton, NJ: Princeton University Press, 2012.

Ghosh, Kaushik. "Between Global Flows and Local Dams: Indigenousness, Locality, and the Transnational Sphere in Jharkhand, India." *Cultural Anthropology* 21, no. 4 (2006): 501–34.

———. "A Market for Aboriginality: Primitivism and Race Classification in the Indentured Labor Market of Colonial India." In *Subaltern Studies X,* ed. Gautam Bhadra, Gyan Prakash, and Susie Tharu, 8–48. New Delhi: Oxford University Press, 1999.

Gill, Navyug. "Limits of Conversion: Caste, Labor, and the Question of Emancipation in Colonial Panjab." *Journal of Asian Studies* 78, no. 1 (2019): 3–22.

Gorringe, Hugo. "Afterword: Gendering Caste: Honor, Patriarchy and Violence." *South Asia Multidisciplinary Academic Journal* 19 (2018), https://doi.org/10.4000/samaj.46.

Govindrajan, Radhika. *Animal Intimacies: Interspecies Relatedness in India's Central Himalayas.* Chicago: University of Chicago Press, 2018.

Guha, Ramachandra. *Savaging the Civilized: Verrier Elwin, His Tribals, and India*. Chicago: University of Chicago, 1999.

Guha, Ranajit. *Elementary Aspects of Peasant Insurgency in Colonial India*. New Delhi: Oxford University Press, 1983.

Gupta, Akhil. "Blurred Boundaries: The Discourse of Corruption, the Culture of Politics, and the Imagined State." *American Ethnologist* 22, no. 2 (1995): 375–402.

Gupta, Charu. "Intimate Desires: Dalit Women and Religious Conversions in Colonial India." *Journal of Asian Studies* 73, no. 3 (2014): 661–87.

———. "Writing Sex and Sexuality: Archives of Colonial North India." *Journal of Women's History* 23, no. 4 (2011): 12–35.

———. "Hindu Women, Muslim Men: Love Jihad and Conversions." *Economic and Political Weekly* 44, no.51 (2009): 13-15.

Haggis, Jane. "Ironies of Emancipation: Changing Configurations of 'Women's Work' in the 'Mission of Sisterhood' to Indian Women." *Feminist Review* 65, no. 1 (2000): 108–26.

Handler, Richard. "Debating Authenticity: Concepts of Modernity in Anthropological Perspective." *American Anthropologist* 116, no. 1 (2014): 205–6.

Hansen, Thomas Blom. *The Saffron Wave: Democracy and Hindu Nationalism in Modern India*. Princeton, NJ: Princeton University Press, 1999.

Haraway, Donna J. *Staying with the Trouble: Making Kin in the Chthulucene*. Durham, NC: Duke University Press, 2016.

Hardenberg, Roland. *Fierce People of the Mountains: Society, Ritual and Cosmology of the Orissa Hills*. Muenster: University of Muenster, 2005.

Hardiman, David. "Christianity and the Adivasis of Gujarat." In *Development and Deprivation in Gujarat: In Honour of Jan Breman*, eds. Ghanshyam Shah, Mario Rutten, and Hein Streefkerk, 175–95. New Delhi: Sage, 2002.

———. *The Coming of the Devi: Adivasi Assertion in Western India*. Delhi: Oxford University Press, 1987.

———. "A Subaltern Christianity: Faith Healing in Southern Gujarat." In *Medical Marginality in South Asia: Situating Subaltern Therapeutics*, ed. David Hardiman and Projit Bihari Mukharji, 126–51. Abingdon, U.K.: Routledge, 2012.

Hart, Keith. "The Ethnography of Finance and the History of Money." *New Perspectives in Economic Ethnography: Modalities of Exchange and Economic Calculation*. Rio de Janeiro: Museu Nacional, 2011.

Harvey, David. *A Brief History of Neoliberalism*. Oxford: Oxford University, 2005.

Herdt, Gilbert, ed. *Moral Panics, Sex Panics: Fear and the Fight over Sexual Rights*. New York: New York University Press, 2009.

Herzfeld, Michael. "It Takes One to Know One: Collective Resentment and Mutual Recognition among Greeks in Local and Global Contexts." In *Counterworks: Managing the Diversity of Knowledge*, ed. Richard Fardon, 118–36. London: Routledge, 1995.

Hirschkind, Charles. *The Ethical Soundscape: Cassette Sermons and Islamic Counterpublics*. New York: Columbia University Press, 2006.

———. "The Ethics of Listening: Cassette-Sermon Audition in Contemporary Egypt." *American Ethnologist* 28, no. 3 (2001): 623–49.

Hota, Pinky. "Populist Panics: Sex as Excess in Right Wing India." *Anthropology Quarterly* 93, no. 3 (2020): 377–400.

Huberman, Jennifer. *Ambivalent Encounters: Childhood, Tourism, and Social Change in Banaras, India.* New Brunswick, NJ: Rutgers, 2012.

Hubert, Henri, and Marcel Mauss. *Sacrifice: Its Nature and Functions.* Chicago: Chicago University Press, 1981.

Inden, Ronald. *Imagining India.* Bloomington: Indiana University Press, 1990.

Jaffrelot, Christophe. *The Hindu Nationalist Movement and Indian Politics: 1925 to the 1990s.* New Delhi: Penguin, 1999.

———. "The Hindu Nationalist Reinterpretation of Pilgrimage in India: The Limits of Yatra Politics." *Nations and Nationalism* 15, no. 1 (2009): 1–19.

———. "The Sangh Parivar between Sanskritization and Social Engineering." In *The BJP and the Compulsions of Politics in India*, ed. Christophe Jaffrelot and Thomas Blom Hansen, 22–71. Delhi: Oxford University Press, 1998.

Jaoul, Nicolas. "Beyond Citizenship: Adivasi and Dalit Political Pathways in India." *Focaal* 76 (2016): 3–14.

Jangam, Chinnaiah. *Dalits and the Making of Modern India.* Oxford: Oxford University Press, 2019.

Jauregui, Beatrice. "Provisional Agency in India: Jugaad and Legitimation of Corruption." *American Ethnologist* 41, no. 1 (2014): 76–91.

Jena, Mihir K., Padmini Pathi, Kamala K. Patnaik, and Klaus Seeland. *Forest Tribes of Orissa: Lifestyle and Social Conditions of Selected Orissan Tribes*, vol. 2, *The Kuttia Kondh.* New Delhi: D. K. Printworld, 2006.

Kakar, Sudhir. *Intimate Relations: Exploring Indian Sexuality.* Chicago: University of Chicago Press, 1990.

Kamat, Sangeeta. *Development Hegemony: NGOs and the State in India.* New Delhi: Oxford University Press, 2002.

Kanungo, Pralay. "Hindutva's Entry into a 'Hindu Province': Early Years of RSS in Orissa." *Economic and Political Weekly* 38, no. 31 (2003): 3293–3303.

Karlsson, Bengt G. "The Social Life of Categories: Affirmative Action and Trajectories of the Indigenous." *Focaal* 65 (2013): 33–41.

Kaur, Ravinder. *Brand New Nation: Capitalist Dreams and Nationalist Designs in Twenty-First Century India.* Stanford, CA: Stanford University Press, 2020.

Kaur, Ravinder, and Thomas Blom Hansen. "Aesthetics of Arrival: Spectacle, Capital, Novelty in Post-Reform India." *Identities* 23, no. 3 (2016): 265–75.

Kaur, Raminder, and William Mazzarella, eds. *Censorship in South Asia: Cultural Regulation from Sedition to Seduction.* Bloomington: Indiana University Press, 2009.

Keane, Webb. *Christian Moderns: Freedom and Fetish in the Mission Encounter.* Berkeley: University of California Press, 2007.

Kent, Eliza. *Converting Women: Gender and Protestant Christianity in Colonial South India.* New York: Oxford University Press, 2004.

Kohn, Eduardo. *How Forests Think: Toward an Anthropology beyond the Human.* Berkeley: University of California Press, 2013.

Kulke, Hermann. "Kshatriyaization and Social Change: A Study in Orissa Setting." In *Aspects of Changing India: Studies in Honour of Prof. G. S. Ghurye*, ed. S. Devadas Pillai, 398–409. Bombay: Popular Prakashan, 1976.

Kumar, Aishwary. "What Is Dalit Studies: A Review." *Indian Economic and Social History Review* 56, no. 2 (2019): 227–45.

Kuper, Adam. "The Return of the Native." *Current Anthropology* 44, no. 3 (2003): 389–402.

Lancaster, Roger N. *Sex Panic and the Punitive State.* Berkeley: University of California Press, 2011.

Latour, Bruno. *We Have Never Been Modern.* Cambridge, MA: Harvard University Press, 1993.

Lee, Joel G. *Deceptive Majority: Dalits, Hinduism and Underground Religion.* New York: Cambridge University Press, 2021.

———. "Disgust and Untouchability: Towards an Affective Theory of Caste." *South Asian History and Culture* 12, nos. 2–3 (2021): 310–27.

———. "Lāl Beg Underground: The Passing of an 'Untouchable God.'" In *Objects of Worship in South Asian Religions: Forms, Practices and Meanings*, ed. Knut A. Jacobsen, Mikael Aktor, and Kristina Myrvold, 143–62. London: Routledge, 2014.

———. "Odor and Order: How Caste Is Inscribed in Space and Sensoria." *Comparative Studies of South Asia, Africa and the Middle East* 37, no. 3 (2017): 470–90.

Li, Tania Murray. "Indigeneity, Capitalism, and the Management of Dispossession." *Current Anthropology* 51, no. 3 (2010): 385–414.

Lock, Margaret. "Cultivating the Body: Anthropology and Epistemologies of Bodily Practice and Knowledge." *Annual Review of Anthropology* 22, no. 1 (1993):133–55.

Lorenzen, David N. "Who Invented Hinduism?" *Comparative Studies in Society and History* 41, no. 4 (1999): 630–59.

Mannheim, Bruce. "Iconicity." *Journal of Linguistic Anthropology* 9, nos. 1–2 (1999): 107–10.

Mathur, Nayanika. "Eating Money: Corruption and Its Categorical 'Other' in the Leaky Indian State." *Modern Asian Studies* 51, no. 6 (2017): 1796–1817.

———. "Effecting Development: Bureaucratic Knowledges, Cynicism, and the Desire for Development in the Indian Himalaya." In *Differentiating Development: Beyond an Anthropology of Critique*, ed. Soumhya Venkatesan and Thomas Yarrow, 193–209. New York: Berghahn Books, 2012.

Markell, Patchen. "Recognition and Redistribution." In *The Oxford Handbook of Political Theory*, ed. John S. Dryzek, Bonnie Honig, and Anne Phillips, 450–69. Oxford: Oxford University Press, 2008.

Marriott, McKim. *Hindi Transactions: Diversity without Dualism.* Chicago: University of Chicago, 1976.

Maurer, Bill. "The Anthropology of Money." *Annual Review of Anthropology* 35 (2006): 15–36.

Mazzarella, William. "The Anthropology of Populism: Beyond the Liberal Settlement." *Annual Review of Anthropology* 48, no. 1 (2019): 45–60.

———. *Censorium: Cinema and the Open Edge of Mass Publicity.* Durham, NC: Duke University Press, 2013.

McClintock, Anne, Aamir Mufti, and Ella Shohat, eds. *Dangerous Liaisons: Gender, Nation, and Postcolonial Perspectives.* Minneapolis: University of Minnesota Press, 1997.

McIntosh, Janet. *The Edge of Islam: Power, Personhood and Ethnoreligious Boundaries on the Kenya Coast.* Durham, NC: Duke University Press, 2009.

McNay, Lois. *Against Recognition.* Cambridge: Polity, 2008.

Melamed, Jodi. "Racial Capitalism." *Journal of Critical Ethnic Studies* 1, no. 1 (2015): 76–86.

Menon, Kalyani Devaki. *Everyday Nationalism: Women of the Hindu Right in India.* Philadelphia: University of Pennsylvania Press, 2010.

Meyer, Birgit. "Introduction: From Imagined Communities to Aesthetic Formations: Religious Mediations, Sensational Forms, and Styles of Binding." In *Aesthetic Formations: Religion/Culture/Critique*, ed. Birgit Meyer, 1–28. New York: Palgrave Macmillan, 2009.

Meyer, Birgit, and Peter Pels, eds. *Magic and Modernity: Interfaces of Revelation and Concealment.* Stanford, CA: Stanford University Press, 2003.

Middleton, Townsend. "Across the Interface of State Ethnography: Rethinking Ethnology and Its Subjects in Multicultural India." *American Ethnologist* 38, no. 2 (2011): 249–66.

———. *The Demands of Recognition: State Anthropology and Ethnopolitics in Darjeeling.* Stanford, CA: Stanford University Press, 2015.

Moodie, Meghan. *We Were Adivasis: Aspiration in an Indian Scheduled Tribe.* Chicago: University of Chicago Press, 2015.

Morris, Rosalind C. "The Mute and the Unspeakable: Political Subjectivity, Violence Crime, and 'the Sexual Thing' in a South African Mining Community." In *Law and Disorder in the Postcolony*, ed. John L. and Jean Comaroff, 57–101. Chicago: University of Chicago Press, 2006.

Mosse, David. "Caste and Development: Contemporary Perspectives on a Structure of Discrimination and Advantage." *World Development* 110 (2018): 422–36.

———. *Cultivating Development: An Ethnography of Aid Policy and Practice.* London: Pluto, 2014.

———. "The Modernity of Caste and the Market Economy." *Modern Asian Studies* 54, no. 4 (2020): 1225–71.

———. "Outside Caste? The Enclosure of Caste and Claims to Castelessness in India and the United Kingdom." *Comparative Studies in Society and History* 62, no. 1 (2020): 4–34.

Nehru, Jawahar Lal. *The Adivasis*. Delhi: Ministry of Information and Broadcasting, 1955.

Nelms, Taylor C., and Bill Maurer. "Materiality, Symbol, and Complexity in the Anthropology of Money." In *The Psychological Science of Money*, ed. Erik Bijleveld and Henk Aarts, 37–70. New York: Springer, 2014.

Nigam, Sanjay. "Disciplining and Policing the 'Criminals by Birth,' Part 1: The Making of a Colonial Stereotype—The Criminal Tribes and Castes of North India." *Indian Economic and Social History Review* 27, no. 2 (1990): 131–64.

Nilsen, Alf Gunvald, and Srila Roy. *New Subaltern Politics: Reconceptualizing Hegemony and Resistance in Contemporary India*. Oxford: Oxford University Press, 2013.

Otten, Tina, and Edward Simpson. "F. G. Bailey's Bisipara Revisited." *Economic and Political Weekly* 2, nos. 26–27 (2016): 25.

Padel, Felix. *The Sacrifice of Human Being: British Rule and the Konds of Orissa*. Delhi: Oxford University Press, 1995.

Padel, Felix, and Samarendra Das. *Out of This Earth: East India Adivasis and the Aluminum Cartel*. New Delhi: Orient BlackSwan, 2010.

Panda, Harihar. "History of Orissa." *Cuttack, 1997* (2008): 272.

Pandey, Gyanendra. "The Time of the Dalit Conversion." *Economic and Political Weekly* 41, no. 18 (2006): 1779–88.

Pandian, Anand. *Crooked Stalks: Cultivating Virtue in South India*. Durham, NC: Duke University Press, 2009.

———. "Tradition in Fragments: Inherited Forms and Fractures in the Ethics of South India." *American Ethnologist* 35, no. 3 (2008): 466–80.

Parry, Jonathan. "'The Crisis of Corruption' and the 'Idea of India': A Worm's Eye View." In *The Morals of Legitimacy: Between Agency and System*, ed. Italo Pardo, 27–56. Oxford: Berghahn Books, 2000.

Pati, Biswamoy. *Identity, Hegemony, Resistance: Towards a Social History of Conversions in Orissa, 1800–2000*. New Delhi: Three Essays Collective, 2003.

Patnaik, Nihar Ranjan. *Economic History of Orissa*. New Delhi: Indus, 1997.

Peake, Linda. "Gender, Race, Sexuality." In *The Sage Handbook of Social Geographies*, ed. Susan J. Smith, Rachel Pain, Sallie A. Marston, and John Paul Jones III, 55–77. Los Angeles: Sage, 2009.

Piliavsky, Anastasia. "The 'Criminal Tribe' in India before the British." *Comparative Studies in Society and History* 57, no. 2 (2015): 323–54.

Piliavsky, Anastasia, ed. *Patronage as the Politics of South Asia*. New York: Cambridge University Press, 2014.

Postone, Moishe. "Anti-Semitism and National Socialism: Notes on the German Reaction to 'Holocaust.'" *New German Critique* 19 (1980): 97–115.

———. *Time, Labor, and Social Domination: A Reinterpretation of Marx's Critical Theory*. Cambridge: Cambridge University Press, 1993.

Povinelli, Elizabeth. *The Cunning of Recognition: Indigenous Alterities and the Making of Australian Multiculturism*. Durham, NC: Duke University Press, 2002.

Prakash, Gyan. "The Impossibility of Subaltern History." *Nepantla: Views from South* 1, no. 2 (2000): 287–94.

Putnam, Hilary. *Mind, Language and Reality*. Cambridge: Cambridge University Press, 1975.

Rajagopal, Arvind. *Politics after Television: Hindu Nationalism and the Reshaping of the Public in India*. Cambridge: Cambridge University Press, 2001.

Ramaswamy, Sumathi. *The Goddess and the Nation: Mapping Mother India*. Durham, NC: Duke University Press, 2010.

Rao, Anupama. *The Caste Question: Dalits and the Politics of Modern India*. Berkeley: University of California Press, 2009.

Rath, Govinda Chandra, ed. *Tribal Development in India: The Contemporary Debate*. New Delhi: Sage, 2006.

Rawat, Ramnarayan S., and K. Satyanarayana, eds. *Dalit Studies*. Durham, NC: Duke University Press, 2016.

Roberts, Nathaniel. *To Be Cared For: The Power of Conversion and Foreignness of Belonging in an Indian Slum*. Oakland: University of California Press, 2016.

Robinson, Cedric. *Black Marxism: The Making of the Black Radical Tradition*. Chapel Hill: University of North Carolina Press, 1983.

Robinson, Rowena, and Joseph Marianus Kujur, eds. *Margins of Faith: Dalit and Tribal Christianity in India*. New Delhi: Sage, 2010.

Rotman, Andy. *Thus Have I Seen: Visualizing Faith in Early Indian Buddhism*. New York: Oxford University Press, 2009.

Rubin, Gayle. "Thinking Sex: Notes for a Radical Theory of the Politics of Sexuality." In *Pleasure and Danger: Exploring Female Sexuality*, ed. Carole S. Vance, 267–93. London: Pandora, 1992.

Rycroft, D. J., and S. Dasgupta, eds. *The Politics of Belonging in India: Becoming Adivasi*. Abingdon, U.K.: Routledge, 2011.

Sangari, Kumkum. "Politics of Diversity: Religious Communities and Multiple Patriarchies." *Economic and Political Weekly* 30, no. 51 (1995): 3287–3310.

Sarkar, Sumit. *Beyond Nationalist Frames: Postmodernism, Hindu Fundamentalism, History*. Bloomington: Indiana University Press, 2002.

———. "Conversions and Politics of Hindu Right." *Economic and Political Weekly* 34, no. 26 (1999): 1691–1700.

Sarkar, Tanika. *Hindu Wife, Hindu Nation: Community, Religion and Cultural Nationalism*. New Delhi: Permanent Black, 2003.

———. "Rebellion as Modern Self-Fashioning: A Santal Movement in Colonial Bengal." In *The Politics of Belonging in India: Becoming Adivasi*, ed. D. J. Rycroft and S. Dasgupta, 65–81. Abingdon, U.K.: Routledge, 2011.

———. "View from outside the Field: An Afterword." *Indian Economic and Social History Review* 53, no. 1 (2016): 155–57.

Satyanarayana, K. "Dalit Reconfiguration of Caste: Representation, Identity and Poli-
    tics." *Critical Quarterly* 56, no. 3 (2014): 46–61.
Schnepel, Burkhard. "Durga and the King: Ethnohistorical Aspects of Politico-Ritual
    Life in a South Orissan Jungle Kingdom." *Journal of the Royal Anthropological Insti-
    tute* 1, no. 1 (1995): 145–66.
Seeland, Klaus. "Indigenous Knowledge of Trees and Forests in Non-European Societ-
    ies." In *Nature Is Culture: Indigenous Knowledge and Socio-Cultural Aspects of Trees
    and Forests in Non-European Cultures*, ed. Klaus Seeland, 101–12. London: IT, 1997.
Sen, Uditi. "Developing *Terra Nullius*: Colonialism, Nationalism, and Indigeneity in
    the Andaman Islands." *Comparative Studies in Society and History* 59, no. 4 (2017):
    944–73.
Shah, Alpa. *In the Shadows of the State: Indigenous Politics, Environmentalism, and Insur-
    gency in Jharkhand, India*. Durham, NC: Duke University Press, 2010.
Shah, Alpa, and Judith Pettigrew. *Windows into a Revolution: Ethnographies of Maoism
    in India and Nepal*. Abingdon, U.K.: Social Science Press, 2012.
Shah, Alpa, and Sarah Shneiderman. "The Practices, Policies, and Politics of Transform-
    ing Inequality in South Asia." *Focaal* 65 (2013): 3–12.
Shah, Svati P. "Sedition, Gender, and Gender Identity in South Asia." *South Asia Multi-
    disciplinary Academic Journal* 20 (2019), https://doi.org/10.4000/samaj.4925.
Sharma, Smriti. "Caste Based Crimes and Economic Status: Evidence From India." *Jour-
    nal of Comparative Economics* 43, no. 1 (2014): 204–26.
Simmel, Georg. *The Metropolis and Mental Life*. New York: Free Press, 1950.
Simpson, Audra. *Mohawk Interruptus: Political Life across the Borders of Settler States*.
    Durham, NC: Duke University Press, 2014.
———. "Settlement's Secret." *Cultural Anthropology* 26, no. 2 (2011): 205–17.
Simpson, Edward, et al. "A Brief History of Incivility in Rural Postcolonial India: Caste,
    Religion, and Anthropology." *Comparative Studies in Society and History* 60, no. 1
    (2018): 58–89.
Singh, Bhrigupati. "Agonistic Intimacy and Moral Aspiration in Popular Hinduism: A
    Study in the Political Theology of the Neighbor." *American Ethnologist* 38, no. 3
    (2011): 430–50.
Singh, Nikhil Pal. "On Race, Violence and So-Called Primitive Accumulation." *Social
    Text* 34, no. 3 (2016): 27–50.
Sinha, Mrinalini. *Colonial Masculinity: The "Manly Englishman" and the "Effeminate
    Bengali" in the Late Nineteenth Century*. Manchester: Manchester University Press,
    1995.
———. "Reading Mother India: Empire, Nation, and the Female Voice." *Journal of Wom-
    en's History* 6, no. 2 (1994): 6–44.
Skaria, Ajay. "Shades of Wildness: Tribe, Caste, and Gender in Western India." *Journal of
    Asian Studies* 56, no. 3 (1997): 726–45.
Smith, Katherine. "Rhetoric and the Everyday—Fairness as Rhetorical Force and the
    Micro-Politics of Intentionality in a North Manchester Town." In *Rhetoric in British*

Politics and Society, ed. Judi Atkins, Alan Finlayson, James Martin, and Nick Turnbull, 160–72. London: Palgrave Macmillan, 2014.

Srinivas, Mysore Narasimhachar. *Social Change in Modern India*. Berkeley: University of California Press, 1969.

Starn, Orin. "Here Come the Anthros (Again): The Strange Marriage of Anthropology and Native America." *Cultural Anthropology* 26, no. 2 (2011): 179–204.

Still, Clarinda. "The State in the Palli: Dalit Perspectives on the State in Andhra Pradesh." *Contemporary South Asia* 19, no. 3 (2011): 315–29.

———. "'They Have It in Their Stomachs but They Can't Vomit It Up': Dalits, Reservations, and 'Caste Feeling' in Rural Andhra Pradesh." *Focaal* 65 (2013): 68–79.

Subramanian, Ajantha. *The Caste of Merit: Engineering Education in India*. Cambridge, MA: Harvard University Press, 2019.

Sundar, Nandini. *The Burning Forest: India's War in Bastar*. Delhi: Juggernaut, 2016.

———. "Debating Dussehra and Reinterpreting Rebellion in Bastar District, Central India." *Journal of the Royal Anthropological Institute* 7, no. 1 (2001): 19–35.

———. "Teaching to Hate: RSS's Pedagogical Program." *Economic and Political Weekly* 39, no. 16 (2004): 1605–12.

Tanabe, Akio. "Ethnohistory of Land and Identity in Khurda, Orissa: From Pre-Colonial Past to Post-Colonial Present." *Journal of Asian and African Studies* 56 (1998): 75–11.

Taussig, Michael T. *Mimesis and Alterity: A Particular History of the Senses*. New York: Routledge, 1993.

Teltumbde, Anand. *Republic of Caste: Thinking Equality in the Time of Neoliberal Hindutva*. New Delhi: Navayana, 2018.

Thapar, Romila. "The Image of the Barbarian in Early India." *Comparative Studies in Society and History* 13, no. 4 (October 1971): 408–36.

Trouillot, Michel-Rolph. "Anthropology and the Savage Slot: The Poetics and Politics of Otherness." In *Recapturing Anthropology: Working in the Present*, ed. R. Fox, 17–44. Santa Fe, NM: School of American Research Press, 1991.

Tylor, Edward Burnett. *Primitive Culture: Researches into the Development of Mythology, Philosophy, Religion, Art, and Custom*, vol. 2. Cambridge: Cambridge University Press, 2010.

Valiani, Arafaat A. "Physical Training, Ethical Discipline, and Creative Violence: Zones of Self-Mastery in the Hindu Nationalist Movement." *Cultural Anthropology* 25, no. 1 (2010): 73–99.

Velaskar, Padma. "Theorising the Interaction of Caste, Class, and Gender: A Feminist Sociological Approach." *Contributions to Indian Sociology* 50, no. 3 (2016): 389–414.

Viswanath, Rupa. "The Emergence of Authenticity Talk and the Giving of Accounts: Conversion as Movement of the Soul in South India, ca. 1900." *Comparative Studies in Society and History* 55, no. 1 (2013): 120–41.

———. *The Pariah Problem: Caste, Religion, and the Social in Modern India*. New York: Columbia University Press, 2014.

Vishwanathan, Gauri. *Outside the Fold: Conversion, Modernity, and Belief.* Princeton, NJ: Princeton University Press, 1998.

Vitebsky, Piers. *Living Without the Dead: Loss and Redemption in a Jungle Cosmos.* Chicago: University of Chicago Press, 2017.

Wakankar, Milind. "Body, Crowd, Identity: Genealogy of a Hindu Nationalist Ascetics." *Social Text* 45 (1995): 45–73.

Wankhede, Harish. "The Political Context of Religious Conversion in Orissa." *Economic and Political Weekly* 44, no. 15 (2009): 33–38.

Willerslev, Rane. *Soul Hunters: Hunting, Animism, and Personhood among the Siberian Yukaghirs.* Berkeley: University of California Press, 2007.

Witsoe, Jeffrey. "Corruption as Power: Caste and the Political Imagination of the Postcolonial State." *American Ethnologist* 38, no. 1 (2011): 73–85.

Wolfe, Patrick. "Land, Labor, and Difference: Elementary Structures of Race." *American Historical Review* 106, no. 3 (2001): 866–905.

Xaxa, Virginius. "Protective Discrimination: Why Scheduled Tribes Lag Behind Scheduled Castes." *Economic and Political Weekly of India* 36, no. 29 (2001): 2765–72.

INDEX

Adibasis: Desia Kandhas, 99; Hinduism and, 101; indigeneity and, 2, 178n2; land veneration and, 127; Panas as, 35, 85; religious fanaticism (*dharmic katarta*) and, 90; religious practices and, 112; simplicity tropes and, 52; terminology and, 173n1, 178n2. *See also* Adivasis

Adivasi-Hindu affinity: Adivasi indigeneity and, 101–2, 124; Adivasi religious leaders and, 106; belief and practice distinctions, 112; caste Hindu traditions and, 109–10; economic victimization and, 158; generational perceptions and, 111–13; hearts-and-minds formulation, 112; Hindu kingship and, 107–10, 115; invented traditions and, 110, 114; Kandha ambivalence and, 107–13, 116; Kandha marginalization and, 107–9; Kandhas as *kar sevaks*, 108, 187n52; kinship language, 92, 110, 114, 119, 122, 124; mythology and, 110; nature-culture relationalities and, 118–19, 167, 170; political alliances and, 122; polysemic practices and, 103–5; precolonial history, 89; recognition and, 109; religious practices and, 100–101, 110–13, 122, 124–25, 127–29, 135; reterritorialization and, 130–31; sacred regard for land and, 122–25, 127–32; Sanskritization and, 99–100, 115, 130; shared heritage and, 105, 116; social hierarchies and, 102–4, 186n38

Adivasi indigeneity: abjuration of capital, 41, 152–53, 156; authenticity and, 12, 38–39, 86–87, 89, 92–93, 114–15, 124, 139, 152–53, 170; caste capitalism and, 5, 12, 42, 169; casteist racialization and, 22–24, 42; Christian cementing of, 75; classification and governance of, 22–23;

Dalit Otherness and, 22, 172; distinctiveness of, 54; embodied religiosity and, 88, 91, 94, 98, 115; Hindu ethnonationalism and, 5, 17, 22, 91–92, 99, 128, 196n20; Hindutva and, 89, 91–94, 102, 115, 138, 183n5, 184n19; identity formation and, 171, 181n5; land veneration and, 17, 91, 93, 115, 117, 122–25, 127–32, 139, 172; money and value in, 45; neo/colonial imaginaries, 12, 22, 40, 89, 94, 170; political identity and, 58, 64, 89, 92–93, 169–71; recognition of, 39; romantic racialization of, 170; savagery tropes and, 17, 20, 22, 155; Scheduled Tribe category, 5; sovereignty and, 106

Adivasiness: authenticity and, 170, 196n20; Hinduism and, 105; Hindu primacy and, 116, 167; identity politics and, 15, 92; as indigenous assimilation, 130; land entitlements and, 126; political-economic abjection and, 15; racialization and, 66, 170; shape-shifting, 12, 169

Adivasis: *bajaar* (marketplace) and, 55; ban on slash-and-burn cultivation, 39, 50, 179n31; caste hierarchies and, 41; casteist racialization and, 16, 22–24, 42; conversion and, 84, 182n16; development projects and, 43–44, 52; economic exploitation of, 32, 47–48, 50, 53; economic marginality and, 8, 24, 45, 49, 52, 168; embodied religiosity and, 89, 91; ethnonationalism and, 16, 88–90; ethnoreligious hostilities and, 1, 3; exclusion from capital, 40, 48; governance and, 179n34; Hinduization and, 99–100, 137; indentured labor and, 39–40; land dispossession and, 39–40; land rights and, 9, 35, 41, 131; mastery of money discourse,

nature-culture beings: Adivasi-Hindu shared
regard, 122–23, 128–29; Bharat Mata
as, 124–28; cycles of reciprocity and, 25,
120–22; Kandha cosmology and, 17, 25,
93, 117–23, 128, 131; Kandha-Hindutva
reframing of, 118–19; land as, 17, 25,
93, 117–19, 124, 128, 130–31, 135–36,
138–39; material expectations from,
120–22, 128; as political actors, 118, 126;
reterritorialization and, 130–31. *See also*
Dharini Pennu
Nehru, Jawaharal, 7, 47
Nelms, Taylor, 53
Neo-hindutva, 196n20
neoliberalism: accrual of capital and, 45,
56; Adivasi land entitlement, 126; anti-
Christian violence and, 4; anti-Dalit
violence and, 6; caste and, 157; caste
inequality in, 10, 131, 158; democratic
exclusion in, 166; economic inequality
and, 152, 160; ethnonationalist violence
and, 11; Indian reforms and, 48; indigeneity and, 116, 188n71, 191n37; minority
gains under, 5; nature-culture beings and,
118; Odisha state and, 14; populism and,
145; racial inequality and, 10
Nigam, Sanjay, 41

Odia language, 13
Odisha state: Adivasi population in, 13–15;
anti-conversion laws, 149; anti-Pana
rhetoric, 38–39; British administration
of, 13; Dalits and, 15; distrust *dhaga*, 38;
ethnonationalism and, 15; ethnonationalist violence in, 3; Hindu ethnonationalism and, 89; Hinduism in, 15, 109–10;
Kandhas and, 25; mining and extraction
industries in, 13–14; neoliberal capitalism
in, 14; socioeconomic change in, 13–15;
Sora-Pano relations in, 176n27
Orientalism, 41
Orissa Freedom of Religion Act (1962), 77
Orissa Province, 13
Orissa Tribal Empowerment and Livelihood
Program, 51
Other: Adivasis as, 93, 119; British colonialism and, 47, 137; Dalits as, 5, 12, 17, 22,
168; embodied religiosity, 89; indigeneity
and, 17, 19, 22, 34, 40, 42, 168; Kandhas
as, 27, 91–92, 109–10, 114; kin-making

and, 92; Panas as, 19, 25, 34, 42, 73;
protections and provisions for, 7; religious
mediation of, 151; sexuality of vilified,
143–46, 158; tribal as, 7, 46–47
Other Backward Caste, 64

Padel, Felix, 26–28, 107–8, 188n71
Pana derecognition: anti-conversion laws
and, 17, 68, 70–71; erasure of Dalitness,
69–70; ineligibility for quotas, 70, 86;
Kandhariya Pana reclassification, 5,
16–17, 34, 123, 164; landlessness and, 135;
perceptions of economic status, 8, 67, 86,
142; political disempowerment and, 59,
69–70; purification and, 68; socioeconomic marginalization and, 10, 19
Panas: Adibasi identity, 35; administrative
employment, 30–31; Ambedkarite politics
and, 68–69; anti-Christian violence
against, 1–6, 147–48, 161–66; benefits of
Christian conversion, 78–80; as canny
mercenaries, 29, 32–34, 38–39, 41, 49, 62,
73, 120, 152; caste hierarchy and, 28–31,
69, 133; casteist racialization and, 33–34;
Christian capital rhetoric, 18, 84–86, 132,
150; criminality motifs, 34–35; derecognition and, 8, 16, 19, 59, 84–85, 135; disgust
for, 153–54; as Dom traders, 27–28,
36; economic exploitation of Kandhas,
62–64; as economic liaisons, 23, 27–32,
49, 63–64; economic marginalization
and, 35–38; ethnoreligious hostilities
and, 1–3, 73, 161; feminized materialism and, 161; indigenous recognition
and, 37, 44, 58, 61–63, 65, 133–34, 164;
Kating, 33–34; Kui Samaj movement and,
20–21; landlessness and, 36–37, 59, 72,
76, 135, 165; market economy and, 49;
materialism and, 18, 20, 23, 32–33, 73–76,
78, 84–85, 135, 150, 152–53; mimetic
movement toward Kandhas, 24, 35–36;
mission schooling and, 30, 32, 65, 76–78,
151; negative dimensions of capital and,
18, 25, 29, 32; as Other, 19, 25, 34, 42, 73;
pejorative burdens of identity, 33; perceptions of economic status, 8, 67; political
power and, 63; politicization as Dalits,
69; pollution taboos, 26, 31, 34–35, 42,
73–75, 81, 102, 133, 163; pride in heritage,
68–69; procurement of meriah victims,

ACKNOWLEDGMENTS

Many debts are incurred during the long, labyrinthine making of an academic book. Only some of these can be acknowledged, and none can be truly repaid. My time in Nagpur, Maharashtra, and in Kandhamal, Odisha, became possible with permission from the Rashtriya Swayamsevak Sangh, Akhil Bharatiya Vanvasi Kalyan Ashram, and the Vishwa Hindu Parishad, secured with the help of Professor Atanu Mohapatra and Swami Laxmananda Saraswati. Further assistance was provided by Professor A. B. Ota, director of the Scheduled Castes and Scheduled Tribes Research and Training Institute, as well as the staff at the Odisha State Archives in Bhubaneswar. I gratefully acknowledge funding from the University of Chicago Committee on South Asian Studies, the Wenner-Gren and Charlotte W. Newcombe Foundations, and Smith College. The perilous fieldwork I conducted in Kandhamal would not have been possible without the assistance of Animesh Mohapatra, as well as the guidance of Uday Nath Behera, Shyam Sundar Patmajhi, and Sujit Mahapatra. I am forever indebted to my Kandha and Pana informants for speaking with me during an extraordinarily difficult time in their lives. By showing how a destructive casteism reengineers relations between Adivasis and Dalits, my hope is that both will increasingly build coalitions to articulate a common politics of resistance in the Indian nation-state—Johar and Jai Bhim.

My years at the University of Chicago were a transformational time in my life. My committee members Richard Shweder, Jennifer Cole, and William Mazzarella shaped me, and this work, in crucial ways. Rick was the first to observe similarities in the Jewish and Pana formations, planting the seed for an analysis of comparative racializations. Jennifer insisted that clarity and storytelling were critical while relaying ambitious ideas. William nurtured conceptual ambition and heterodox explanatories. My friends in Human Development were encouraging guides and mentors. In particular, I would like to thank Kimberly Walters, Christine Nutter El Ouardani, Amy Cooper, Amy Sousa, Lara Braff, Michael Kaufman, Lara Perez-Felkner, Barnaby

Reidel, James Goss, Elizabeth Fein, Jessica Whitham, Nicole Martinez, Jacob Hickman, John Davy, Bianca Dahl, Hallie Kushner, Lainie Goldwert, Greg Thompson, Ben Smith, Deanna Barenboim, Julia Cassaniti, Julia Kowalski, and Erin Moore. Conversations with Mudit Trivedi, Tarini Bedi, and Dipesh Chakrabarty were also valuable while I was writing my dissertation. Perhaps my biggest teacher during this time was the South Side of Chicago itself. Riding the number 55 bus, exploring historic neighborhoods, and training at Cook County Hospital provided a humbling education that sowed the desire to build bridges between caste and race.

My editors at Penn Press, especially Sharika Thiranagama and Jenny Tan, supported and encouraged the ideas presented in this book and ushered it to its final form. I thank them, Tobias Kelly, and two anonymous reviewers whose input strengthened my arguments. As developmental editor, Hollianna Bryan encouraged me to more fully lean into my ideas in order to claim my argument and her help with formatting and referencing enabled the completion of the manuscript after long bouts of sickness and family crises. I thank Vikrant Bhise for allowing me to use his powerful art for the cover image. Thanks also to Jon Caris, Tracy Tien, and most especially Kate Nash, who created the maps used here, at Smith's Spatial Analysis Lab.

I have benefited from presenting this material at the University of North Carolina at Chapel Hill, the Harvard South Asia Institute, the State University of New York at Albany, Union College, Reed College, the Columbia South Asia Institute, Williams College, the Caste and Race Conference at University of Massachusetts, Amherst, as well as the university's Legal Studies Workshop. For their support of the ideas presented here, I thank Townsend Middleton, Anand Vaidya, Shankar Ramaswami, Parimal Patil, Sheetal Chhabria, Rupa Viswanath, Suraj Yengde, Banu Subramaniam, Amrita Basu, Svati Shah, Sareeta Amrute, Jeff Kahn, Elif Babul, Robert Samet, Joel Lee, Uday Chandra, Anagha Tambe, and Chad Bauman.

This book's analysis is inspired by a rich tradition of Dalit scholarship and activism that builds bridges between caste and race struggles and solidarities. It is also shaped by my work with students in the Smith classroom who are most familiar with race in the American context. Teaching them, I learned from global accounts of right-wing populism, indigeneity, and blackness to demonstrate just how minority issues in India might inform these debates. My students' queries and concerns clarified the biggest stakes of my analysis. These ideas were further encouraged by current and former members of, and speakers at, the Five Colleges, including Jessica Cattelino, Nusrat Chowdhury, Uditi Sen, Hiba Bou Akar, Elif Babul, Robert Samet, Mona Oraby, Kiran Asher, Banu Subramaniam, Amrita Basu, Svati Shah, Iyko Day, Krupa Shandilya, Yael Rice, Chris Dole, Deborah Gewertz, Debbora Battaglia, Priyanka Srivastava, Deepankar Basu, Colleen Woods, Onni Gust, Navyug Gill, Jennifer Hamilton, Hannah Holleman, Roopa Krithivasan, and Tim Malacarne. At Smith, conversations with Christen Mucher, Andy Rotman, Kevin Quashie, Colin Hoag, Fernando Armstrong Fumero, and Caroline Melly informed the book. My department members—Suzanne Gottschang, Caroline Melly, Elizabeth Klarich, Fernando Armstrong Fumero, and Colin Hoag—expressed faith in me at crucial junctures. The South Asian Studies faculty members at Smith, particularly Andy Rotman, Elisabeth Armstrong, Ambreen Hai, Jay Garfield, Nalini Bhushan, and Payal Banerjee, continually encouraged me. Banu, Lisa, and Andy have supported me in ways I hope to emulate to lift up others.

Nusrat Chowdhury used tough love to urge me to pick myself up and move forward after many a fall—I look forward to more years of good food and debate with her. Christen Mucher has tolerated all my ramblings on indigeneity and more; without her as my neighbor in Dewey Hall, this book and I would be bereft. Vanitha Virudachalam and Raj Mehta provided refuge when I needed it most. Ginetta Candelario, Jennifer Guglielmo, Michelle Joffroy, Jeff Ahlman and Mehammed Mack offered friendship and advice. And Caroline Melly has modeled courage, reinvention, and growth in the face of adversity.

My love and gratitude to Gayatri Moorthi, Aditi Subramaniam, and Arpita Chatterjee who have lifted me up for more than twenty years, and along with them Vikram Balasubramanian, Shyam Venugopal, and Debraj Ghosh. I hope my work makes Rajeshwari Ramanan, Varun Ramanan, and Shweta Gupta as proud of me as I am of their accomplishments. No words are adequate to convey my enormous love and respect for Vinayak Ramanan whose care and companionship have kept me going in the darkest of times. The loves of my life, Akila and Amay Ramanan, are my muses and partners in all that I do. This work is as much theirs as it is mine, and I hope it encourages them to think deeply, create fearlessly, and challenge all forms of inequality.

I was fortunate to be raised by four women without whom I would not be here. Since childhood, my mother, Rama Hota, endured great hardships while forging a pioneering path, but my admiration for her has been cemented over the past decade as she has endured immense losses to show me the meaning of true resilience. My grandmother Kadambini Misra modeled an insatiable appetite for good food and learning in equal measure. My greatest debt, above all, is to my sisters, my heroes, Monali and Rupali Hota—parents, siblings, wards, and champions. Every word in this book is wrought by the immeasurable grief of their loss. I hope they know how much they mean to me, and how grateful I am for them. This book is dedicated to their memory.

www.ingramcontent.com/pod-product-compliance
Lightning Source LLC
Chambersburg PA
CBHW030313270326
41926CB00010B/1340